AKBAR AND THE JESUITS

PLATE 1

AKBAR
About the year 1602

[*front.*

Akbar and the Jesuits

An Account of the Jesuit Missions to the Court of Akbar

by

Father Pierre Du Jarric

Translated with Introduction and Notes by

C H Payne

Low Price Publications

2014

First Published 1926
Reprinted in **LPP** 1999, 2008, 2014

ISBN 10: 81-7536-444-0
ISBN 13: 978-81-7536-444-8

Published by
Low Price Publications
A-6, 2nd Floor, Nimri Commercial Centre,
Ashok Vihar Phase 4, Delhi 110052 (INDIA)
tel.: +91-11-27302453 fax.: +91-11-47061936
url: www.LPPindia.com e-mail: info@LPPindia.com

Printed at
D.K. Fine Art Press Pvt. Ltd.
Delhi

PRINTED IN INDIA

THE BROADWAY TRAVELLERS

EDITED BY SIR E. DENISON ROSS
AND EILEEN POWER

AKBAR AND THE JESUITS

AN ACCOUNT OF THE JESUIT MISSIONS TO THE COURT OF AKBAR BY FATHER PIERRE DU JARRIC, S.J.

Translated with Introduction and Notes by C. H. Payne

Published by

GEORGE ROUTLEDGE & SONS, LTD.
BROADWAY HOUSE, CARTER LANE, LONDON

PREFACE

THE early Jesuit missionaries wrote so sparingly and withal so modestly of their adventures by sea and land that we are unaccustomed to think of them as travellers. Yet few men of their day have a better right to the designation; while one at least of them is entitled to a place amongst the foremost travellers of the world. We point with pride to the narratives of Fitch, Hawkins, Coryat, Roe, and other of our merchant heroes who, in the opening days of the seventeenth century sowed the seeds of British influence in the East; and the daring and enterprise of these sturdy pioneers may well kindle our admiration. But they went nowhere where the Fathers had not been before them. The latter were, in fact, the first, and with the exception of Ralph Fitch's flying visit to the court of Jahangir in 1585, the only Europeans who found their way into the Mogul empire in the sixteenth century. Moreover, theirs was no flying visit. They spent more years at Akbar's court than the others did months, and, in the course of their missionary labours, traversed his dominions from end to end, from Lahore to Kabul, and from Kashmir to the Deccan. It must be allowed, therefore, that they are fully qualified for admission even into so distinguished a company as the Broadway Travellers.

PREFACE

I have dealt in the Introduction with the character and scope of Father du Jarric's *Histoire*, the manner of its composition, and the nature and value of the historical testimony which it furnishes. I need only add, or rather repeat, here that its peculiar value lies in the fact that it reproduces or faithfully summarises nearly all the most valuable of the letters of the missionary Fathers written prior to the year 1610. The inaccessibility of these records adds greatly to the value of du Jarric's work. The original Jesuit letters are jealously preserved and widely dispersed. Age has rendered many of them almost illegible; while their translation demands an extensive acquaintance with the languages of medieval Europe. Even such of them as have been translated and published in English have a limited and exclusive circulation, and are accessible only to those who live within reach of one or other of the few libraries in which they are to be found. It is not surprising, therefore, that the contents of these letters are little known, and that Jesuit testimony has hitherto received little attention at the hands of the historian.

Du Jarric's *Histoire* is as scarce and inaccessible as the records on which it is based. A gap of more than two and a half centuries separates the only two English writers who make any considerable reference to it. The first of these was John Ogilby, whose description of the kingdom of 'Mogor', contained in the first volume of his *Asia*, published in 1673, includes numerous references to 'Jarrick', and quotations from his book. The other was the late Mr Vincent

Smith, who used the *Histoire* as one of his authorities for the later years of Akbar's life. Count von Noer made use of the first two volumes of the *Histoire* in writing his *Kaiser Akbar*, but never saw the complete work, which appears to be as little known on the Continent as it is in England.

It was my original intention to translate the whole of that portion of the *Histoire* which relates to the Mogul empire. But the undertaking proved a longer and more arduous one than I had anticipated, and as the death of Akbar seemed to provide a convenient halting place, I decided to confine myself to the reign of that emperor, leaving his successor to be dealt with in a subsequent volume, should my readers manifest any desire for Father Pierre's further acquaintance. The account of the Missions to the court of Akbar, of which this is the first English version, is based entirely on the letters and reports written by the Fathers while on service with the Missions. The first eight chapters were compiled and published within six, and the remaining chapters within nine years of Akbar's death. The account thus possesses all the value of a contemporary narrative; while it has an additional and unique claim to our attention as the earliest European description of the Mogul empire.

A word as to the illustrations. These are reproductions of the works of contemporary artists, and are amongst the best extant examples of the Mogul art of the period. Nos. I and VIII are, I believe, the only two that have been reproduced before. Nos. III and IV are from a contemporary manuscript copy of the *Akbarnama* of Abul Fazl, now in the Victoria and Albert Museum, South Kensington. The manuscript, which bears Jahangir's autograph, is illustrated by more than a hundred paintings, executed by the court artists of Akbar's reign. The two here reproduced are interesting examples of the collaboration of two or more artists in the production of a single picture, a common feature of the art of the period. No. V, which shows Akbar holding a New Year's Day durbar, is from an album which was looted from the library of the Rohilla leader, Hafiz Rahmat, by one of Shuja-ud-Daulah's sepoys, from whom it was purchased by a British officer. It came into the possession of the British Museum in 1858. Among the many interesting features of this picture are the representations of the Sun, to whose worship Akbar was addicted, suspended on either side of the imperial pavilion. Four of the artists represented in my small gallery, namely Lal, Sanwalah, Madhu, and Muskin, are mentioned by Abul Fazl in the *Ain-i-Akbari* as 'among the forerunners on the high road of art'. I am much indebted to the Librarian of the British Museum Library, and to the Curators of the Indian Section of the Victoria and Albert Museum, for the facilities afforded me in obtaining copies of these pictures.

In the case of proper names, I have preserved the spelling of the original French version of the *Histoire*, from which my translation has been made. In many cases Eastern names and words are shockingly distorted, sometimes beyond all recognition. For this, du Jarric is not to be held responsible. Possessing no knowledge of Eastern tongues, he could not do otherwise than follow the spelling of his authorities. Amongst the latter there was no uniformity, and consequently, in the pages of the *Histoire*, a particular name does not always wear the same disguise. Thus Akbar appears as 'Echebar', 'Achebar', or 'Aquebar': the king of Khandesh as 'Miram', or 'Miran': Hindustan as 'Indostan', or 'Industan': Kabul as 'Cabul', or 'Chabul': etc. Even in the spelling of the names of the Jesuit Fathers there is no uniformity; and we get such variations as 'Monserrat' and 'de Monserrat', 'Pignero' and 'Pigneiro', 'de Goës' and 'de Goïs.' These inconsistencies, however, are not without their value; for they afford considerable assistance in the identification of du Jarric's authorities, which in most cases are not named. In the notes, I have endeavoured to conform to modern principles; that is to say, I have followed the spelling of the best modern scholars, pleasing myself where they disagree. I have omitted all diacritical marks, as being unnecessary for those who are familiar with Oriental names, and embarrassing rather than helpful to others.

My grateful thanks are due to Sir E. Denison Ross for the interest he has taken in the production of this volume, as well as for much assistance both in the translation and in the preparation of the notes. I have also to thank Dr F. W. Thomas and Mr C. A. Storey for kind assistance in the solution of du Jarric's linguistic enigmas, and Mr E. Marsden for placing his valuable library at my disposal. I have given a list of the chief works I have consulted, to all of which I am beholden. I am under special obligations to Sir E. D. Maclagan's monograph, *The Jesuit Missions to the Emperor Akbar*, equally valuable as a critical study of the Jesuit campaign, and as a guide to the literature of the subject: to the writings of the Rev. H. Hosten, S.J., particularly those relating to the works of Father Monserrate: and to the late Mr Vincent Smith's *Akbar, the Great Mogul*, a work of uneven value, but the most detailed and comprehensive survey, so far attempted, of the reign of Akbar. Lastly, I desire to express my indebtedness to the Superintendent of the library of the British Museum for the help he has given me in tracing elusive authorities, and for permitting me the continuous use of du Jarric's *Histoire*, and numerous other scarce works. I know of no other library in which a complete copy of the original edition of the *Histoire* is to be found.

C. H. PAYNE.

CONTENTS

PAGES

LIST OF AUTHORITIES xix

INTRODUCTION xxiii

CHAPTER ONE

AKBAR, THE GREAT MOGUL

The early Moguls—Tamerlane—Babur—Humayun—Akbar's conquests—Limits of his empire—Its fertility and wealth—Military strength—War-elephants—Personal appearance of Akbar—His temperament, tastes, and recreations—Methods of hunting deer—Public audiences—Administration of justice—Punishments 1–13

CHAPTER TWO

THE FIRST MISSION TO MOGOR

Akbar's first contact with Christianity—Antoine Cabral—Pierre Tavero—Father Julien Pereira—The priest and the Mullas—Akbar sends for Jesuit Fathers—The first Mission—Its composition, despatch, and arrival at Fathpur—Favourable reception at court—Debates with the Mullas—Their effect on Akbar 14–23

CHAPTER THREE

'WHAT IS TRUTH?'

Residence of the Mission—The royal Princes—Akbar visits the oratory—His leanings towards Christianity—Doctrinal difficulties—The ordeal by fire—Abul Fazl—Revolt in Bengal—The Kabul campaign—The Fathers lose favour—Akbar defends his Mullas . . . 24–34

CONTENTS

CHAPTER FOUR

FATHER RUDOLF AQUAVIVA

PAGES

The Fathers regain Akbar's favour—Hostility of the Saracens—The Mission breaks up—Father Rudolf alone at the Mogul court—His influence over Akbar—The Mullas seek his life—His prayers and austerities—Loved and respected by all classes—His return to Goa . . . 35–43

CHAPTER FIVE

THE SECOND MISSION

Akbar celebrates the feast of the Assumption—Displays his contempt for Islam—Leon Grimon arrives at court—Carries the King's letters to Goa—Jesuit Fathers again invited to the Mogul court—Arrangements for their journey—Akbar's letter to the Fathers—The Mission at Agra—Its failure and recall 44–50

CHAPTER SIX

DISPATCH OF THIRD MISSION

Dispatch of third Mission—Arrival at Cambay—First fruits—Meeting with Prince Murad—Travelling with a caravan—At Ahmadabad—A Yogi—A wonderful tomb—Pilgrims on their way to Mecca—The feast of the Passover—Arrival at Lahor 51–61

CHAPTER SEVEN

THE FATHERS AT COURT

Welcomed by the King and the Prince—The King's library—A vassal Prince pays homage to the Great Mogul—Gifts fit for a king—Renewed hopes of the King's conversion—His reverence for Christianity and contempt of Islam—He founds a new religion—The Fathers open a school at Lahor—The King grants them permission to make converts . 62–71

CONTENTS

CHAPTER EIGHT

ON TOUR WITH THE KING

PAGES

Akbar's eclecticism—The royal palace on fire—The Fathers accompany Akbar to Kashmir—The country described—Illness of Father Xavier and of the King—Famine—The return journey—Prince Salim's adventure with a lioness—Celebrating Christmas at Lahor—The Fathers pay a visit to Akbar—A strange experiment—Facing a storm—The price of baptism—The King, accompanied by Father Xavier, sets out for the Deccan—Public baptism of converts at Lahore—A brave proselyte . . . 72–96

CHAPTER NINE

AT THE SEAT OF WAR

Akbar marches to Burhanpur—Father Corsi joins the Mission—His adventurous journey from Cambay to Burhanpur—The Deccan Campaign—The investment of Asirgarh—Submission of king Miran—The Governor of the fortress commits suicide—The defenders are bribed, and the fortress is surrendered 97–109

CHAPTER TEN

AN EMBASSY TO GOA

Father Pigneiro comes to the royal camp—He pays his respects to the King—Akbar's designs against the Portuguese—An ambassador is sent to the Portuguese Viceroy—His reception at Goa—Akbar's letter to the Viceroy . . 110–117

CHAPTER ELEVEN

FATHER PIGNEIRO AT LAHORE, 1600–1

Work amongst the people—Opposition of the Brahmans—A friendly Viceroy—Father Pigneiro as peace-maker—Vice-regal state—Mogul death duties—The Kotwal stands by the Fathers 118–121

CONTENTS

CHAPTER TWELVE

THE CONFIDENCE TRICK

PAGES

Father Pigneiro entertains a thief unawares—He is drugged and robbed—His misfortune arouses general indignation and sympathy 122–126

CHAPTER THIRTEEN

SOME NOTABLE CONVERSIONS

Christmas celebrations—A pastoral play—The Viceroy and other great lords attend the festival—Many are converted to Christianity—Some notable cases described—Some Armenian converts—Death of an Armenian bishop—An eclipse of the sun 127–136

CHAPTER FOURTEEN

A BRAVE CHAMPION

A Brahman convert—Persecuted by his parents—Takes refuge in the Fathers' house—The Fathers are charged with abduction—The Chief Judge acquits the Fathers and defends the Christian faith—The case is referred to Pagan judges—The neophyte is ill-used and insulted—He defies the 'Coxi'—Is taken before the Kazi—His courage remains unshaken—He resigns his worldly possessions, and is left in peace—The Chief Judge commends his constancy 137–151

CHAPTER FIFTEEN

AN IMPERIAL FARMAN

Akbar returns to Agra—Benoist de Goës joins the Mission—An unfriendly Viceroy—'The King was in his counting-house'—The Fathers obtain a farman from Akbar permitting his subjects to embrace Christianity—The Saracens put obstructions in the way—Mogul red tape—A friend at court—The farman is issued 152–159

CONTENTS

CHAPTER SIXTEEN

A MIRACULOUS PICTURE

PAGES

A picture of the Madonna del Popolo is placed in the church at Agra—Great crowds press to see it—Its miraculous influence—It is taken to the King's palace—The King's painters try to copy it—The Queen-mother sends for it—Also Aziz Khan and the ex-king of Kandahar . . . 160–172

CHAPTER SEVENTEEN

EVENTS OF THE YEAR 1602

The Fathers rescue and baptise a number of Portuguese prisoners—Some other noteworthy baptisms—The remarkable case of a Greek Christian and his wife—Fifty shipwrecked Portuguese are sent as prisoners to Akbar—With much difficulty the Fathers procure their freedom . . 173–181

CHAPTER EIGHTEEN

PRINCE SALIM

The Prince in rebellion—Murders Abul Fazl—Displays great affection for the Fathers and respect for Christianity—Jacques Philippe—Death of the Queen-mother—The Prince makes submission to Akbar—Is placed in confinement and afterwards released—His reverence for Christ and the Virgin—Makes provision for a church at Agra . 182–191

CHAPTER NINETEEN

PERSECUTION OF THE FATHERS

Saracens and Gentiles make vows and bring offerings to the Virgin—A Saracen of note dedicates his child to the Church—The Prince's physician is baptised—The perils of preaching the Gospel—Troubles at Lahore—The Viceroy's hostility—A Gentile conspiracy—Providence intervenes—Retribution overtakes the Viceroy and the chief conspirators 192–202

CONTENTS

CHAPTER TWENTY

THE DEATH OF AKBAR

PAGES

Akbar's fatal illness—The Fathers are refused admission to the palace—The Prince visits his dying father—Akbar's last moments—His character and manner of life—His conquests and good fortune—Funeral rites . . 203–208

NOTES 209–280

INDEX 281–288

LIST OF ILLUSTRATIONS

I. *Akbar at the Age of Sixty.* (*Wantage Collection, Victoria and Albert Museum.*) *Part of a group picture by the artist Manohar* . . *Frontispiece*

FACING PAGE

II. *Title-page of the original Edition of the* HISTOIRE . XXXVI

III. *Akbar Hunting Antelope.* (*From a manuscript copy of the* AKBARNAMA *of Abul Fazl illustrated by contemporary painters, and now in the possession of the Victoria and Albert Museum, South Kensington.*) *Artists: Lal* (*outline*), *Sanwalah* (*painting*) 10

IV. *A Vassal Prince doing Homage to Akbar.* (*From the same source as the preceding.*) *Artists: Muskin* (*outline*), *Sarwan* (*painting*), *Madhu* (*eight portraits*) . . 64

V. *The* Bargah-Nauroz, *or New Year's Day Darbar.* (*British Museum, Add. MS.* 22470.) *The picture is unsigned. Akbar* (*aged about* 45) *is surrounded by his chief officers of state, whose names are inscribed in tiny characters on their costumes. The seven figures on his right hand are* (*commencing from the left of the picture*), *Shaikh Faizi* (?), *Asaf Khan, Abul Fazl, Aziz Koka, Raja Man Singh, the Khan-Khanan, and Aka Shah. The aged Todar Mal is seen on the right of the picture, with hands folded* . . 74

VI. *Prince Salim attacked by a Lioness.* (*British Museum, Stowe* Or. 16.) *Unsigned* . . . 80

VII. *The Magdalen.* (*Wantage Collection, Victoria and Albert Museum, South Kensington.*) *Copied from an Italian picture by one of Jahangir's court artists* . . 190

VIII. *Jahangir shortly after his Accession.* (*Victoria and Albert Museum, South Kensington.*) *Part of a group picture by the artist Govardhan* (?) . . . 204

LIST OF PRINCIPAL AUTHORITIES CONSULTED

ABUL FAZL. *Akbarnama.* Translation by H. Beveridge. Published by the Asiatic Society of Bengal. Calcutta, 1897, &c.

—— *Ain-i-Akbari.* Translation by H. Blochmann. Calcutta, 1873.

BADAONI (Abd al-Kadir). *Muntakhab-ut-tawarikh.* Translation published by the Asiatic Society of Bengal. Calcutta, 1898, &c.

BARTOLI (Father Daniel, S.J.). *Missione al gran Mogor,* &c. Rome, 1714.

CATROU (F. F.). *A History of the Mogul Dynasty in India.* London, 1826.

DALGADO (S. Rodolfo). *Glossário Luso-Asiático.* Lisbon, 1919.

DANVERS (F. C.). *The Portuguese in India.* London, 1894.

DE BACKER (A.). *Bibliothèque des Écrivans de la Compagnie de Jésus.* Paris, 1869.

DELLA VALLE (Pietro). *Travels in India.* Hakluyt Society, 1892.

DE SOUSA (Father Francisco, S.J.). *Oriente Conquistado,* &c. Lisbon, 1710.

ELPHINSTONE (The Hon. Mountstuart). *The History of India.* London, 1889.

FAIZI SIRHINDI. *Akbarnama.* Extracts translated in Elliot and Dowson's *History of India,* Vol. VI.

AUTHORITIES CONSULTED

FARIA Y SOUSA (Manoel). *The Portuguese Asia.* Translated by J. Stevens. London, 1695.

FIRISHTA. *Tarikh-i Firishta.* Translated by John Briggs. 1829.

FOSTER (Sir W.). *Early Travels in India.* London, 1921.

FRYER (John). *A New Account of East India and Persia.* London, 1698.

GOLDIE (Father Francis, S.J.). *The First Christian Mission to the Great Mogul.* Dublin, 1897.

GUERREIRO (Father Fernam, S.J.). *Relacam annal das cousas,* &c. *Vide* Introduction, p. xxxii.

GUZMAN (Father Luis de, S.J.). *Historia de las Missiones,* &c. Alcala, 1601.

HAY (John). *De Rebus Japonicis, Indicis,* &c. Antwerp, 1605.

HERBERT (Sir Thomas). *Some Yeares Travels into Divers Parts of Asia and Afrique.* London, 1638.

HOSTEN (Rev. H., S.J.). See MONSERRATE, Father A.

HUGHES (Thomas Patrick). *A Dictionary of Islam.* London, 1885.

JAHANGIR. *Tuzuk-i-Jahangiri.* Translated by A. Rogers. London, 1909–1914.

MACLAGAN (Sir Edward). *Jesuit Missions to the Emperor Akbar.* Published in the *Journal* of the Asiatic Society of Bengal, Vol. LXV.

MANDELSLO (J. A.). *Voyages and Travels into the East Indies.* London, 1669.

MONSERRATE (Father Anthony, S.J.). *Mongolicæ Legationis Commentarius.* Published (with Introduction and Notes by the Rev. H. Hosten, S.J.) in the *Memoirs* of the Asiatic Society of Bengal, Vol. III, 1914.

AUTHORITIES CONSULTED

MONSERRATE (Father Anthony, S.J.). *Relaçam do Equebar.* Published (with translation and notes by the Rev. H. Hosten, S.J.) in the *Journal and Proceedings* of the Asiatic Society of Bengal, 1912.

MORELAND (W. H.). *India at the Death of Akbar.* London, 1920.

MUNDY (Peter). *The Travels of Peter Mundy in Europe and Asia.* Hakluyt Society, 1914.

MURRAY (Hugh). *Historical Account of Discoveries and Travels in Asia.* London, 1820.

NOER (Count von). *Kaiser Akbar.* Translation by Annette S. Beveridge. Calcutta, 1890.

OGILBY (John). *Asia.* London, 1673.

ORANUS (Joannes). *Japonica, Sinensia, Mogorana,* &c. Liège, 1601.

ORME (Robert). *Historical Fragments of the Mogul Empire,* &c. 1805.

PERUSCHI (Giovanni Battista). *Informatione del Regno e Stato del gran Rè di Mogor.* Brescia, 1597.

PIMENTA (Father Nicolo, S.J.). *Nova Relatio Historica de Rebus in India Orientali,* &c. Maintz, 1601.

—— *Exemplum Epistolae . . . ad R. P. Claudium Aquavivum.* Maintz, 1600.

ROE (Sir Thomas). *Embassy to the Court of the Great Mogol.* Hakluyt Society, 1899.

SEWELL (R.). *A Forgotten Empire.* London, 1900.

SMITH (V. A.). *Akbar, The Great Mogul.* Oxford, 1919.

SPITILLI (Gasparo). *Brevis et compendiosa narratio missionum,* &c. Antwerp, 1593.

SUAU (Pierre). *Les bienheureux martyres de Salsette.* Bruges, 1893.

AUTHORITIES CONSULTED

TAVERNIER (Jean Baptiste). *Travels in India.* Translation by V. Ball. London, 1889.

TEIXEIRA (P. Pedro). *Relaciones . . . de los Reyes de Persia,* &c. Amberes, 1610.

TERRY (Edward). *A Voyage to East India.* London, 1717.

THEVENOT (Jean de). *Voyages and Travels* (tr. Lovell). London, 1687.

VARTHEMA (Lodovico di). *Travels.* Hakluyt Society, 1863.

YULE (Sir Henry). *Cathay and the Way Thither.* Hakluyt Society, 1913.

—— AND BURNELL (A. C.). *Hobson-Jobson.* London, 1903.

INTRODUCTION

Father Pierre du Jarric was born at Toulouse in 1566. He entered the Society of Jesus in 1582, with the intention of becoming one of the missionaries of the Order. This intention, owing to circumstances which were, apparently, beyond his control, he was never able to fulfil; and he spent the major portion of his life as professor of philosophy and moral theology at Bordeaux. He never ceased to regret his inability to engage in active missionary work; and his leisure and his pen were ungrudgingly devoted to the cause he had at heart. He died at Saintes in 1617, three years after the completion of the third volume of his *Histoire*.

The following is the complete title of du Jarric's *magnum opus*:[1]

Histoire des choses plus memorable advenes tant ez Indes Orientales, que autres païs de la descouuerte des Portugais, en l'establissement et progrez de la foy Chrestienne et Catholique: et principalement de ce que les Religieux de la Compagnie de Iésus y ont faict, & enduré pour la mesme fin; depuis qu'ils y sont entrez jusques à l'an 1600. [*Le tout recueilly des lettres, & autres*

[1] Du Jarric's only other literary work was a translation from the Latin of *The Soul's Paradise*, by Albertus Magnus. It was entitled *Le Paradise de l'âme ou Traité des Vertus composé en latin par Albert le Grand, et traduit en françois (par P. du Jarric, de la Compagnie de Iesus)*, and was published at Bordeaux in 1616 by S. Millanges.

Histoires, qui en ont esté escrites cy deuant, & mis en ordre] *par le P. Pierre du Jarric Tolosain, de la mesme Compagnie.*

In the titles to Parts II and III, the portion of the last sentence, which I have placed in brackets, is omitted, and is replaced in the former by the words *Dediée av Roy tres-chrestien de France & de Nauarre Lovis XIII*, and in the latter by *Dediée à la Royne Regente, mère du Roy.* Part I was dedicated to *Henri IIII.* In Part III the words *depuis* . . . 1600 are replaced by *depuis l'an* 1600 *jusques à* 1610.

The *Histoire* consists of three Parts, each containing two Books. Books I and II give an account of the life and work of St. Francis Xavier, and of the Missions in India (Travancore, Cochin, Calicut, Vijayanagar, Bengal, etc.), Pegu, and the Molucca Islands, down to the close of the year 1599. Books III and IV, i.e. Part II, give accounts, down to the same date, of the Missions in Africa (Congo, Angola, Monomotapan, etc.), Brazil, China, and the Mogul Empire; and Books V and VI, i.e. Part III, carry on the accounts of the same Missions, bringing them, in most cases, down to the year 1610. The first eight chapters of the translation contained in this volume belong to Book IV of Part II (Chapters VIII–XV), and the remaining chapters to Book V of Part III (Chapters IV–XV).

As its title indicates, the *Histoire* is not an original account of the Jesuit missions, but a compilation. The circumstances in which it was composed, and the sources whence its materials were drawn, are thus set forth by the Compiler in his preface *au lecteur Chrestien:*

'Although, dear reader, divers authors have written histories of the East and the West Indies, very few of them have dealt with the progress of the Christian religion in those parts. Maffee[1] has indeed written with as much judgment, eloquence, and accuracy, as any author of our time, an account of what the Portuguese have done in the East and South, whether for the increase of their territories, or for the enlargement of the kingdom of Jesus-Christ. But his history covers only 16 or 17 years of the preaching of the Holy Gospel; for it ends with the reign of John III, king of Portugal, who died in the year 1557; and the work of converting the Infidels did not commence before the year 1540. Tursellin,[2] again, has written very admirably and fully of the labours of the blessed Father François Xauier, who was the first of all the Company of Jesus to preach the Christian faith in the East. But he did not attempt more than this; and his account ends with the death of the blessed Father, which took place on the 2nd of December, 1552. There is, likewise, a Commentary on what has been done

[1] Joannes Petrus Maffeus, S.J. (1536–1603), was one of the best of the Jesuit writers. He wrote in Latin, and prided himself on the purity and elegance of his style. His two principal works are, *Historiarum Indicarum Libri XVI* (Florence, 1585), and *Vita Ignatii Loyolæ* (Venice, 1585). The first of these took twelve years to complete; but as the author is said to have spent hours, even days, in modelling a single sentence, the wonder is that he ever did complete it. So great was Maffeus' reverence for *la belle Latinité*, that he used to repeat his breviary in Greek, so as to avoid contaminating his style.

[2] Tursellin, or Torsellino, was born at Rome in 1545. His chief work, *De Vita Sancti Francisci Xaverii*, was published in 1595. He also wrote an Epitome of the history of the world, which, in 1761, was publicly burnt in Paris by order of Parliament, as containing *maximes dangereuses.*

in the East by those of the said Company, by Emmanuel Acosta,[1] a Portuguese writer; but it is brief and condensed, and omits much that is to be found in the writings of Maffee, Tursellin, and others. Moreover, since his time, many noteworthy things have taken place in connection with the establishment and progress of the faith in these lands, of which we should know little or nothing, were it not for the letters and reports which those of the Company have written almost every year to Europe. Although, however, these letters are from time to time printed in Latin, or other languages, there are many of them which have been seen only by a very few

Since it would be no easy task to make a collection of all these letters, while the labour of reading the many volumes they would fill would be very great, many who are anxious to inform themselves of the growth of Christianity in these countries have expressed the desire that some one should undertake a history of the same.

There came into the hands of our reverend Father Provincial a history written in Spanish by the Father Louys de Guzman,[2] entitled the *History of the Missions undertaken by*

[1] Acosta's *Hist. rerum a Soc. Jesu in Oriente gestarum* was published in Paris in 1572.

[2] Luis de Guzman, a Spanish Father of great virtue, was born in 1544. He joined the Society in 1565, was Rector of many colleges, and had charge of the provinces of Andalusia and Toledo. He died at Madrid in 1605. His *Historia*, written in Spanish, was published at Alcala in 1601. Its full title is: *Historia de las Missiones de la Compania de Jesus, para predicar el Sancto Evangelico en la India Oriental, y en los Reynos de la China y Japon, escrita por el Padre Luis de Guzman, Religioso de la misma Compania.* The portion of the *Historia* relating to the Mogul empire gives a general sketch of the three Jesuit Missions to the court of Akbar. It is based on original Jesuit writings of the period, the contents of which are, however, much condensed. The account will be found in Vol. I, pp. 240–271, of the Alcala edition. The second volume deals only with the Mission to Japan.

the Religieux of the Company of Jesus to preach the Holy Gospel in the East Indies & the Kingdom of China; and this having been entrusted to me to translate into our language, I devoted to the work what little leisure remained to me after my daily lectures on theology. Now, as I came to read other histories treating of the same subject, I began to see that my author had made no reference to many important matters that were dealt with by the others; and being at a loss to understand this, and finding other difficulties also in his book, I wrote to him for enlightenment. Whether he ever received my letters, or whether he died before they reached him (his death took place soon after he became Provincial of the province of Toledo), I do not know; in any case, I received no reply from him. I then addressed myself to a certain Father of Portugal, who, I had been told, was well versed in these matters. This was Father Fernand Guerreiro, who is at the present time Superior of the house of the Profes at Lisbon, and who has written three or four books in Portuguese treating of what has taken place in the East Indies since the year 1599, at which date the history of Guzman closes. Having received my letter, he not only answered, as I think very pertinently, the questions I asked, but promised to send me some books in which I should find information on many important matters, which would greatly enhance the value of my history. He added that his advice, and that of many other Fathers, as well as of certain laymen of learning and judgement, who had read the books of Guzman, was that I should take in hand the writing of a history, instead of confining myself to the translation of a single author; and he told me that he could supply me with books and memoirs which would greatly assist me in my task. This advice did not at first commend itself to me, partly because I did not think to have sufficient leisure to follow it, and partly because I had already advanced far with my translation, having completed the first four volumes, which cover all the Missions except that to Japan; while many persons, to whose opinions I attached weight, having seen the greater portion of what I had translated, considered that the portion already completed should be given to the public, whilst the history of Japan was in preparation.

It was just when I had made up my mind to revise my translation, that the books and memoirs which had been promised to me arrived. Amongst them were some notes on the history of Guzman, made by Albert Laertius,[1] an Italian Father, who is at present Provincial of India. These notes, which are in his own handwriting, I have made use of in many places, regarding them as very valuable; for he is a man of wide experience, who has lived long in these regions, and who was, as he himself states, an eye-witness of many of the events recorded. I likewise received, through the same channel, the letters received from Japan, commencing with the year 1549, when the rays of our faith first shone upon that country, and ending with the year 1590, the whole printed in Portuguese in two large volumes. Another history which came to me contained, in ten Books, an account of what Father Xauier, and other *Religieux* of the same Company, had done in India. This was written by a Portuguese Father, Iean de Lucena,[2] an accomplished writer, and, as his

[1] Albert Laertius (or Laerzio, as de Backer calls him) was Provincial of Malabar during the early years of the 17th century. "The Province of the Indies (*Provincia Indicarum*, with headquarters at Goa) was split into the Province of Goa and the Province of Malabar in 1610. Malabar had become a vice-Province in 1601. The latter division, writes Fr. L. Besse, S.J., had been negotiated in Rome by Fr. Alb. Laerzio, who returned to India in 1602" (*J.A.S.B.*, 1910, p. 446).

[2] Jean de Lucena was born in 1548, and died in 1600. His *Historia da vida da Francisco de Xavier* is still regarded in Portugal as a classic. Faria y Sousa, however, who cites Lucena as one of his authorities, remarks: "He sticks not to the rules of history, but in his way of writing deserves esteem for his judgment, elegancy, and way of reasoning" (*Asia Portuguesa*, tr. J. Stevens, III, p. 437).

work shows, a man well versed in both religious and general literature. Laſtly, I received a number of books dealing with what has taken place in these regions since the year 1600, compiled from the letters which came therefrom, by the said Father Fernand Guerreiro, who, besides supplying me with these and other aids, and giving me much valuable advice, has continued to put into my hands the volumes he has published of the letters arriving year by year from India, so that I am now in possession of all of these down to the year 1606.

As it became apparent to me from reading these books, that my author had omitted almoſt as many circumſtances, both noteworthy and authenticated, as he had recorded; and finding too that Lucena, except occasionally and, as it were, *en passant*, confined himself to the life of the blessed Father Xauier, and that he dealt with the same at great length, including in it many discourses which, though very learned and excellent, seemed better suited to the requirements of a preacher than of an hiſtorian, I decided to follow the counsel of the Fathers of Portugal, and to take from one what was omitted by the other. I have, however, kept to the plan of my firſt author, by means of which, it seemed to me, the growth of Chriſtianity in each country, could be moſt easily followed[1]; but in regard to matters dealt with by both, I have preferred to rely on Lucena, since he had better oppor-

[1] In his Introduction du Jarric writes: 'Or jacoit que nous suyuions l'ordre des temps en chaque contrée, de laquelle nous traictons icy, remarquans tout ce qu'il y a eu de plus signalé, concernant le faict de la Religion, despuis que les nostres y ont mis le pied jusques en l'an 1600: toutesfois pour dõner plus de clarté à l'Histoire nous auons jugé qu'il seroit meilleur d'auoir esgard à l'ordre des lieux. Car si nous faisions un meslange de tout ce, qui est arrivé en une mesme annee au Japon, à la Chine, aux Indes, au Brasil, & autres païs icy comprins, cõme ont faict quelques uns, qui ont escrit les gestes des Portugais en tous ces quartiers là, ce seroit à mon aduis causer une merueilleuse confusion en l'esprit du lecteur, à raison de la grande distance des lieux, desquels il faut parler; & l'on ne pourroit pas si bien cognoistre le progrez que la religion Chrestiẽne y a fait en chacun d'iceux.'

tunities of ascertaining the truth, having, as he himself says, had in his charge the authentic copies, made by order of the king of Portugal, Iean IIII, of the reports relating to the work of the blessed Father Xauier, as well as the originals of many of the letters from India, which are carefully preserved in the College of Coimbra. In short, he had every facility for studying these documents; and that he diligently availed himself of the same is manifest from his writings. He was, moreover, as his writings also show, well versed in cosmography; and I am informed that his History is highly esteemed in Portugal, and is accepted as an authoritative work.

I have been the more emboldened to begin my task over again even at this late hour, seeing that—a circumstance that I deeply deplore—our studies have been interrupted by the contagious sickness which for some years has afflicted this city, and in consequence of which, I find myself with more leisure than I had anticipated. As for those who have urged me to publish what I have already translated, I think it better to keep them waiting a little longer, rather than offer them an imperfect work. Nor will they lose anything thereby. For, besides the works of the best historians, such as Osorius and Maffee, I have examined the yearly letters and reports which have come from these parts, from which, and particularly from those I have mentioned above as having been sent to me, I have drawn, with all the care and fidelity of which I am capable, the materials of which my history is composed. I can confidently assert that I have set down nothing in these pages which I have not derived from the works of approved authors, or from the letters of persons worthy of credit. My chief regret is that so rich a subject has not been dealt with by a worthier pen. But since the choice was not given to me, but rather the command, I hope, dear reader, that you will not judge too harshly the labours which have been undertaken on your behalf. If I know that what I have written has your approval, I shall have the more courage to complete my story, in the continuation of which I shall, with God's help, tell you many things of no less interest than those here presented. Year by year, as the letters from the Indies arrive, I shall have a new dish to set before you, moving you thereby to praise continuously the Infinite Goodness that never ceases to work marvels on earth and in heaven.'

The above refers more especially to Parts I and II of the *Histoire*, which deal with events prior to the year 1600. In a short preface to Part III, which covers the period 1600–1610, du Jarric mentions Guerreiro as his main authority, referring to him as a man ' of ripe and solid judgment, and very learned in these histories, who every two years has collected, and compiled into a single volume, the letters from the Indies, to the great edification of those who desire to study the progress of the Christian faith in foreign lands. . . . Since the year 1600, he has published 5 or 6 volumes which he has had the kindness to place in my hands, and from which, in the main, I have taken that which I have here set down in writing.'

Stated briefly, therefore, du Jarric's authorities for events prior to the year 1600, which include the three Missions to the court of Akbar,[1] were Guzman's

[1] The first Mission arrived at the Mogul court in 1580, the second in 1591, and the third in 1595. No definite date can be assigned for the termination of the third Mission. It was despatched in response to Akbar's request for further instruction in the Christian religion, and, so far as this particular purpose was concerned, it can hardly be said to have extended beyond the close of the century; but the Fathers remained at the Mogul court, and continued their missionary labours for several years after the death of Akbar.

Historia, supplemented by the notes of Father Laertius, Lucena's life of St. Francis Xavier, and such of the materials supplied to him by Guerreiro as related to this period. The latter included many of the letters and reports received in Europe from those who organised and conducted the Missions. For the events of the succeeding eight years he relied almost wholly on the last-named writer. Indeed, the third Part of the *Histoire* is largely a translation from Guerreiro's narrative.

A work on which so considerable a portion of the *Histoire* is based calls for more particular notice. Of its author I have discovered nothing beyond what du Jarric tells us in his preface, and the few bare facts given by De Backer in his *Bibliothèque des Ecrivains de la Compagnie de Jesus*, namely, that he was born at Almodovar in Portugal in 1550, that he entered the Company of Jesus in 1567, and that he died in 1617 having held many honourable posts. The work itself, the nature of which du Jarric has sufficiently indicated, consists of five parts, and covers the period 1600–1608. Its title is, *Relaçam Annal das Cousas que fizaram os Padres da Companhia de Jesu nas partes da India Oriental, & em alguas outras da conquista deste Reyno nos annos de [604 & 605], & do processo de conversam & Christandade daquellas partes. Tirade das cartas dos mesmos Padres que de la vieram, pello Padre Fernam Guerreiro da mesma Companhia, natural de Almodour de Portugal.* It was published between the years 1603 and 1611, as follows:

Part I	(1600–1601)	published at Evora	by Manoel de Lyra	in 1603
„ II	(1602–1603)	„ Lisbon	by Iorge Rodrigues	in 1605
„ III	(1604–1605)	„ „	by Pedro Crasbeeck	in 1607
„ IV	(1606–1607)	„ „	by „ „	in 1609
„ V	(1607–1608)	„ „	by „ „	in 1611

Each Part is divided into Books. Part I consists of two, Part V of five, and each of the other Parts of four Books. A Spanish translation of Part I, made by Father Antonio Colaço, S.J., was published at Valladolid in 1604. The original work is of extreme rarity. The library of the British Museum has all five parts; and this is, I believe, the only complete copy of the work to be found in this country. The same library has Colaço's Spanish version of Part I, of which there is also a copy in the library of All Souls College.

Owing to its inaccessibility, the *Relaçam* is practically unknown to students of Indian history. I have met with only two modern works in which it is referred to, namely Count von Noer's *Kaiser Akbar*, and Mr. Vincent Smith's *Akbar, the Great Mogul.* Neither of these writers, however, had more than a fragmentary acquaintance with Guerreiro's work, and both, in consequence, came badly to grief in their references to it. In justice to von Noer, it must be remembered that the second volume of *Kaiser Akbar* was published four years after his death, under the editorship of Dr. Gustav von Buchwald, to whom his papers and notes were made over. It is, therefore, the latter writer who must be held responsible for the mishandling of material which this volume reveals. Of the *Relaçam*, a portion of Part V appears to have been all that came into Buchwald's hands, and it would have been well for him if he had never seen even this. Knowing nothing of Guerreiro or his work, he mistook the *Relaçam* for a personal narrative, and, what was far more disastrous, he failed to discover that the Mogul emperor depicted in this Part is not Akbar, but his successor Jahangir. Hence, in the fifth chapter of his book, he attributes to Akbar a method of sealing letters with the images of Christ and the Virgin which was invented and adopted by Jahangir after he became emperor; and on this impossible foundation he constructs an elaborate theory that Akbar regarded himself as of higher rank than Christ. In a subsequent passage (Chapter XI), he makes Akbar the chief speaker in a discussion on the divinity of Christ which took place two years after his death. This discussion he antedates by some twelve years, making it occur on the 5th May, 1595, the date on which the third Jesuit Mission reached Akbar's court; and not content with this, he makes Guerreiro himself, who was not a missionary and was never in the East, one of the disputants. The latter blunder is the more inexcusable since, in the first volume of *Kaiser Akbar*, the names of the Fathers who composed the third Mission are correctly stated. His mistake in regard to the identity of the emperor, though much more serious, is less difficult to account for. In this Part of the *Relaçam*, Guerreiro does not mention Jahangir by name, but refers to him throughout as 'el Rey.' The period dealt with (1607–1608) is stated on the title-page; but in a short extract, unaccompanied by the title-page, it is quite possible there might be no actual clue to the identity of 'el Rey.' Mr. Vincent Smith's references are equally misleading and inaccurate. The most serious of his misstatements is referred to in the notes at the end of this volume (*vide* p. 252). He would have avoided this particular blunder had he taken the trouble to glance through the first few pages of Part I of the *Relaçam*, Colaço's Spanish version of which he had at his disposal; whilst a single visit to the library of the British Museum, or even a reference to the catalogue, would have enabled him to write an accurate, instead of an inaccurate, note on the scope of Guerreiro's work and the form in which it was published. The perfunctory nature of Mr. Smith's investigations is the more astonishing in view of the immense weight he attached to Jesuit testimony.

But to resume. The original French edition of the *Histoire* was published at Bordeaux (not at Arras, as erroneously stated by Mr. Smith) in three quarto volumes, which appeared successively in 1608, 1610, and 1614.[1] It was produced by S. Millanges, *Imprimeur Ordinaire du Roy*. In 1611, a new edition of Part II was published at Arras (*chez* Gilles Bauduyn), and was reissued by the same publisher in 1628, being entitled this time, *Nouvelle Histoire des choses, &c.* Part II was also published in 1611 at Valenciennes (*chez* Jean Vervliet). It was a copy of this edition that was used by Count von Noer, when writing his

[1] In some cases Part I also bears the date 1610. The illustrated title-page does not appear in the earlier issue of this Part.

Kaiser Akbar (see Mrs. Beveridge's translation, Vol. I, p. 296). A Latin translation of the entire work, by M. Matthia Martinez, entitled *Thesaurus rerum Indicarum, &c.*, was published in 1615 at Cologne (*Coloniæ Agrippinæ, sumptibus Petri Henningy*). The *Thesaurus* is bound both in four, and in two volumes. In the former case, Books V and VI, which are considerably longer than the earlier Books, are in separate volumes; and in the latter case, the first volume contains Parts I and II, and the second contains Part III. The illustrated title-page of the Bordeaux edition is reproduced in the *Thesaurus*. The subjects represented are the martyrdoms of seven Fathers who gave up their lives on the mission field.

Both the French and the Latin versions of du Jarric's work, more especially the former, are extremely scarce, though not to the extent imagined by Mr. V. A. Smith (see his *Akbar*, p. 468), who was evidently unaware that in the library of the British Museum, du Jarric is represented by no less than eighteen volumes. These include two copies of the original Bordeaux edition, complete in all three Parts; a copy of the Arras edition of Part II, published in 1611, and of the reprint of the same issued in 1628; two complete copies of the *Thesaurus*, one in four volumes and the other in two; another copy of the former, but lacking the third volume (i.e. Book V), and another copy of the first volume only. Of the two copies of the Bordeaux edition, one has been rebound, the other is in the original binding. The latter has the arms of the Rt. Hon'ble Thomas Grenville on the inside of the cover,

PLATE II

SECONDE PARTIE

DE L'HISTOIRE

DES CHOSES PLVS MEMORABLES ADVENVES

tant ez Indes Orientales, que autres païs de la descouuerte des Portugais,

En l'establissement & progrez de la foy Chrestienne & Catholique:

Et principalement de ce que les Religieux de la Compagnie de IESVS y ont faict, & enduré pour la mesme fin,

Depuis qu'ils y sont entrez iusqu'à l'an 1600.

DEDIEE AV ROY TRES-CHRESTIEN de France & de Navarre LOVIS XIII.

Par le P. PIERRE DV IARRIC, Tolosain, de la mesme Compagnie.

A BOVRDEAVS,

Par SIMON MILLANGES Imprimeur ordinaire du Roy. 1610.

TITLE-PAGE OF THE *HISTOIRE*

[*face p. xxxvi*

and on a slip of paper attached to the fly-leaf of Vol. I, the following words are written in ink: "The 3rd volume is so scarce that it is said no other copy is to be found in this country except in the library of Lord Bute. The same work is translated into Latin. I have a copy of it." The incomplete copy of the *Thesaurus* mentioned above is also stamped with the Grenville arms, and is evidently the copy referred to on the slip. The Bodleian Library has the first volume of the Bordeaux edition, and a copy of the *Thesaurus* in four volumes. There is also a copy of the latter in the library of the India Office.

The *Thesaurus* has no independent value. Its importance lies in the scarcity of the original work. It is, on the whole, a faithful translation, though by no means free from inaccuracies. To some of these I have drawn attention; but I have come across others; and I have little doubt that, if a careful comparison of the two versions were made, a good many more would be brought to light. Mr. Vincent Smith, who made extensive use of du Jarric's work in his *Akbar*, relied mainly on the Latin version, and was 'let down' more than once in consequence.

Du Jarric, as is plain from his preface, makes no claim to rank as an historian, or a man of letters. His *Histoire* is in no sense an original work, nor is it a great literary achievement. It is, from first to last, a compilation, a series of extracts and abstracts from the writings of others. Its importance consists in its being an accurate reproduction of a large store of first-hand evidence, much of which is not available elsewhere. Other writers made collections from the Jesuit records; but du Jarric not only collected on a more extensive scale, but wove his materials into a series of continuous narratives, covering the whole field of Jesuit missionary enterprise in the sixteenth, and the opening years of the seventeenth centuries. I have compared the chapters relating to the Mogul Empire with the corresponding portions of the *Historia* of Guzman, the *Relaçam* of Guerreiro, and with such other of the Jesuit writings used in their composition as I have had opportunities of consulting; and in every case I have found that du Jarric used his authorities with fidelity, either literally translating, or carefully summarising. Except for an occasional reflection, or moral 'aside,' he never obtrudes himself on his readers. Errors of translation are here and there to be met with; but in a work covering close on two thousand five hundred quarto pages, compiled from materials written in at least four different languages, and available in many cases only in manuscript form, our wonder is, not that du Jarric made errors, but that he made so few.

In estimating the historical value of the *Histoire* it is necessary to bear in mind the purpose of the compiler, and the nature of the materials he had at his disposal, as well as the fact that accuracy of reproduction is not, in itself, a guarantee of the accuracy of the information reproduced. We may safely assume that du Jarric exercised as much care in the selection, as in the use of his authorities; but his choice was naturally determined by the object he had in view, which was to compile a history of the Jesuit Missions, not of the countries in which they were located. In defining the scope of his undertaking, he is careful to disclaim any intention of dealing exhaustively or precisely with the events and affairs of the outside world. In his *avant propos* (Part I, p. 10) he writes: 'Quant aux faicts-d'armes, & autres affaires d'estat, nous n'en traicterons point, sinon qu'il soit necessaire, pour entendre les choses qui concernent la religion: parce qu'il y a beaucoup d'autres qui se sont employez à cela avec grande loüange & fidelité.' His *Histoire*, therefore, is essentially a religious work, religious both in theme and treatment; and as such, and not as a treatise on general history, it must be regarded.

The account here reproduced of the Missions to the court of Akbar, is based on the letters of the Fathers by whom the Missions were conducted, and the reports sent to the General of the Society at Rome by the Provincials at Goa. The Fathers who resided at the Mogul court were men of learning and culture, and in most cases accomplished writers. They were also keen, shrewd, and, as far as their religious prejudices permitted, sympathetic observers. Had they, therefore, chosen to devote more attention to, and to write more fully of, the concerns of the empire, their letters would have held a place amongst the most valuable and the most authoritative of the world's historical records. But it was no part of their business to collect materials for a history of the reign of Akbar. Their mission was to convert that monarch to Christianity, and to sow the seed of the Gospel in his dominions; and to these aims their interests and their energies were almost wholly confined.

The range of their outlook naturally determined the range of their letters. These were written for the purpose of keeping the superiors of their Order in touch with the Missions, and informed as to the progress that was being made. They may, in fact, be described as progress reports, or collectively, as 'official correspondence.' The references they contain to the public affairs of the day are, in consequence, few in number, and relate, with rare exceptions, only to circumstances that came under the personal observation of the writers, or had a direct bearing on their lives, or the work of their calling. The information contained in such references is sometimes detailed and of great value: in other cases, and these are unfortunately the more numerous, it is disappointingly meagre and vague. In regard to matters that had no bearing on *les choses qui concernent la religion*, the Fathers were either altogether silent, or merely passed on, for what they were worth, any odds and ends of information that chanced to come their way.

For the student of Indian history, however, the outstanding interest of du Jarric's compilation lies not so much in the references it contains to contemporary events, as in the intimate light it sheds on the character and mind of Akbar, in the portraits it presents of the royal Princes and other notable figures of the time, and in the insight it affords into the general conditions of life under Mogul rule.

The Fathers had abundant opportunities of studying Akbar. Besides occupying a privileged position at the imperial court, they were in frequent and close attendance on his person. At the public assemblies they were assigned places very near his throne: they accompanied him on his campaigns: they educated his children: and they were often the companions of his leisure hours. On the occasions when they visited him in private, he frequently laid aside all reserve, opening, and even unburdening his heart to them, and discussing freely and frankly the various problems of life on which, in his more serious moments, he was wont to ponder. As a result of such constant and familiar intercourse, the Fathers came to know Akbar very thoroughly. They saw him in every variety of mood, and watched his behaviour under every variety of circumstance; and their impressions of him from one aspect or another, which are scattered through du Jarric's pages, make up a likeness that is at once complete and intimate. The *odium theologicum* has, it is true, left its lines across the picture; but these are too unmistakable to interfere seriously with our view: we see the real Akbar behind them as plainly as we see the lion through the bars of his cage.

Hardly less intimate is the portrait we get of Prince Salim; indeed, during the later chapters of his narrative, the beam of du Jarric's searchlight plays oftener on the Prince than on the King. If the portrait in this case interests us less, it is not through any fault in the drawing, but because the subject of it is less worth studying. From time to time, the beam traverses the great hall of audience, resting momentarily on other notable personages. Of these, especially of such men as Abul Fazl and Aziz Koka, we could have been well content to see more, and of the Prince less. But to the Fathers of the third Mission, the latter was the most important person in the empire. The goal of their desires was to see a Christian prince seated on the Mogul throne; and as the prospect of Akbar's conversion waxed dim, their attentions and their efforts became more and more concentrated on the son who was to succeed him.

Our glimpses of the world outside the purlieus of the court become more numerous as the story proceeds; for it was only after the despatch of the third Mission, that the spreading of the Gospel amongst the people at large was seriously taken in hand. A considerable portion of du Jarric's account of this Mission is devoted to stories of conversions, baptismal ceremonies, religious festivals, and other circumstances illustrating the work of evangelization, the progress made, and the difficulties encountered. These stories, though sometimes confused and rambling, and though the interest attaching to the incidents they describe is mainly religious, have a very real historical significance. As contemporary records, they are redolent of the atmosphere of the period. They familiarise us with the common sights and the little everyday occurrences which are seldom part of the stock-in-trade of the professional historian, but which do more than any thing else can do to bridge the gulf between the present and the past. Incidentally they bring us into touch with the administrative machinery of Akbar's kingdom, and introduce us to various types of state officials, such as Viceroys, Nawabs, Kotwals, Kazis, Eunuchs, etc., shedding many interesting sidelights on the duties they performed, and on the manner in which the law of the land was administered. At the same time they illustrate, better than any other part of the *Histoire*, the daily life and surroundings of the humbler classes of the people.

It is, therefore, as a guide to the spirit rather than to the events of the time, to the characters of men rather than to their actions, that du Jarric's account of the Missions to Akbar merits a high place amongst our authorities for the history of India. These were matters on which the Jesuit Fathers, both on account of their training and of their opportunities, were eminently qualified to enlighten us, and on which they wrote with knowledge gained from personal observation and experience. The scarcity of contemporary accounts of India in the days of Akbar lends additional importance to their letters, which not only give us information unobtainable from other sources, but contain the earliest impressions of the Mogul empire ever recorded by European writers; for the Fathers were the first, and with the exception of the English traveller Ralph Fitch, the only Europeans who visited Northern India in the sixteenth century. The letters likewise contain a considerable amount of miscellaneous information about current events. But, as already pointed out, the attitude of the Fathers towards the general affairs of the empire was one of indifference; and on this account, and for the reasons previously given, the *Histoire*, in so far as it relates to the action of the political drama of the period, needs to be read and used critically, and with caution.

The termination of the third Mission to the court of Akbar marked the close of the first and most interesting phase of the Jesuit campaign in Northern India. Whilst the Missions were in progress, the political element, which entered so largely into the later phases of the movement, though present, was in abeyance; and the Fathers who had charge of the Missions devoted themselves, as I have said above, almost exclusively to the work of evangelization. It may be presumed that, from the outset, they were expected to do anything they could to further the interests of their country at the Mogul court, and to pass on to Goa any information likely to be of use to the Portuguese authorities; but we have only to read the letters they wrote during this period to realise how completely their religious duties outweighed these and all other considerations.

The Portuguese authorities, whether at Goa or Lisbon, were by no means lacking in missionary zeal. Though fully alive to the political advantages which might accrue from the conversion of Akbar, they welcomed his appeal for instruction in the doctrines of Christianity as much for the religious as for the political opportunities which it offered; and had Akbar's conversion been a matter of no political concern whatever to them, we need not doubt that the

Missions would still have been despatched. It has been maintained that the Portuguese had, from the first, no belief in the conversion of Akbar, and that the object of the Missions was entirely political. I think du Jarric's narrative will convince the reader that neither of these views is tenable. There was both a religious and a political motive behind the Missions; and the existence of the latter in no way implies the insincerity of the former. As Mr. W. H. Moreland has rightly pointed out, it is this combination of religious and political motives which 'is the key to the activities of the Portuguese during the sixteenth century, and much of their conduct which is inexplicable from the traders' point of view finds an excuse, though not always a justification in the missionary zeal by which the rulers of the country were distinguished' (*India at the Death of Akbar*, p. 200).

Akbar's attitude towards the Missions closely resembled that of the Portuguese authorities. Like them, he was influenced by both religious and political motives, and the former were quite as strong and real in his case as in theirs. In his case, too, it may confidently be said, that if all political inducement had been lacking, he would still have invited the Fathers to his court. The Missions, however, did offer him political advantages, and he naturally welcomed them none the less on that account. Chief amongst these were the opportunities, or excuses, which they afforded him of sending letters and farmans to Goa, the bearers of which were able to bring him much useful intelligence regarding the state of affairs in the Portuguese settlements, towards which he had long been casting covetous eyes.

It cannot be said that Akbar's motives did him great credit, in as much as they were directly hostile to those whose friendship he was cultivating; but their baseness was appreciably discounted by the fact that he took little or no pains to conceal them. Looked at from his own point of view, his hostile attitude was neither unnatural nor unprovoked. As a race he held a high opinion of the Portuguese: he was strongly attracted by their religion; he admired their civilization; and he took delight in the society of their learned doctors. At the same time, he regarded them as intruders. Their domination of the Indian seas was a constant offence to him, and was rendered the more intolerable by the humiliating control which it enabled them to exercise over his maritime ventures. More than all, he resented their settlements on the outskirts of his territories, which effectually barred his access to the West Coast ports. In short, the Portuguese were a very troublesome thorn in Akbar's side, and one of the dearest wishes of his heart was to turn them neck and crop out of India.

The open participation of the Jesuit missionaries in political concerns commenced with the efforts made by the Fathers Xavier and Pinheiro to frustrate the plans of the English merchant-adventurer, Mildenhall, who visited Akbar's court in 1603, with the object of obtaining trading facilities for himself and his countrymen. In the reign of Jahangir, their employment in affairs of a kindred nature became a matter of course.

For this, the Portuguese authorities at Goa were mainly responsible. The aim of Portugal's Eastern policy at this period was not the acquisition of new territories, but the extension of her commerce; and the chief item in her programme was the capture, or, failing that, the control, of India's trade with Europe. It was a policy of greed; and its success depended on the ability of the Viceroys at Goa to win and retain the good-will of the Great Mogul, and to prevent its extension to other European countries. For the purpose of influencing the mind of the Emperor the Fathers were in a position of peculiar advantage; and hence it was largely on them that the task of securing these essential conditions devolved.

The use thus made of the Fathers, while it did little to retard the decay of Portuguese commerce, was wholly detrimental to the cause of the Gospel. Whatever progress that cause had hitherto made was the direct outcome of the purity of life, the singleness of purpose, and the fearless devotion exhibited by the pioneers of the missionary campaign. Such qualities have always commanded admiration in India; and it was their possession in a pre-eminent degree by Monserrate and Rudolf Aquaviva that enabled those Fathers to win the heart of Akbar, and the respect of his subjects, whether Moslim or Hindu. But a continuous supply of men of this stamp was not to be looked for; and the Fathers who followed them, though equally zealous for the spread of the faith, were not endowed with the same saintliness of character; while the work they were called upon to do in the political arena, and, it may be added, in a very unsavoury corner of that arena, was not conducive to the display of the nobler Christian virtues. The stories of Jesuit intrigues told by Mildenhall, Hawkins, Finch, and other travellers who found their way to the court of the Great Mogul, are probably overdrawn; but when all due allowance has been made for the bias of the writers, they leave little room for doubt that, in their endeavours to outwit these intruders, the Fathers had frequent recourse to measures which sorted ill with their religious calling, and which must have done much to discredit the Christian faith in the eyes of the people. From the time the Fathers openly assumed the rôle of political agents, their religious influence began steadily to wane. In the reign of Shah Jahan its decline was rapid; and before the end of the reign of Aurangzeb it had ceased to exist.

Akbar and the Jesuits

CHAPTER I[1]

Akbar, the Great Mogul

This beautiful, rich, and spacious province, which the Romans called *India citerior*, or *India intra Gangem* (India on this side of the Ganges), and which we call Indostan, is to-day in the possession (at least, for the most part) of a powerful monarch who is generally known as the Great Mogor,[2] his ancestors having been termed Mogores by the inhabitants of that part of India which first came under their sway.

This monarch is of the lineage of the great Tamerlane or Tamberlan, the Tartar king whom men have called the scourge of God; the same who, having made war upon Bajazet, the emperor of the Turcs, and first of that name, defeated him in a pitched battle, and having taken him prisoner, kept him, like some wild bird, in an iron cage, and fed him as though he had been a dog with the remnants from his own table. Similarly, when he wished to mount his horse, he compelled his captive to offer his back as a mounting-step, and for this purpose led him whithersoever he went by a chain of iron, or, as some say, of gold.[3]

From this man was descended, in a direct male line, he of whom we are about to speak. He was the seventh descendant [*sexiesme nepueu*[4]] of Tamerlan, or, as others say, the eighth king after him, which means the same thing. He was born in the province of Chaquata [Chaghatai],[5] which extends on the south to Indostan, on the west to Persia, and on the north to the country of the Tartars. Howbeit, the inhabitants resemble Turcs rather than Tartars or Persians, and, for the most part, they speak the language of the former, though not with the elegance and purity of the Turcs themselves. The gentlefolk, and others who follow the court, speak Persian, but their pronunciation differs from that of the Persians, and they use many foreign words. This king had a brother who was prince, or king of Cabul,[6] a kingdom lying to the north of Cambaya, between Persia and India, and which is believed by many to be the Arachosia[7] of the ancients. This is the sole kingdom which the successors of Tamberlan have retained in their possession, having been driven from all the other kingdoms, provinces, and principalities which their ancestors had conquered, though they afterwards regained some of these which they now hold, with the addition, as we shall presently see, of other newly acquired territories.

The immediate successors of the great Tamberlan, lacking the spirit and prowess of their ancestor, were unable to resist the repeated onslaughts of the Patanes (who are the same as the Parthes), and, in the end, were expelled from all their inherited possessions except the province or kingdom of Cabul. But the great-grandchildren and successors of the same, finding themselves driven to bay in a small corner of their ancestral domains, turned so fiercely on their enemies that they not only drove them from the countries of which they themselves had been dispossessed, but made themselves masters of all that now comprises the kingdom of the Great Mogor.

It was the king Baburxa [Babur Shah], grandfather of him of whom we are speaking, who invaded this part of Indostan, and driving the Parthes before him, confined them to the islands of Bengala.[8] But on the death of Baburxa, the Parthes regained their courage, and made fierce war upon his son Emmaupaxda [Humayun Padshah], attacking him with such vigour that he was driven back with dishonour to Cabul.

Seeing that he had no force capable of resisting such powerful enemies, Emmaupaxda appealed to the king of Persia[9] to aid him in the recovery of his estates and seignories. The Persian promised him assistance, provided that he was willing to embrace the law of Mahomet as taught by Hali,[10] which the Persians follow. Emmaupaxda having accepted this condition, the Persian king sent him many thousands of soldiers, with whose aid he recaptured all his father's possessions, driving the Parthes from every part of the Mogor kingdom. He was succeeded by him who is the subject of our present inquiry. The name of this king was Echebar, or, as some call it, Achebar, but, as we shall see, he styled himself in his royal letters, Mahumet Zelabdin Echebar [Muhammad Jalalu-d din Akbar].

Echebar continued the war which his predecessor

had waged against the Parthes (or Patanes, as they are now called in India). He invaded the kingdom of Bengala, of which they had taken possession, expelling them from all but a few islands; though, as we shall see, they subsequently gave him much trouble. He next captured Cambaya, and after that many other of the kingdoms of Indostan. He continued his conquests as long as he lived, so that his sway extended almost to the territories of the kings of Narsinga, Calecut, and other countries bordering the sea, even to the Island of Goa, so that he was greatly dreaded in all these lands. His court was attended by many kings, some of whom he had reduced by force of arms, while others had tendered their submission voluntarily, that they might not be deprived of their kingdoms. Sometimes as many as twenty kings were to be seen at his court, each having the right to wear a crown, and the least of whom was as powerful as the king of Calecut. Besides these, there are many others who stay in their kingdoms, and who, in order that they may be exempt from personal service, pay a larger tribute than those who attend at court. Some of these kings are Pagans, and others Mahometans; but Echebar, although he professed, at least outwardly the Mahometan faith, placed more trust in the former than the latter.

As to the limits of his empire, these cannot yet be stated with accuracy; for until the time of his death, which took place on the 27th of October, 1605, he was constantly making new conquests. We are told that in the year 1582 his territories stretched westward to the Indus, and further north to the confines of Persia. The eastern boundaries were the same as those of the kingdom of Bengala, of which he was master. On the north was Tartarie, and on the south the sea which washes the shores of Cambaya.[11] Nowhere else, except in Bengala, did his empire extend to the sea; for the kings of the Malabars, the Portuguese, the king of Narsinga,[12] and certain others, hold, in addition to their other possessions, all the maritime ports. The rest belongs to the great Mogor, whose territories, all included, are estimated to have been, at that time, six hundred leagues in length, and four hundred in breadth; but since then he has annexed the kingdom of Caximir [Kashmir], and several others.

The country is, for the most part, fruitful, producing the needs of life in abundance; for between the two famous rivers, the Indus and the Ganges, which wind over the greater portion of it, watering it like a garden, there are nine others which empty themselves into these two; namely, the Taphy [Tapti], the Heruada [Narbada], the Chambel, and the Tamona [Jumna], flowing into the Ganges,[13] and the Catamel [Sutlej], the Cebcha [Beas], the Ray [Ravi], the Chenao [Chenab], and the Rebeth [Jhilam], flowing into the Indus, which the people call the Schind. From this we can judge of the fertility of this region, and of the wealth of the great Mogor. For all the kingdoms and provinces which he conquers he holds as his own, appointing his captains, or the kings whom he has dispossessed, as his lieutenants over them. From these he takes a third portion of the revenues, the remainder being for their personal needs, and the maintenance of the soldiers, horses, and elephants which each of them is bound to keep in readiness for any emergency that may arise. The wealth of these provinces is increased by the extensive trade which is carried on in drugs, spices, pearls, and other precious things, and also in civet, cotton cloth, cloth of gold, woollen stuffs, carpets, velvet and other silken fabrics, as well as in every kind of metal. Horses also are brought in large numbers from Persia and Tartary.

But his military strength is even more formidable. For in the various provinces throughout his empire he has in his pay captains dependent on him, each of whom commands twelve or fourteen thousand horse. These they are compelled to maintain, as has already been stated, out of the revenues of the provinces which the king has assigned to them.[14] Besides these, there are others of inferior rank who maintain seven or eight thousand horse, as well as a number of elephants trained for warfare. The king has in his stables five thousand of these elephants, all ready to march at his will. As to the number of elephants in the whole of the kingdom, it has been estimated that he can put into the field fifty thousand, all well armed, in the manner about to be described.[15] In a war with his brother, the Prince of Cabul, who marched in great force against him, Echebar took the field with fifty thousand cavalry, all chosen men, and five thousand fighting elephants, besides innumerable infantry; and this is leaving out of account the thousands of followers, mounted and on foot, whom he left in garrisons, or in other places requiring protection. In time of war, he recruited his army from all classes of the people, Mogores, Coronans [Khurasanis], Parthes, Torquimaches, Boloches, Guzarates, and other Industans, whether Pagans or Mahometans.

He goes into battle with many pieces of artillery, which are placed in the front line. The elephants are kept in the rear, and are armed in the following fashion. To protect the head from blows, it is covered with a plate of iron, or tough hide. A sword is attached to the trunk, and a dagger to each of the long tusks which protrude from the mouth. Each animal bears on his back four small wooden turrets,[16] from which as many soldiers discharge their bows, arquebusses, or muskets. The driver is protected by a cuirass, or by plates of metal overlapping like scales. Elephants thus equipped are not placed in the front line, as they would shut out the enemy from the view of the soldiers, and would, when wounded, break the ranks of the soldiers, and throw the army into disorder. They are kept in the rear of the force; and should the enemy penetrate so far, this formidable troupe is brought suddenly into action, to bar his further progress. These beasts, even when unarmed, can do great damage. They seize with their trunks those whom they find in their path, and raising them in the air as high as they are able, dash them to the ground and trample them under their feet. At other times they attack with their iron-sheathed heads, butting after the manner of rams.

The city of Delhi had formerly been the residence

of the kings of Mogor. Echebar, however, first took up his abode at another city called Agra; and when two of his children died there,[17] he caused another city of great beauty to be built, which was named Pateful, or Fatefur. But after his conquest of the kingdom of Lahor, he made its capital city, Lahor, his usual residence.

It was in the year 1582[18] that his court was first visited by Fathers of the Company. He was then about forty years of age, of medium stature, and strongly built.[19] He wore a turban on his head, and the fabric of his costume was interwoven with gold thread. His outer garment reached to his knees, and his breeches to his heels. His stockings were much like ours; but his shoes were of a peculiar pattern invented by himself. On his brow he wore several rows of pearls or precious stones. He had a great liking for European clothes; and sometimes it was his pleasure to dress himself in a costume of black velvet made after the Portuguese fashion[20]; but this was only on private, not on public occasions. He had always a sword at his side, or at any rate so near by that he could lay his hand upon it in a moment. Those who guarded his person, and whom he kept constantly near him, were changed each day of the week, as were his other officers and attendants, but in such a manner that the same persons came on duty every eighth day.

Echebar possessed an alert and discerning mind; he was a man of sound judgment, prudent in affairs, and, above all, kind, affable, and generous. With these qualities he combined the courage of those who undertake and carry out great enterprises. He could be friendly and genial in his intercourse with others, without losing the dignity befitting the person of a king. He seemed to appreciate virtue, and to be well disposed towards foreigners, particularly Christians, some of whom he always liked to have about him. He was interested in, and curious to learn about many things, and possessed an intimate knowledge not only of military and political matters, but of many of the mechanical arts. He took delight in watching the casting of pieces of artillery, and in his own palace kept workmen constantly employed in the manufacture of guns and arms of various descriptions. In short, he was well informed on a great variety of matters, and could discourse on the laws of many sects, for this was a subject of which he made a special study. Although he could neither read nor write, he enjoyed entering into debate with learned doctors. He always entertained at his court a dozen or so of such men, who propounded many questions in his presence. To their discussions, now on one subject, now on another, and particularly to the stories which they narrated, he was a willing listener, believing that by this means he could overcome the disadvantage of his illiteracy.

Echebar was by temperament melancholy, and he suffered from the falling-sickness;[21] so that to divert his mind, he had recourse to various forms of amusement, such as watching elephants fight together, or camels, or buffaloes, or rams that butt and gore each other with their horns, or even two cocks. He was also fond of watching fencing bouts; and on certain occasions, after the manner of the ancient Romans, he made gladiators fight before him; or fencers were made to contend until one had killed the other.[22] At other times, he amused himself with elephants and camels that had been trained to dance to the tune of certain musical instruments, and to perform other strange feats. But in the midst of all these diversions —and this is a very remarkable thing—he continued to give his attention to affairs of state, even to matters of grave importance.

Often he used to hunt the wild animals that abound in these regions. For this purpose he employed panthers[23] instead of hunting-dogs; for in this country panthers are trained to the chase as we train dogs. He did not care much for hawking, though he had many well-trained falcons and other birds of prey; and there were some expert falconers amongst his retainers. Some of these were so skilful with the bow that they very rarely missed a bird at which they shot, even though it was on the wing, and though their arrows were unfeathered.

To catch wild deer he used other deer which had been trained for this purpose. These carried nets on their horns in which the wild deer that came to attack them became entangled, upon which they were seized by the hunters who had been lying in concealment near by. When on a military campaign, he used to hunt in the following manner. Four or five thousand men were made to join hands and form a ring round a piece of jungle. Others were then sent inside to drive the animals to the edge of the enclosure, where they were captured by those forming the ring. A fine

PLATE III

THE CHEETA'S SPRING
A hunting scene from the *Akbarnama*

[face p. 10

was levied on those who fled [illegible] without [illegible] through [illegible] escape.

So much for the King's treatment [illegible] turn to [illegible] matters. [illegible] perhaps be able to [illegible] Mogul. [illegible] Echebar appeared [illegible] daily [illegible] audience to all classes [illegible] made use of two large [illegible] which was placed [illegible] throne. [illegible] access, and there [illegible] with him. But [illegible] the customs [illegible] ambassadors, who came [illegible] with him on affairs [illegible] men of experience and good [illegible] stant attendance on him. [illegible] tioned the days of the week [illegible] special day for [illegible] audience. [illegible] tials of all [illegible] ceremony [illegible] were foreigners [illegible] and how [illegible] on these occasions [illegible] the custom [illegible] the king on [illegible] king is also [illegible] duty is [illegible] This is a custom [illegible] Persia, and other eastern [illegible] was levied on those who allowed an animal to break through and escape.

So much for the king's recreations. We will now turn to more serious matters. That any person might be able to speak to him on business of importance, Echebar appeared twice daily in public, and gave audience to all classes of his subjects. For this purpose he made use of two large halls of his palace, in each of which was placed on a raised dais a splendid and costly throne. To the first of these halls all his subjects had access, and there he listened to all who sought speech with him. But to the second none was admitted but the captains and great nobles of his kingdom, and the ambassadors who came from foreign kings to confer with him on affairs of importance. Eight officers, men of experience and good judgment, were in constant attendance on him. Amongst these he apportioned the days of the week, so that each had his special day for introducing those who desired an audience.[24] It was their duty to examine the credentials of all such persons, and to act as masters of ceremony, instructing them, more especially if they were foreigners, how to make reverence to the king, and how to comport themselves in his presence; for on these occasions much ceremony is observed, it being the custom, amongst other things, to kiss the feet of the king on saluting him. When giving audience, the king is also attended by a number of secretaries, whose duty is to record in writing every word that he speaks.[25] This is a custom much practised by the princes of Persia, and other eastern countries.

For the administration of justice, there are magistrates whose judgement is final, and others from whom there is an appeal. In every case the proceedings are verbal, and are never committed to writing.

The king of whom we are speaking made it his particular care that in every case justice should be strictly enforced. He was, nevertheless, cautious in the infliction of punishment, especially the punishment of death. In no city where he resided could any person be put to death until the execution warrant had been submitted to him, some say, as many as three times. His punishments were not, ordinarily, cruel; though it is true that he caused some who had conspired against his life to be slain by elephants, and that he sometimes punished criminals by impalement after the Turkish fashion. A robber or sea-pirate, if he had killed no one, suffered the loss of a hand; but murderers, highwaymen, and adulterers were either strangled or crucified [*attachez en croix*],[26] or their throats were cut, according to the gravity of their crimes. Lesser offenders were whipped and set free. In brief, the light of clemency and mildness shone forth from this prince, even upon those who offended against his own person. He twice pardoned an officer high in his service, who had been convicted of treason and conspiracy, graciously restoring him to favour and office. But when the same officer so far forgot himself as to repeat his offence a third time, he sentenced him to death by crucifixion.[27]

Echebar seldom lost his temper. If he did so, he fell into a violent passion; but his wrath was never of long duration. Before engaging in any important undertaking, he used to consult the members of his council; but he made up his own mind, adopting whatever course seemed to him the best. Sometimes he communicated his intentions to his councillors, to ascertain their views. If they approved, they would answer with the words "Peace be to our lord the King." If anyone expressed an adverse opinion, he would listen patiently, answer his objections, and point out the reasons for his own decision. Sometimes, in view of the objections pointed out to him, he changed the plans he had made. Persian is the language usually spoken at his court, but learned men and the priests of Mahomet speak Arabic.

This is what we have been able to ascertain about the Great Mogor and his state.

CHAPTER II[1]

The First Mission to Mogor

That we may the better understand the motives which led the Great Mogor to summon the Fathers of the Company from Goa, we must bear in mind that the Viceroy in India of the Portuguese king, had, in the year 1578, sent as ambassador to his court a Portuguese gentleman named Antoine Cabral,[2] who was accompanied by several others of the same nation. Whilst they were at his court, Echebar closely watched their behaviour and manner of life, gaining thereby some idea of other adherents of the Christian religion, of which he had heard so much. He was very favourably impressed by what he saw of these persons; and showed himself so anxious to know something of the law they followed, that the ambassador did his best to explain to him its main principles, telling him also of the Fathers of the Company who were preaching it in India. The King had already heard of two Fathers of the same society who had gone in the year 1576 to the kingdom of Bengala,[3] and he had been told that there were in India many others of the same order who were labouring to spread the law of Jesus-Christ in all the countries of the East. Finally a certain Portuguese, named Pierre Tauero,[4] a man of substance and intelligence, who had for some years resided at his court, enlightened him still further on certain aspects of the Christian law, with the result that, being told of a Christian priest, renowned for the sanctity of his life, who was then in his kingdom of Bengala, he sent for him forthwith, that he might receive from him a complete exposition of the faith which he professed.

About the month of March in the year 1578, the good priest, whose name I have not discovered,[5] reached Pateful, where the King then held his court, and was received with much kindness. It was not long before his Majesty told him the reason why he had sent for him, which was, he said, that he might clear his mind of certain doubts which prevented him from deciding whether it was better to follow the law of the Christians or the law of Mahomet. The priest, accordingly, expounded to him the main principles of our faith, at the same time opening his eyes to the worthlessness of the law of Mahomet.

Echebar heard these things with evident gladness; and so strongly was he moved to abandon his faith that, one evening while conversing with his Caziques,[6] or Mullas, as the priests of the Mahometan religion are called, he told them frankly that he had decided to follow the counsel of the good priest, and pray to God for light to see the truth, and the path to salvation. At this discussion, his Soldan of Mecque[7] [Mecca], the chief of all his Mullas or Caziques, was present, who, the moment these words fell from the King's lips, said, "Your Majesty follows a good law, and has no reason to doubt it, or to seek another." On hearing this, the King rose to his feet and exclaimed, " May God help us! May God help us!" repeating the words as if to imply that he was far from satisfied with the law that he followed, and that he would gladly have knowledge of a better.

A few days later, he asked the same priest to teach him to speak Portuguese; for he had a great desire (or so he said) to know that tongue, that he might the better understand his exposition of the Christian law. This the priest commenced to do with much care and zeal; and the first word that he taught the King was the sweet name of Jesus. The King found such pleasure in this holy word that he repeated it at each step as he walked up and down in his house.

One evening the same priest was disputing with the Mullas in the royal ante-chamber, while the King sat listening in his private apartment. In the course of the dispute, the priest said that the law of Mahomet was a tissue of errors and lies. This so enraged the Mullas that they were on the point of laying violent hands on him when the King entered and restrained them, appeasing their anger by telling them that it was no unusual thing for one engaged in a disputation to hold his own views to be true, and those of his adversaries to be false.

While conversing with the King, the priest told him one day that there were in the town of Goa some very learned and holy Fathers, who had spread a knowledge of Jesus-Christ in many parts of India; and that if he would communicate his doubts to them, he would learn from them, much better than from himself, all that he desired to know touching the Christian faith, in as much as they were much more learned in the holy scriptures. This made the King very anxious to see and know those of whom he spoke; and not long afterwards he sent an ambassador to India, with a letter addressed to the Fathers of the Company residing at Goa, which, translated into our own language, was to the following effect:—

'Forman of Zelabdin Mahemet Echebar. Reverend Fathers of the Order of Saint Paul:[8] Be it known to you that, holding you in great esteem, I am sending you my ambassador Ebadola, and his interpreter Dominique Briz,[9] to beg you to send to me two Fathers, learned in the scriptures, who shall bring with them the principal books of the law, and of the Gospels; for I have a great desire to become acquainted with this law and its perfection. I earnestly enjoin you not to hinder their coming with these same ambassadors as soon as they shall reach you. Know, also, that the Fathers who shall come here will be received by me with all honour, and that it will be a peculiar pleasure to me to see them. If, after I have been instructed as I desire in their law and its perfection, they wish to return, they will be free to do so whenever it shall seem good to them, and I shall despatch them with great respect and honour. Let them not hesitate to come, for they will be under my care and protection.'

The ambassador and his interpreter having arrived at Goa,[10] delivered the letter of the King to the priests of the said Company dwelling at the college of Saint Paul, who rejoiced greatly at the good news, believing that it was the will of our Lord to manifest to this great Prince the abundance of his mercy and goodness; and each one of them desired the happiness of being sent to him. But the Father Provincial, after submitting the matter to God with many prayers, chose and named for the work the following Fathers, to wit:—the Father Rodolfe Aquauiua,[11] the lawful son of the Duke of Atria, brother of Cardinal Aquauiua, and nephew of R. P. Claude Aquauiua, now General of the same Company; the Father Antoine de Monserrat,[12] who was afterwards despatched to Aethiopie, and was enslaved by the Turcs, as has been narrated in the third book; and the Father François Henriqués.[13]

Having set out from Goa in the company of the ambassador and his interpreter, the three Fathers arrived after twenty days at Surraté, which is a port of the kingdom of Cambaya, above the town of Daman, and which belongs to the Great Mogor. At last, on the 18th day of February in the year 1580, after passing through many difficulties and dangers, they reached the imperial court, then located at Pateful [Fathpur], their entire journey having occupied forty-three days.[14] So great was the King's anxiety to see them that, during this period (as they subsequently learnt), he constantly calculated the number of days necessary for the completion of their journey, and repeatedly asked those about him when they would arrive. The moment he heard that they had come, he summoned them to his palace, where he received them with many marks of friendship, and entertained them in various ways until far into the night. Before they took their leave, a large quantity of gold and silver was brought to be presented to them. The Fathers thanked him very respectfully, but would not take any of the money, courteously excusing themselves on the ground of their calling. As for their livelihood, for which the King urged them to accept what he offered them, they said that it was sufficient happiness for them to enjoy his favour, and that they trusted to God to supply their daily needs. The King was much impressed by their refusal of the money, and for a long time could talk to his courtiers of nothing else.

Three or four days later, the Fathers again visited the King, who received them as cordially as on the first occasion. As he had asked to be shown the books of the law of the Creator (meaning thereby the holy Scriptures), the Fathers took with them and presented to him all the volumes of the Royal Bible, in four languages,[15] sumptuously bound, and clasped with gold. The King received these holy books with great reverence, taking each into his hand one after the other and kissing it, after which he placed it on his head, which, amongst these people, signifies honour and respect. He acted thus in the presence of all his courtiers and captains, the greater part of whom were Mahometans. Afterwards he inquired which of these books contained the Gospels; and when it was pointed out to him, he looked at it very intently, kissed it a second time, and placed it as before on his head. He then gave orders to his attendants that the books were to be conveyed to his own apartment, and ordered a rich cabinet to be made for their reception. The Fathers also presented to him two beautiful portraits, one representing the Saviour of the world, and the other the glorious Virgin Mary, his holy Mother. The latter was a copy of that in the church of Notre Dame la Maieur, in Rome.[16] The King took the portrait of our Saviour in his hands with great reverence, and before putting it down kissed it, and made his children, and several of his courtiers who were present, do the same.

Some time afterwards, he again sent for the Fathers, summoning at the same time his Mullas and Caziques, in order that they might dispute together in his presence, so that he might discover which were in truth the holy scriptures on which to place his faith. The Fathers clearly established the authenticity and truth of the scriptures contained in the Old and New Testaments, laying bare at the same time the falsehoods and fallacies with which the Koran is filled. This first dispute ended in the complete discomfiture of the Mullas and Caziques, who, unable to find any answer to the arguments of the Fathers, took refuge in silence.[17] The King appeared well satisfied with what he had heard; and, after the conference, told the Fathers that their law seemed to him to be good; but that he desired them to explain to him the mystery of the holy Trinity, and how God could have had a son who became a man; for these were the greatest difficulties he found in our belief. The Fathers gave him the explanations for which he asked, and with these he seemed for a time to be satisfied, though not wholly so; for afterwards he advised them to be on their guard when they spoke before the Saracens, " because," he said, " they are not capable of understanding so holy a doctrine as this which you preach."

The priests had brought with them the Koran of Mahomet translated into the Portuguese language, that they might be the better able to refute its errors and demonstrate the false and contradictory statements which it contained, which, by this means, and with the help of their interpreter, they did very effectively.

Three days after the first dispute, another took place concerning the paradise which the Mahometan law promises to its followers. The Fathers assailed the infamous and carnal paradise of Mahomet with arguments so clear and convincing that the Mullas blushed for shame, not knowing what to say in reply. The King, seeing their perplexity, essayed to take up their cause; but he was as little able as they to disprove the incongruities that had been pointed out.

On the Tuesday following, they entered on a third dispute with the Mullas, dealing with the pride and state of Mahomet and the irregularities of his life, all of which they contrasted with the humility and purity of life of Jesus-Christ; and in a like manner they contrasted the truth of the Christian doctrine, which a thousand miracles has confirmed, and the holiness of those who have proclaimed it to the world, with the fables and inconsistencies of the law of Mahomet, which has been spread abroad by means of the sword. In this dispute the Mullas were again put to confusion; and they never, from that time, had the hardihood to meet the Fathers in debate. The latter, however, were treated by the King with the same kindness as before.

The Fathers now became anxious to ascertain what effect these disputes had had on the King, and whether the adoption of the Christian faith was a step that he was seriously deliberating. They accordingly made their way to the palace, the fact that they had not seen the King for some days affording a sufficient excuse for their visit. He received them with his accustomed courtesy and good-will. After some conversation on general subjects, the Fathers begged him to give them private audience; and when this was granted, Father Rodolfe Aquauiua, who was the superior of the others, thus addressed him:—" Your Majesty wrote a letter to our R.P. Provincial demanding that some Fathers of the Company should be sent to you to expound the law of God. We three have, accordingly, been sent; and we count it a peculiar happiness that God has led us to a Prince who is so powerful, and who desires so earnestly to know the divine law. This happiness was intensified when you made known to us that you had no other desire in the world but to discover and to embrace the true law. Our thoughts have been given day and night to this matter, and the means of attaining the end for which we have been sent here; and after earnest consideration, and continual prayers to God for guidance, it seems to us fitting that your Majesty should now, for the sake of your temporal and spiritual welfare, the preservation of your life, the increase of your dominions, the comfort of your conscience, and the salvation of your soul, set apart a time for hearing the interpretation of the divine law, and that, recognizing it to be true, and that there is no other which leads to salvation, your Majesty should adopt it as your own, and renounce that which is preached in all your kingdoms and provinces." In reply to these words, the King said that the matter was in the hands of God, who possessed the power to accomplish what they desired; and that, for his part, there was nothing in the world he desired more. By what he said, he gave them to understand that there were weighty reasons why he should not, at that juncture, declare himself a Christian.

At another time the same Father Aquauiua came to present to the King his *bonne Pasques*, or Easter gift, it being the evening of the resurrection of our Saviour. His Majesty was greatly pleased thereat. He showed the Father much honour, detaining him in conversation until late in the night. He asked him many questions, chiefly concerning the mystery of the Revelation, and also inquired what rules the Christians observed when they made prayers to God. These and other questions having been answered, he dismissed him with much kindness.

CHAPTER III[1]

'What is Truth?'

Sometime after these visits and disputes, Echebar, learning that the house in which the Fathers were lodged was inconvenient for them, owing to the din and bustle of the crowded thoroughfare in which it was situated, provided a more suitable residence for them within the precincts of his own palace. He did this partly from a desire to have them near at hand, so that he could visit them more often, or send for them whenever he wished, or had leisure to see them.

In this lodging the Fathers fitted up, as well as they could, a small chapel, in which they held divine service; and here, on several occasions, they were visited by the King. His Majesty entrusted his second son to them that they might teach him Portuguese, and to read and write after the European style, at the same time instructing him in the mysteries of the Christian faith. It may here be mentioned that in the year 1582, when these Fathers were at his court, Echebar had three sons and two daughters. The eldest son, who has since succeeded him on the throne, was then about 17 or 18 years of age.[2] His proper name was Scieco [*Shaikhu*]; but he was always known as Sciecogio, the word Gio [*Ji*] being added as a title of honour, just as in certain parts of Europe the word

Dom is placed before the names of persons of rank or distinction. In the language of these people, Gio signifies 'soul'; so that Sciecogio is equivalent to the soul, or the person, of Scieco. The second son, whose name was Pahari, was 13 years of age. It was he who was placed under the Fathers to learn Portuguese and the rudiments of Christianity, to the study of which he showed himself well inclined. He was a lad of considerable promise, being both intelligent and docile.[3] The last of the three was called Dan, which is the same as Daniel.

But, to resume. On one occasion, the King, having come to see what his son was learning, bade him read aloud to him the exercise which the Fathers had given him to write. The exercise commenced with the words 'In the name of God,' on hearing which his Majesty at once told him to add the words 'and of Jesus Christ the true prophet and son of God'; and this was done then and there in his presence.[4] He then entered the chapel, where the Fathers daily said mass for the benefit of the Portuguese connected with the court; for there were several who had made their homes in this country, and others who had journeyed there for the purpose of trade. The King entered the oratory unaccompanied by any of his guards or courtiers, and having removed his turban from his head, fell upon his knees and prayed, first of all in our fashion, then in his own, that is to say, after the manner of the Saracens of Persia, whose law he still outwardly observed, and lastly in the fashion of the Gentiles. "God," he said, as he rose from his devotions, "ought to be adored with every kind of adoration." After that, he seated himself on a cushion on the floor; and when the Fathers had also seated themselves, he told them that he did not doubt that our law was the best of all, and that he beheld something more than human in the life and miracles of Jesus-Christ; but that it was beyond his comprehension how God could have a son. On a subsequent visit, after talking on sundry topics, he said: "Fathers, you have, by your discourses, taught me many things about your law, which please me more than all that I have been able to learn of other laws, whether of the Saracens, or the Gentiles; and, for my part, I regard the law of the Saracens as worse than any other."

Eight days later, he again came to the oratory, accompanied this time by his three sons, and some of the chief nobles of his court. For a while he stood apart, looking attentively at the various objects in the chapel, and expressing his admiration of them in the presence of his courtiers. He then removed his shoes from his feet, and ordered his sons and all who were with him to do likewise, this being the custom observed by Moslims when entering their mosques. He showed great reverence for the pictures of our Saviour and the blessed Virgin, and even for those of other saints; and he ordered his painter to make copies of those which the Fathers had placed in their chapel. He also ordered his goldsmith to make for him a casket of gold with a richly carved lid, similar in shape to the copper casket in which the Fathers carried the images of our Saviour and the Virgin. Before leaving, he told the Fathers that their law appealed to him very strongly; but that there were two points in it which he could not comprehend, namely, the Trinity and the Incarnation. If they could explain these two things to his satisfaction, he would, he said, declare himself a Christian, even though it cost him his kingdom.[5]

Although his mind was not wholly made up, he used every endeavour to implant in those who served him an admiration for the Christian law, which he preached to them himself, extolling it on all occasions, and manifesting his strong desire that many should embrace it. Sometimes he would spend the entire day maintaining, in debate with his Mullas, the inferiority of the law of Mahomet. The Mullas are very ignorant, and can neither defend their own false prophet, nor render reason for the things that are written in his Koran. They admit, and accept as inspired scriptures, the Books of Moses, the Psalms of David, and the Evangels. But these they are expressly forbidden by Mahomet either to possess, or to read.[6] The Fathers were, therefore, able to convict them out of their own mouths. For if, said they, your Koran is an inspired book, there ought to be no antagonism between it and the Books of Moses, the Psalms of David, and the Evangels, which you admit to be inspired; for if there is antagonism, it is certain that one or the other must be false. And since you hold it to be blasphemy to say that there is any falsehood in the Books of Moses, the Psalms of David, and the Evangels, it must necessarily follow that your Koran is false, since it is in so many points antagonistic to these books.

The force of these arguments was not loſt upon the King, who ceased to have any respect for the law of Mahomet, or for his Mullas, and openly declared as much. At the same time, his respect for the law of Christianity increased, and he favoured those who followed it in every way he could. Amongst the latter, there were in his country some who had been enslaved by his subjects,[7] and who, to regain their freedom, had renounced the Christian faith (for very often the Saracens offer liberty to the Christians whom they capture, on condition that they abandon their faith). It happened at this time that some of the latter desired to revert to their own religion, and, that they might be able to practise the same without molestation, begged from the King permission to return to their own country, that they might live amongst Christians. His Majesty at once granted their request; and when one of them expressed a desire to remain in Indostan, he not only permitted him to live and clothe himself after the Christian manner, but received him into the service of his own household.

It was about this time that, at the request of the Fathers, he gave permission that a certain Portuguese, who had died, should be given a public funeral with Christian rites, that is to say, with lighted candles, and preceded by the cross. The funeral procession passed through the middle of the city, to the great wonderment of the infidels, who were strongly impressed by reverent respect shown by the Portuguese towards their dead; and many even of the Saracens uttered prayers for the deceased, and offered to assist in the interment.[8]

But although such acts as these seemed to show that the King held the Christian faith in high esteem, there were, nevertheless, many things which stood in the way of his embracing it. The first was his unwillingness to accept the doctrines of the Trinity and the Incarnation without being able to comprehend them; so that he was kept in a state of perpetual irresolution, not knowing where to fix his faith. "For the Gentiles," he said, "regard their law as good; and so likewise do the Saracens and the Christians. To which then shall we give our adherence?" Thus we see in this Prince the common fault of the atheist, who refuses to make reason subservient to faith, and, accepting nothing as true which his feeble mind is unable to fathom, is content to submit to his own imperfect judgement matters transcending the highest limits of human understanding.

Another obstacle consisted in the innumerable duties and occupations in which he was generally plunged. These left him little leisure for private meditation, and made it impossible for the Fathers to find convenient opportunities for explaining to him the doctrines of our faith with the fullness and exactness that they demanded. To overcome this obstacle, the Fathers put before him the example of certain Kings and Princes of Iapon, who, having no leisure during the day for self-examination and religious instruction, set apart for that purpose a considerable portion of the night. But though he signified his readiness to follow this example, he never did so. He also had this bad habit: whilst one of his questions was being answered, he would suddenly, and before there had been time to deal with it, ask another. He had not the patience to hear one explanation at a time; but in his eagerness for knowledge, tried to learn everything at once, like a hungry man trying to swallow his food at a single gulp.

But, in the eyes of many, that which constituted the greatest hindrance to his conversion to our faith was the multitude of wives which the Mahometan law permitted him to keep. There were in his seraglio as many as a hundred women; and it was doubtful if he would ever be willing to renounce all of these but one, and to live with that one in lawful wedlock, as the Christian law demands.

Lastly, he had a great desire to witness a miracle; and several times he suggested that, to prove which of the two laws was the better, that of the Christians or that of the Saracens, the Fathers and the Mullas, the former holding their holy scriptures, and the latter their Koran, should enter a fire together, and those who were not burnt should be regarded as the possessors of the true law. But it was pointed out to him that it would be presumptuous, and only tempting God, to act thus without His special sanction; and, in the end, the King was convinced by their reasoning, and gave up the idea of this strange test.[9]

But notwithstanding all these things, many began to desire a knowledge of the religion for which the King displayed so much admiration, and whose priests he held in such high esteem. Amongst others, one of his own priests, named Abdulfasil, a man greatly beloved by his Majesty, who looked upon him as a kind of Grand Chaplain, expressed a desire to be instructed in the Christian faith; though whether he did so with a view to embracing it, or in order to please the King, and to be able to discuss it with him on suitable occasions, no one can say. However this may be, the King, on hearing of his desire, treated him with increased affection, and told the Fathers that they could talk with him on any matter they chose with as much confidence, and as freely, as though they were talking to himself. And, in fact, Abdulfasil performed many kind offices for the Fathers, as we shall see later. Another who manifested a desire for enlightenment was the King's physician; and he, too, took every opportunity that presented itself of showing his good-will towards the Fathers.[10]

Seeing that the King remained irresolute, and in order that their time might not be wasted, the Fathers began to devote themselves to the conversion of others; and, to this end, begged permission to baptise all those who desired to become Christians. This his Majesty willingly granted; and sent word to them by Abdulfasil that he was willing they should convert as many as they could; and that if any should attempt to interfere with them in this, they should inform him, and he would cause such persons to be punished according to their deserts. He also gave them permission to build, out of the charitable offerings of the Portuguese, a hospital for the sick. For it had been found in many places that both Pagans and Saracens were frequently persuaded to embrace Christianity, by witnessing the charitable deeds of its followers.

These and other means adopted to advance the glory of God, together with the King's affection for the Fathers, and his favourable treatment of Christians, aroused in many of those who served his Majesty a desire to embrace the Christian faith. Indeed, so great was the number of catechumens enrolled, that the Fathers were scarce able to undertake their instruction. But it was then that the Devil, ever working against the salvation of mankind, set himself to shuffle the cards, and, to prevent the reaping of this rich harvest, stirred into rebellion against the King the Parthes, or Patanes, who, as we have already told, had been confined to the islands of Bengala.

These people having heard (as they said afterwards, in excuse for their revolt) that it was the King's intention to abandon the law of his ancestors, that is to say, Mahometanism, and to follow another, raised a rebellion in the kingdom of Bengala, killing the Viceroy, or Governor, whom the King had placed there.[11] They had also, it was said, negotiated with the King's half-brother, the Prince of Chabul, who simultaneously invaded the other side of his kingdom, which he penetrated with a large army to a distance of three hundred leagues.

These events greatly perturbed the King; while his Mullas, who were fallen so low in his credit, were quick to interpret them as a punishment for his contempt of themselves and their law. This, and much more to the same effect, which the Mullas daily poured into his ears, made so strong an impression on him, that he began little by little to avoid the company of the Fathers, and to abate his former enthusiasm for the Christian faith. His changed attitude was plainly shown; for he refused to see the Fathers when they came to condole with him on the loss of the kingdom of Bengala; and for a period of some months they were not once summoned to his presence.[12]

The King marched to meet his brother at the head of 50,000 horse, and 5000 fighting elephants, besides infantry too numerous to be estimated.[13] Seeing so vast a force coming against him, his brother gradually withdrew. The King followed him, continuing the pursuit till he had shut him up in his own territories, which were on the other side of the Indus. After this, he put down without difficulty the revolt stirred up by the Patanes in Bengala.

When, after the pacification of his dominions, he returned to his capital, the Fathers requested him, through his chaplain Abdulfasil, to inform them whether he desired to be more fully instructed in matters touching our faith, in as much as it was to this end that they had been sent to him, and they counted their time as wasted when it was not employed in ministering to his spiritual welfare. After some days had passed, the King sent for them; but all that he did was to ask them a number of questions of a curious, rather than of a profitable nature. At last, the Fathers suggested that, as the previous disputes had not made clear to him the difference between the law of Jesus-Christ and that of Mahomet, he should again arrange a public debate between themselves and the Mullas, so that he might be able to make up his mind once for all which was the better religion to follow. This suggestion was not greatly to the King's liking, for he feared the Mullas would again be defeated; but as the Fathers urged him very strongly, he assigned the coming Saturday for the dispute.

On this day, at the hour arranged, the Fathers went to the palace; but the King, who had no desire that the conference should take place, announced, with many excuses, his inability to be present. In a short time, however, he realised that he had done wrong to break his promise; and, to repair his mistake, gave orders that the debate should be held on the Monday following. On this occasion, he not only attended himself, but brought with him all the Captains and lords of his court, besides a large number of his Mullas. The latter strove to uphold their false prophet; but they were so hard pressed by the Fathers, that they were able neither to explain his sayings in the Koran, nor to maintain what they advanced in his defence. The King, perceiving the futility of their arguments, tried to bring his own knowledge into play, and to cover their shame; but he too was put to equal confusion, with the result that almost all who were present saw clearly the false and impious character of the Mahometan law.

CHAPTER IV[1]

Father Rudolf Aquaviva

Seeing the earnestness with which the King, in this last dispute, had defended his Mullas and their law, the Fathers realized how greatly he was changed, and decided to ask his permission to return to Goa, whence he had called them. This was tactfully done by Father Rodolfe. " I do not doubt," he said to the King, " that your Majesty has a great desire to hear the interpretation of the true law, and also to embrace it; but you consider it would be unwise to alarm your subjects by making this known. This being the case, it seems to us that our labours at your court are no longer as profitable as they were at first." The King at once understood his meaning, and said that he derived great pleasure from having them at his court, and that in speaking thus they were only seeking an excuse for going away. The Father replied that his Majesty knew from experience that it was their desire to serve him; and that if it would please him to listen earnestly to their interpretation of the divine law, it would be a great happiness to them to remain in his territories. To that the King made no answer; but withdrew without a word to his chamber, evidently much displeased at their desire to return.

As the Fathers were anxious to know the reason why

the King wished them to remain at his court, since he showed no intention of embracing the Christian faith, they put the question to Abdulfasil. In reply, the chaplain gave them to understand that the King, having a desire for all kinds of knowledge, and liking to show his greatness, delighted to have at his court people of all nations; and that he was particularly pleased with them, the Fathers, both on account of their conduct, and their law, which appealed to him more than any other. He told them also that on the day previous he had taken the Holy Bible which they had given to him, and with great reverence had placed it on his head, adding that he had not done the same with the book of Mahomet, which had been presented to him on the same day, and which was far more richly bound.

With their hopes partially revived by these words, the Fathers sought by every means they could think of, to bind the King's affections anew to the Christian faith. When they saw that his anger, which the suggestion of their departure had kindled, was abated, they intimated to him that they would again instruct the princes, his sons, in the Portuguese language, if such were his pleasure. The King gladly consented to this proposal; and the work of instruction was entrusted to Father Antoine Monserrat. His Majesty came often to see what his sons were learning; and this led to renewed intercourse with the Fathers, who were, thereby, able to regain his friendship and esteem. It is very true, however, that when the conversation turned on matters relating to the divine law, he displayed little of his former interest; for he had been greatly disturbed by the ideas which the Mullas had put into his head at the time of the Patane revolt in Bengala. Furthermore, though convinced in his own mind that the law of the Evangelists was superior to all others, he was still held in bondage by the vicious customs and licentious indulgences to which the law of Mahomet gives its sanction.

The Saracens, seeing that he was again drawn towards our religion, showed a disposition to rise against him; and his mother, his aunt, and many of the great lords of the kingdom who attended him, left no stone unturned to discredit the Fathers and their teaching. This they considered themselves bound to do out of loyalty to their sect; while they were further incited thereto by their natural hatred of the Christian religion, which they denounced to the King as the basest and most worthless in the world. His bevy of wives followed their example; for they realised that all of them, save one only, would be abandoned if the King became a Christian; and all their arts and blandishments were employed to divert him from such a step. Finally, his long excursions, the recreations in which he indulged each day, and, more than all, the many urgent affairs of state which demanded his attention, allowed him no opportunities for meditating on his spiritual welfare.

Whilst matters were in this state, the Fathers received a letter from the Father Provincial of India, in which he commanded their return to Goa; since he was desirous, as they could accomplish nothing where they were, to employ them on other enterprises for the advancement of the glory of God. Father Rudolf Aquauiua, having received this letter, took it to the King, that he might show him the order they had received from their Superior and Provincial. The King, with many marks of affection, told him how greatly he would regret his departure. " I love you, Father," he said, " and rejoice to have you near me; for you have taught me many things which have pleased me more than all I have learnt from others. If, however, you wish to go, I shall not constrain you to remain. But your departure is much against my will; and if you forsake me in this state, the sin will be on your head." The Father replied modestly that other Fathers, more learned and worthy than himself, would come, when he should need them, in his place. Upon this, the King manifested much displeasure: " I want no more argument," he said; " for I will never, willingly, consent to your departure." And in this determination he was supported by some of the chief nobles of his court, who were present at the conversation.

Seeing how averse the King was to his departure, and that the nobles likewise urged him to remain, so as not to arouse his Majesty's anger, Father Rodolfe, after commending the matter to God, and consulting with his companions, resolved to abide where he was, pending the receipt of instructions from the Father Provincial. But the other Fathers returned to India as they had been commanded.[2] The King greatly appreciated Father's Rodolfe's courteous compliance with his wishes, and from that day bestowed on him the highest marks of his affection. He again entered into familiar discourse with him on his difficulties, and even showed signs of again desiring to hear the exposition of the Christian faith, which gave rise to a similar desire on the part of many of the gentlemen and nobles of his court.

The Mullas, seeing that Father Rodolfe had regained the King's goodwill, and fearing that he might win for Jesus-Christ not only his Majesty, but the chief lords and captains of the court, sought secretly for an opportunity to compass his death. The King, on becoming aware of their evil design, spoke about it to the Father. " The Mullas," he said, " are traitors and rogues. I am therefore going to appoint some of my own people to guard you and accompany you wherever you go, so that no evil may befall you." In reply, the Father reminded him that when he and his fellow-priests came to his court, the Viceroy of India had demanded hostages for their safety; but that they themselves had opposed this " because," he said, " it is our glory to die for the faith which we preach; and if your Majesty were now to provide me with a guard, I should not be placing my sole reliance on God, which in all circumstances it is my duty to do." "Assuredly," said the King, " there is reason in what you say; but I regard it as my duty to provide for your safety, since you are here under my protection and safe-guard." Shortly afterwards, while in conversation with his Captains and courtiers, he told them how the Father had said that he would count it a happiness to shed his blood in defence of the law which he preached, praising his courage, and adding that his own Mullas had no desire to die in defence of their law.

Father Rodolfe did all in his power to persuade the King to declare himself a Christian; for neither would his subjects be persuaded whilst they saw him perplexed and in doubt. But his utmost efforts were unavailing; for the King knew well that such a step would mean the abandonment of his numerous wives, as well as of other vicious customs incompatible with the Christian law.

For the rest, so long as the Father remained there, and especially during the last year, when he had none of the Company with him, he led a life like that of the ancient Fathers of the desert; for he ate nothing but a little dry bread, and water was his only drink. He slept on the bare ground, and practised many other severe penances. The greater portion of the day and night he devoted to prayers and orisons, the constant burden of which was that God would illumine with His divine light the darkened mind of the King. He learnt the Persian language that he might the more easily expound to him the mysteries of our faith. He had always devoted much time to prayer; but during these last days amongst the barbarians, he prayed more than ever before. Sometimes he remained on his knees the entire day; for he never left his lodging except to visit the King; and often the dawn would discover him on the same spot where he had knelt to pray the evening before.

So great were his labours, and so severe the austerities he practised,[3] that at last he fell grievously sick, and it was thought that he would die. But the consolation which he received from God so completely outweighed his afflictions and alleviated his sufferings, that he was able to say, with the Apostle Paul, *cum infirmor, tunc fortior sum*, when I am sick and infirm, then am I most strong. Indeed, he was often heard to say, especially in these days, that he had lived as he had wished to live, and that he was then experiencing greater peace of mind than he had known in all his previous life; from which it can be seen that our Lord was, little by little, preparing him for the glory that is reserved for the martyr, and which was his shortly afterwards. On his arrival at Goa, he seemed like one who had passed through a school of righteousness, rather than one who had sojourned long in a heathen land. On account of his virtues and the many rare qualities and graces with which God had endowed him, he won the respect both of Pagans and Saracens. Though the Mullas regarded him with mortal hatred because, in the debates which took place before the King, he had always reduced them to shameful silence, yet so great was the learning he displayed in these night-long encounters, and such was the modesty of his demeanour, that even the Gentiles were wont to speak of him as the 'Angel.'

But although the treacherous Mullas were constantly plotting the death of Father Rodolfe, their fear of the King's wrath deterred them from carrying out their evil design. For the virtues, and particularly the humility, of the Christian priest, had completely won the heart of his royal patron, who regarded him with the strongest feelings of affection and esteem. At the same time, however, the views which the King held, the corrupt customs which he followed, and still more his arrogant desire to be regarded as some God, or great Prophet,[4] prevented him from following the counsel which the Father gave him; so that the latter, seeing that there was nothing further to be achieved, intimated to the Father Provincial that it was labour wasted to sow in so barren a field, where no fruit could be looked for. In reply the Father Provincial instructed him to ask the King's permission to return, and, having obtained it, to set out for Goa as soon as possible.

The King, though at first he would not listen to the Father's request, desiring to keep near him one whose manner of life so greatly pleased him, yielded at last to his earnest entreaties. Before letting him go, however, he made him promise that he would obtain the Father Provincial's consent to his making another visit to his court. This the Father promised, and the King then allowed him to set forth, showing him innumerable signs of his favour and friendship. At the moment of his departure, he wished to present to him a large sum of money in gold and silver; but the Father would accept nothing, saying that he was a monk, and that such things belonged to the world which he had abandoned. One boon, however, he asked, which was that his Majesty would permit him to take back to Goa a Muscovite Christian and his wife and children, who had been kept in bondage for a long time, and had suffered much, so that they were now hardly to be distinguished from the Saracens amongst whom they dwelt. The Queen Mother was very unwilling that these people, who were in her service, should be allowed to go. But the King, to show his affection for the Father, granted his request, so that he took the Muscovite family with him to Goa, where they lived from that time as good Christians. This was all the treasure that Father Rodolfe took away with him from the court of this great monarch.

CHAPTER V[1]

THE SECOND MISSION

SEVEN or eight years after Father Rodolfe Aquauiua had left the court of the Great Mogor, it seemed to be the will of our Saviour again to rouse this great monarch from the deep sleep of obstinacy, and to inspire him to emerge from the shades of unbelief into the light of the true faith, and to spread the same throughout his kingdom. This, we may without impiety believe was through the intercession of the blessed Virgin Mary, towards whom this Prince had always been powerfully attracted. It was in the year 1590 that, on learning that the Christians were celebrating the feast of the Assumption, he determined that he, too, would celebrate it in his own way. To this end, he caused a high throne to be erected, upon which he placed the picture of the blessed Virgin which Father Rodolfe had given to him, commanding all his princes, captains, and courtiers to do it reverence, and to kiss it. The chief lords of the court demanded that the eldest son of the King should first set them the example, and this he at once and very willingly did. The most distinguished of the officers showed themselves the readiest to honour the Virgin.

On the same occasion the King caused all the Alcorans in the town in which he then held his court to be razed to the ground. By the word 'Alcoran'[2] is signified not only the law of Mahomet, but certain high towers from which the ministers of the sect of Mahomet, in a loud voice, invoke their false prophet, and from which they summon the people to prayer. The mosques also, which are the temples of the same deceiver, were by his order converted into stables for horses and elephants; and since one of the greatest of his former difficulties had been the multitude of his wives, he abandoned them all save one, giving them in marriage to various lords and gentlemen of his court.[3] He also made proclamation, by sound of trumpet, that, from that time forward, no Mahometan should circumcise his male children until they had attained the age of 15 years, so that they might choose for themselves the law which they desired to follow.

About this time, there arrived on the scene a Greek sub-deacon named Leon Grimon,[4] who was to pass through Goa on his way to his own country. The King was very glad to see him, and asked him many questions about what he had done in different parts of the world; for, whenever anyone came to his court from a foreign land, he was anxious to learn from him all that he had seen and heard in the course of his travels. The sub-deacon was a man of intelligence, who had seen many things; and the King was so pleased with his conversation, that he resolved to employ him as his ambassador to the Viceroy of India, and to send through him a request that Fathers of the Company of Jesus might again be sent to him. He, accordingly, entrusted him with a letter and some gifts for the Viceroy, and a second letter (which is given below) with other gifts, for the Fathers of the Company, the latter being addressed to the Father Provincial. He also proposed to send, at the same time, five thousand crowns for distribution amongst the poor Christians at Goa; and when the sub-deacon suggested that it would be better if he distributed this sum amongst the poor of his own kingdom, he replied that he had no wish to do so, as they were all slaves of Satan. When, however, the sub-deacon made a further remonstrance, pointing out the risk involved in carrying so large a sum on so long a journey, he gave orders that, instead of money, he should be given precious stones and other articles of value, representing two thousand crowns, which being of little weight, he could more easily carry to the poor at Goa. The gift came at a time when the city was stricken with famine, and afforded relief to many who were in dire distress.

In order that the Fathers whom he desired to come to him might travel in safety, the King despatched letters-patent to the Viceroy of Cambaya, and to the governors of other provinces, the contents of which were as follows:

'The Command of the exalted Mahomet, great King and Lord of the Fosliere,[5] to all the Captains, Viceroys, Governors, Treasurers [*receueurs*], and other officers of my realm.

'You are to know that I have greatly honoured and favoured Dom Leon Grimon; and it is my will and intention that the Captains and other officers of my kingdom should do likewise; for I hope, by his means, to ensure the despatch of certain other Fathers whom I have invited to come to me from Goa, and through whose holy doctrine I hope to be restored from death to life, even as their master, Jesus-Christ, who came down from heaven to earth, raised many from the dead, and gave them new life.[6] On this occasion, I am summoning the most learned and the most virtuous of the Fathers, that they may help me to a true knowledge of the Christian law, and of the royal highways by which they travel to the presence of God. I, therefore, command all these my officers to honour and cherish both Dom Leon Grimon, and the Fathers for whom I am sending, in every town of my kingdom through which they shall pass, furnishing soldiers to escort them safely from town to town, and providing them, at my expense, whatsoever is necessary for themselves and their beasts, and all else that they may need. It shall be their duty to conduct them safely to my presence, and to see that they suffer no harm by the way, nor loss of aught that they may bring with them.

'It shall be the duty of my Captain Canchena[7] to conduct them safely to Captain Raizza who, with all the other captains, shall do likewise, until they reach my court. It shall be the duty of Giabiblica, captain of Cambayetta, to furnish all their requirements, both for their coming and for their return. Furthermore, I forbid my customs officers to exact or demand anything from the said Fathers on account of the baggage which they bring with them, whatsoever it may be, but to allow it to pass free of all dues or tolls. The aforesaid officers shall pay careful heed to these my instructions, so that the Fathers shall suffer no molestation either of their persons or their effects. If they make any complaint against you, you shall be severely punished, even to the loss of your heads. For I desire that everything shall be done according to these my orders, both as regards their persons and their effects, so that they may pass freely through all my towns without paying any impost, and that they may be accompanied by a sufficient and trustworthy guard throughout the whole of their journey.

'They are to be conducted from Cambayetta to the town of Amanadab [Ahmadabad], and from thence to Paian [Pattan], and thence to Gelu [? Jalor], from Gelu to Guipar, from Guipar to Bicanel [Bikanir], passing from there to Bitasser [? Jalasir]. From Bitasser they shall go to Multum [Multan], and from Multum to Lahor, the place where we reside. This is the route by which I desire the Fathers to travel. I hope, by God's grace, to see them soon at my court, where they shall be received by me and mine as their quality deserves.'

The ambassador, Dom Leon Grimon, having reached Goa, delivered, first to the Viceroy, and then to the Fathers, the letters which the King had written to them. That which was addressed to the Fathers may be translated into our language as follows:

'*In the name of God.*

'The exalted and invincible Echebar, to those who have been received into the grace of God, and have tasted of His holy Spirit, and who obey the spirit of the Messiah, and lead men to God: learned Fathers, whose words are heeded by all as coming from men who have retired from the world, and have eschewed earthly honours and greatness: Fathers, who walk in the path of truth: be it known unto Your Reverences that I have knowledge of all the faiths of the world, both of those of the Gentile of various sorts, and the law of Mahomet, excepting only that of Jesus-Christ which is the law of God, and as such is accepted and followed by many. Now, in as much as I have a strong inclination for the friendship, and society of the Fathers, I desire that through them I may receive instruction in this law.[8]

'There has recently come to this our court and royal palace a certain Dom Leon Grimon, a person of great merit and sound discourse, whom I have questioned on divers subjects. His answers have been much to the purpose, and have given satisfaction to myself and to my doctors. He has assured me that there are in India several Fathers of great prudence and learning. If this be so, your Reverence, on receipt of this letter, will be able, with every assurance, to send some of them to my court, to the end that they may dispute with my doctors, and that I, by comparing the knowledge and other qualities displayed on either side, may be able to see the superiority of the Fathers over my own learned men, whom we call Caziques,[9] and who by this means may be taught to know the truth. If the Fathers are willing to remain at my court, I will build a residence for them, where they shall live and enjoy greater respect and favour than any of the Fathers who have hitherto come to my country [*ce pays cy*]. When they desire to return, they will be free to do so, and they shall be despatched with all honour. It behoves you, therefore, to accede to my request; and to do so the more readily because I make it in this my letter, written at the commencement of the moon of June.'

The Father Provincial, who was at Goa when the ambassador arrived, having read this letter, and being informed by the ambassador that the King seemed strongly disposed to become a Christian, decided to comply with the request thus made to him. He accordingly despatched to the King the Fathers Edoüard Leïoton, and Christofle de Vega, with another who was not a priest. These three set out together and arrived at Lahor, where the King was in the year 1591. The King received them with a great display of good-will, lodging them in his palace, and treating them with much respect and attention. Shortly after their arrival, he expressed his desire that a school should be built in which the sons of the principal lords and captains of his court, as well as a son and grandson of his own, might be taught to read and write Portuguese. The Fathers remained for some time at his court, encouraging themselves, like their predecessors, with the hope of his conversion. But seeing, as time went on, that he had no intention of making up his mind, they desired to return to Goa. The Father Provincial, however, sent an express order to Father Edoüard Leïoton that he was not to leave Lahor, but permitted the return of Father Christofle de Vega. The King had become much attached to Father Christofle, and did not allow him to depart until he had made him swear to return, if permitted to do so. When, therefore, he reached Goa, the Provincial considered the advisability of sending him back.[10] But, in the end, seeing how little hope there was of the King's conversion, and that the Fathers, whom he was anxious to employ elsewhere, were labouring to no purpose, he recalled them all; and they returned to Goa, having accomplished nothing of what they had intended.[11]

CHAPTER VI[1]

Dispatch of the Third Mission

ALTHOUGH the King Echebar appeared, on the one hand, to be strongly attached to the Christian faith and to those who preached it, being convinced, as we may suppose, of its manifest truth; yet, on the other hand, he was bound hand and foot by evil desires and depraved habits, so that he could not bend his will to submit to so holy a law. We may, as it seems to me, appropriately apply to him the words of the prophet, *venerunt filij usque ad partum, et virtus non est pariendi*, 'for the children are come to the birth, and there is not strength to bring forth.'

Some years after the departure of the above-mentioned Fathers, namely, in the year 1594, he sent another ambassador to Goa, requesting, for the third time, that Fathers of the same Company might be sent to instruct him, as he expressed it, in the divine law; and he wrote to the Viceroy of India in terms evincing so much eagerness, that the latter at once summoned the Father Provincial, and begged him to comply with the request which this Prince made with so much insistence. The Provincial, who had already seen two Missions go and return without having accomplished anything, was not in favour of compliance; but knowing that it was the desire of the Reverend Father

General of the Company that there should always be some Fathers at the court of so great a monarch, both for the benefit of the Christians who were there, as well as for sundry other considerations, he at last, after consulting with the most eminent Fathers in Goa, gave his consent. As leader of this Mission, he nominated Father Hierosme Xauier Nauarrois, nephew of the blessed Father Xauier, who was at that time the Superior of the house of the Profes at Goa,[2] and who willingly quitted that office to undertake the enterprise now entrusted to him. This duty he had long foreseen (as he then said) would fall to his share, feeling in his soul that God had given him courage to support the labours which it would necessitate; and he, therefore, accepted it as a charge from heaven. Two others of the same Company were sent to assist him, namely, the Father Emmanuel Pignero, a Portuguese, and a Brother coadjutor named Benoist Goës, or de Goïs.[3] They took with them as guide an Armenian who had conducted Father Rodolfe Aquauiua and the others, who were sent the first time.

Thus accompanied, and supplied with what they needed, they set out from Goa in a ship which was bound for Daman, from which place they passed into the kingdom of Cambaya, or Guzarate, where our Saviour gave them a foretaste of the fruits which they hoped to gather on this Mission, granting them so much spiritual consolation that it seemed to be His desire to recompense them in advance for the labours they were to undergo in His service. It was at Christmas, in the year 1594, that they entered the city of Cambaya, otherwise called Cambayetta,[4] capital of this realm; and as the great festival of the birth of the Saviour of the world was about to take place, they resolved to celebrate it in this town, because several Portuguese families resided there.

They accordingly converted a large room of the house in which they were lodged into a chapel, where they erected an altar for the celebration of mass; and this they decorated so beautifully that the Pagans, and even the infidels, came in great crowds to see it. Above all, the Portuguese found great comfort from the sojourn of the Fathers in their town; for they all made confession and received communion, to the great consolation and spiritual benefit of their souls. In particular, there was amongst them one who, having lived long in that country, had turned Iogue [Yogi], the devil holding him entangled in many great and grievous sins. But it pleased God to touch his heart so strongly that he became himself again, and took the path of salvation, greatly repenting his sins, and firmly resolved to live a better life. He straightway prepared to take up his abode amongst the Christians with his legitimate wife, whom he had abandoned.

These and similar happenings so cheered the Fathers that one of them, Father Pignero, wrote that never in all his life had he felt such zeal, though in the midst of barbarism and unbelief. Throughout the time that they were there, they preached daily to the Portuguese in the courtyard of their lodging, and said mass each day. As the chapel was not large enough to hold all the Portuguese at once, some of them attended the first mass, and others the second, so that the former came out as the latter entered; and on no single day was there any lack of people. The Fathers remained there for three weeks, partly for the reasons just mentioned, and partly because the Soldan Morad,[5] the second son of the Great Mogor, arrived there with a large army, which he was leading in his father's name against Melique,[6] King of the Decan. Hearing that the Fathers were there, he sent word to them on the following day, which was Christmas eve, that he desired to see them, and that they would find him at the castle of the said town of Cambaya, where he was about to take up his quarters. The castle was close to where the Fathers lodged; and, accordingly, as soon as they knew that Soldan Morad had arrived with a small party (having left the remainder of his force in camp outside the town), they went to pay their respects to him, and were received with kindness and honour, the Prince, like his father, showing them much goodwill. As it was late in the night, the Prince remained only a short time at the castle, and then withdrew, having first collected two hundred thousand crowns in the town, partly in coin, and partly in ingots of gold.

He marched thence to Surraté, which is a seaport of the same kingdom on this side of the town of Daman. Having travelled a league from Cambaya, he again summoned the Fathers to his presence. It was three hours after midnight when they received the message, which greatly disconcerted them; for they had thought on that day to celebrate with special solemnity the feast of the circumcision of our Lord. Nevertheless, they arose and set forth, after one of them had said mass. They reached the camp at the hour when all the captains were assembled to make their morning salutation to their General, the Soldan Morad, who was standing near an elevated pavilion where all could see him. When the Fathers approached, they also made their reverence in the same fashion as the others, that is to say, bowing their heads before him; after which they took their places amongst the captains and other lords, who were standing, like so many statues, with their eyes fixed on the Prince.

After a while, the Prince entered his pavilion which was placed in the centre of a specially prepared mound, resembling a rampart; it was open on all sides, and contained a small couch. Here he received the Fathers in a more courteous and less formal manner than at first. He chatted with them for some time, asking them many curious questions. Amongst other things, he enquired if there was snow or ice in Portugal, and whether bears, hares, and other wild animals were to be found there, or birds of the chase, such as falcons and hawks. When the Fathers said that all these were to be found, he turned to his captains, and said, "So they have such things as these in Portugal." The captains placed the palms of their hands first on the ground and then on their heads, signifying thereby their gratitude for the honour of being included in the conversation. After answering some more trifling questions, the Fathers proceeded to the small mound of earth by which the Prince mounted his elephant, and there took leave of him. At this moment there were brought to him fifteen hundred *manudes*,[7] which is a kind of money used in those parts; and this sum was equivalent to about six hundred French *livres*. The Prince then turned to the Fathers and said, "I know you do not accept money, or presents of any kind; but because you are poor, and will need help on your journey, I desire you to accept this which I give you as alms." So saying, he sprang on to an elephant, and from thence on to a larger one, which seemed like a tower. Fearing that the Fathers would not take this money, he had left orders with his people that it was to be entrusted to the Armenian who conducted them; so that on their return to their lodging they should find the fifteen hundred *manudes;* and he sent them besides three carts and six bullocks to carry their loads, and three horses for them to ride, all of which were of great service to them, and especially the money; for the Armenian had no passport to conduct them to Cambaya, but to Schind; so that without it they would have been very poorly lodged.

The son of the Great Mogor had with him at that time only four or five thousand horse; but it was said that twenty thousand had already gone on in advance, with four hundred elephants, seven hundred camels, forty or fifty dromedaries, four thousand bullocks, fifteen large pieces of cannon and four small, with some culverins and falconets. He went to this war with a good courage, and with great hopes of gaining possession of the kingdom of the Decan. But he was as yet inexperienced; and as he allowed himself to be guided by the young, paying no attention to the counsels of his elders, his actions were not of the wisest,[8] from which the Fathers prophesied that he would be defeated; and that, as we shall presently relate, is what happened. He was by nature mild, kind, liberal, and good-tempered; but the youthful retainers by whom he was surrounded had already corrupted him. He had no respect for the mosques of Mahomet, which he seldom entered; his sole pleasure was in the chase, in love-making, and in running hither and thither.

After his departure, the Fathers prepared to continue their journey, which they were unable to pursue in the direction of Schind, as commanded by the King, and as they had greatly desired to do, because the Governor of that place was still occupied with his fast; for when they make this fast, they are not allowed to attend to any other affairs. Some fast for the space of twenty or thirty days, others for fifteen, and others again for only eight days.[9] The Fathers were travelling altogether for five months, although from Goa to Lahor, where the Great Mogor resided, was but a two months' journey. They made some two hundred and thirty leagues by land, marching always in the countries under his jurisdiction, but with much difficulty; for the road from Cambaya to Lahor lies, except for the last twenty leagues, where the country is of a better description, mainly through deserts and dry, sandy tracts, where neither springs nor streams are to be found, but only sand everywhere, which is often lifted into the air by the wind, so that people are enveloped in it, and sometimes buried for ever. On this account, and also as a protection against robbers, those who make this journey usually travel in companies, which are known as *cafilas*, or caravans. Like the travellers to Ormuz, of whom mention has been made, they choose a captain to lead and command their troop, which often contains two or three thousand persons. That which the Fathers joined consisted of four hundred camels, a hundred carts, and as many horses, and there were besides many poor folk who followed the others on foot. Before the caravan starts, the captain orders drums to be beaten three times. When the first drums are heard, they all fold up the tents in which they have slept during the night. On the second signal, the camels and carts are loaded; and on the third, the caravan moves forward. When travelling by night, in order that the people may not become separated from one another, the drummers lead the way, beating their drums continuously. They also give the signal when a halt is to be made. Ordinarily the caravan stops at night for repose; but halts are also made in places where it is known that wells have been dug. Such wells are usually forty or fifty fathoms deep; and to raise the water they use the bullocks which draw the carts. One of the Fathers has written that there was great scarcity of water on this journey; for that which they found was frequently as salt as the water of the ocean. "This," he writes, "I should never have credited if I had not experienced it, seeing how far away we were from the sea-coast." They also suffered severely from the heat, while no food was procurable on the way, because the country was a desert.

In the middle of March, they reached a town called Amadaba,[10] where they saw three remarkable things. One was a Iogue, who had established himself in the middle of the great square of the town, whither people flocked from all parts to see him. For he was esteemed a great Saint, because of the austerities which he practised, a custom, as we have elsewhere remarked, followed by the majority of these Iogues, at least for a time. He whom the Fathers saw at Amadaba was so arrogant and conceited, that when the King's son, Soldan Morad, of whom we have spoken above, summoned him to his presence, he contemptuously told those who had been sent to fetch him, that the Prince could come and see him if he chose, " for my holiness well merits it." When the Prince was informed of this reply, he had the Iogue soundly flogged, and banished him from the country in which he then was, which his presumption and conceit richly deserved.

Another notable thing was a superb building which they came upon about a league and a half from Amadaba. It was the tomb of a Cazique who had been the instructor of a certain king of Guzarate, who erected this building in honour of his preceptor, he himself and three others being buried in another chapel. It was constructed entirely of beautiful marble, highly polished. It had three inner courts, in one of which the Fathers counted four hundred and fifty marble pillars, each thirty feet high, with their bases and capitals in the Corinthian style. On one side of it there was a lake larger than the square in Lisbon which is called Rozzio. It was a very elaborate building, and designed with marvellous art. Though in a barbarous land, it was free from all trace of barbarism.[11]

Here too they saw many Mahometans, both men and women, who were going to make the pilgrimage to Meque, and from whom they learnt a very curious and amusing thing, namely that, as unmarried women are forbidden by their false prophet Mahomet to make the pilgrimage, the younger women, who go in as large numbers as the older, all get married beforehand, so as not to break the law. After their return, they are free to part from their husbands, if they have a mind to do so.[12]

The Fathers left Amadaba on the 19th of March, and late on the 24th reached another town called Patana.[13] The following day being the eve of the Passover, they stayed there three days to celebrate the festival. Many Christians who had joined the caravan confessed to them; but a difficulty arose in the case of some Armenians, for these people do not follow the Gregorian calendar. However, whether through fear (for they had to return through Portuguese territory), or because they were convinced of the truth, they joined in the celebration, with the exception of an obstinate old doctor, who said that the Fathers had misreckoned the date by five weeks, so that he made the Passover come on the Sunday that is before the feast of the Ascension. As they continued their journey, they passed through many towns and large cities which were mostly in a state of ruin, particularly the mosques, which had not been rebuilt. Finally, on the 5th of the month of May, 1595, they entered the town of Lahor, having set out from Goa on the 3rd of December of the preceding year.

CHAPTER VII[1]

The Fathers at Court

On being informed that the Fathers had reached Lahor, the King sent one of his captains to welcome them on his behalf, and to tell them how happy he was to hear of their safe arrival. Shortly afterwards they went to pay their respects to him, and met with a very courteous reception. He greeted each of them with a friendly embrace, as did also the Prince his son, who was then thirty-one years of age.[2] The King showed, both by his manner and his words, the pleasure it gave him to see them at his court; and he appointed for their lodging a large house he had once occupied himself, which was close to the river, so that their door was but fifteen yards from its brink. Here they were far removed from the noise and turmoil of the town. Only those to whom they gave permission could pass their lodging; for the King's guards allowed no one to go by that way, because it lay under the windows of the royal palace.

The night following their arrival, his Majesty sent for them, and showed them the pictures of our Saviour and our Lady, which Father Rodolfe had given him, holding them in his arms as reverently as though he had been a Christian. As soon as the Fathers saw the pictures, they fell upon their knees to do them reverence, as was fitting; seeing which the little grandson[3] of the King also knelt down, and clasped his hands together. This greatly pleased the King, who turned with a smile to his son the Prince, and father of the child, and said, "Look at your son." He next showed them his books, which the same Father had left with him. Amongst these were the following: The Royal Bible in four languages, the Concordances, the Summary of the Theology of St. Thomas, in four volumes, the Book against the Gentes, with another against the Jews and the Saracens by the same author, Soto, St. Antonin, the History of the Popes, the Chronicle of St. François, Sylueſtre, Nauarre, Caietain, all in duplicate; and besides these the Ordonnances of Portugal, the Commentaries of Alfonse Albuquerque, the Constitutions of the Company of Jesus, the Spiritual Exercises of the blessed Father Ignace de Loyola, founder of the same Society, the Latin Grammar of Emanuel Aluarez, and many others.[4] He lent the Fathers such of them as they desired to make use of, and they took away with them those mentioned above. For the rest, both the King and his eldest son used the Fathers with much kindness, and it was noticeable that his Majesty showed greater attention to them than to any of those who were about him, though these included the greatest Lords of his kingdom; for he kept them constantly beside him, and even invited them, from time to time, to sit on the cushion, or pillow, which he alone, and his son the Prince, were accustomed to occupy.

One day as he was walking in a gallery which

overlooked the courtyard of the Palace, where all the Governors, Magistrates, and Captains were assembled to speak with him, the Fathers appeared on the scene, having come on purpose to visit him. As soon as the King saw them, he made them approach, and received them with great honour, bowing his head to them in salutation, and assigning them the highest places. None of the kings or princes present received so much honour; though some of them had come for the first time, to make submission as his tributary. There was one who came for this purpose on the 28th of August, 1595, whose reception was much less cordial than that of the Fathers. This King,[5] when he entered the hall where the Great Mogor was seated, and while yet a long way off, bowed himself down, touching the ground with his hands and head; then, advancing little by little, he made the same reverence several times. When he had come near to the King, he was felt all over, to see if he carried arms; after which he advanced and touched the feet of his Majesty, who made no other motion or sign of his goodwill beyond placing his hand on his vassal's neck; and even this was more than he did to others. The new Tributary then rose to his feet and took the place assigned to him, and which he kept from that time forward, amongst the other Princes and Captains of the court.

It may be mentioned in passing that this Tributary made a present to the Great Mogor which was estimated to be worth two hundred thousand crowns. It consisted of a pair of poniards with their sheaths and

PLATE IV

A VASSAL PRINCE PAYS HOMAGE TO AKBAR

[face p. 64

girdles of fine gold covered with precious [illegible] great [illegible] gold; a pair of gold [illegible] with [illegible] another of the same metal, but [illegible] didly furnished. Among all [illegible] precious stones set in gold, together with [illegible] and fifty other horses [illegible] and fifty [illegible] housed in green and crimson velvet and [illegible] carpets, each of which was worth an [illegible] And what [illegible] King was willing to accept this [illegible]

This was [illegible] valuable [illegible] by [illegible] Gujarat [illegible] worth a hundred and fifty thousand [illegible] of gold and a number of [illegible] ments made of [illegible] mother-of-pearl [illegible] other of the most costly things [illegible] At the same time there was brought [illegible] the Viceroy of Bengal, which [illegible] thousand crowns, as well as [illegible] things [illegible] ary than [illegible] Those [illegible] (so writes Father Jarric) [illegible] a million [illegible] in particular [illegible] they call Nauroz [illegible] finity of presents of great value [illegible] from all parts. A single [illegible] was estimated to be worth [illegible] thousand crowns. From this it can be inferred girdles of fine gold covered with precious stones of great value, such as rubies and carbuncles, all set in gold; a pair of good-sized vials, all of gold, and another of the same metal, but larger; a horse splendidly furnished, having all about his harness many precious stones set in gold, together with a hundred and fifty other horses, ten mares, and fifty camels housed in green and crimson velvet; and lastly four carpets, each of which was worth two thousand crowns. And what is more, he deemed it a high favour that the King was willing to accept this present.

This was followed by a second present, of no less value, sent to him by his son Soldan Morad, then at Guzarate. It consisted of fifty elephants, which were worth a hundred and fifty thousand crowns; a chariot of gold, and another of silver; some beautiful ornaments made of *nacre* [mother-of-pearl]; and many other of the most costly things procurable. At the same time there was brought a third present from the Viceroy of Bengala, which was valued at eight hundred thousand crowns; for he sent, in addition to other things, three hundred elephants. It was a very ordinary thing for such presents to be made to the King. Those which he received in the course of a week (so writes Father Pignero) frequently amounted to a million *d'or*. In particular, at the feast which they call Neroza [*nau-roz*, or New Year], an infinity of presents of great value are brought to him from all parts. A single captain made him one that was estimated to be worth at least five hundred thousand crowns. From this it can be imagined how great must be the treasure which this Prince has amassed.

But to turn to other subjects. The King's reverent regard for objects relating to the Christian faith, gave the Fathers great hopes of his conversion. The pictures he possessed of our Saviour and our Lady were some of the best that had been sent from Europe. These he held in high veneration, taking great pleasure in showing them to his friends, often holding them in his arms till he was weary, for they were large and heavy. He came one day to a feast which the Fathers were celebrating, and was present whilst they recited the Litany, throughout which he remained on his knees with his hands clasped, as though he had been a Christian prince. He looked long and attentively at the pictures in the Chapel, and enquired about the mysteries which they represented. He also lent the Fathers, in response to a hint which they had thrown out, his own beautiful pictures for the feast of the Assumption, and sent them in addition some hangings of silk and of gold cloth, with which they decorated their chapel very splendidly. We learn this from a letter written to the reverend Father General of the Company on the 20th of August, 1595, by Father Hierosme Xauier, who added that the King showed special devotion and affection for the glorious Virgin Mary. His eldest son, he stated, showed a similar devotion, and was very angry with those who had conducted the Fathers, because they had not brought him any picture of our Lady from Goa; and speaking to another who was about to set out for those parts, he charged him to buy certain pieces which he desired to have, bidding him above all things not to forget to bring a beautiful picture of our Lady. As the Fathers had brought with them a Portuguese painter, the Prince straightway ordered him to make a copy of the picture of our Lady which they had brought from Goa; and having seen, on the day that he came to the chapel with the King his father, an embossed image of the little infant Jesus, and another of a crucifix, he ordered similar ones to be made for himself in ivory by his own craftsmen. He showed much affection for the Fathers, and obtained for them from the King all that they desired. The first day they spoke with him, he promised to find the means for the erection of a church, and obtained from his father a site for the building. He afterwards confirmed this, and said he would see that some of his father's officers were appointed to take the matter in hand. The King also gave the Fathers permission to baptise all who wished to become Christians. He has, wrote the same Father Xauier,[*] practically banished the sect of Mahomet from this country; so that in the town of Lahor there is not now a single mosque for the use of the Saracens; for those which were formerly there have been, by his orders, turned into stables, or into public granaries for the storage of wheat, rice, and other grain. The Alcorans also have been levelled with the ground. Besides this, the King, on every Friday, which is the day the Saracens regard as holy, has brought before him forty or fifty boars, which are provoked to fight with one another; and he has their tusks mounted in gold. It is said that he does this for the sole purpose of bringing additional contempt on the Saracens, who detest these animals above all things.[7]

By these and similar means he has deprived the Mahometan law of much of its credit in these parts. And yet one does not know for certain what law he follows; for though he is certainly not a Mahometan, as his actions show plainly enough; and though he seems to incline more to the superstitions of the Pagans, Gentiles being more welcome at his court than Mahometans, he cannot be called an Ethnique; for he adores and recognises the true God, the maker of heaven and earth; and yet, at the same time, he worships the sun. It is the opinion of many, says the same Father, that he aims at making a new religion, of which he himself is to be the head; and it is said that he already has numerous followers; but that these are for the most part flatterers, or people who have been bribed by money.[8] It is more or less certain that he has a strong desire to be looked upon, and esteemed as a God, or some great Prophet; and he would have people believe that he performs miracles, healing the sick with the water with which he washes his feet. Many young women pay vows to him to get their children cured, or that they may have children. And if these things come to pass, they bring him offerings, as to a saint, which, though they may be of little worth, are willingly received and highly valued by him. Thus did Father Xauier write of this Prince, showing whither ambition leads those who are unrestrained by the fear of that sovereign Monarch who casts down the mighty from their thrones, and exalts them that are humble. Some think, says the same Father, that he follows the opinions of the Vertéas[9] (of whom we have spoken in Book II). But it seems probable that he is drifting hither and thither, like a ship without a rudder, not knowing what haven to make for. He frequently urges the Fathers to acquire the Persian language, in order that he may discourse with them without an interpreter; and once he sent word to them by a certain person high in his confidence, and whom he employed on matters of a religious nature, that if they understood Persian they could cut the knot by which the bonds that held him fast were secured. It is on this account, and to this end, that the Fathers are studying the Persian tongue. With a similar object they have opened schools in which all who desire it may learn to read and write Portuguese, and by this means may be the more easily taught the doctrines of Christianity. Many of the children of the princes and nobles come to this school, among them three sons of a certain king who is a vassal of the said Echebar.[10] Some of these disciples are anxious to be baptised, and have already begged the Fathers to grant their desire. One of them seeks to become not only a Christian, but a monk. He publicly conducts himself as a Christian; and one day, on entering the chapel, he threw aside his turban, and kneeling down before the altar, said, in a loud voice, these words: "O Saviour, Jesus-Christ, remember me!" Another of their disciples, having been rebuked by a Saracen who came to learn Persian with the Fathers, because he had not fasted on a day on which the Mahometans are accustomed to fast very strictly, said, "Who has commanded this fast?" "Mahomet," replied the Saracen. "And who is Mahomet, if not a false prophet and an impostor?" asked the youth. This so astonished the other that he stopped his ears, so as not to hear such things. But he was obliged to swallow these words however much he disliked them; for the youth was of such calibre that he did not dare to say a word in opposition; but begged his pardon for having rebuked him.

Now though the King and the Prince his eldest son had given permission for the building of a church, the Fathers, for certain reasons, pretended to have forgotten it; and on the 5th of August, 1595, which was the day of our Lady of the Snows, the King again told them to build a church, and to baptise all those who desired, of their own free will, to become Christians. But when the Fathers requested him to publish the same in writing, he answered that this was unnecessary in a place where he resided, in as much as his presence was living writing. Nevertheless, some time afterwards, he sent them letters-patent, which were very clear and sufficient.[11] Further, when Father Xauier called to mind how well-disposed he had found the inhabitants of Cambaya to receive the seed of the Holy Gospel,[12] he asked the King for letters-patent declaring that he permitted the Fathers of the Company to go there and preach the Christian faith, and his subjects to accept the same. This the King likewise granted, and the royal letters were sent. On receiving them, the Fathers sent those relating to Cambaya, or copies of them, to the Provincial of India, who selected and despatched thither certain of the Fathers, as has been told in Book II.[13] In virtue of their own letters,[14] they commenced to preach the faith of Jesus-Christ publicly in the city of Lahor, and to such good purpose that, by the month of September of the same year 1595, there were several persons who had received baptism, and others who were desirous of receiving it; and though these were persons of humble birth, they were souls redeemed by the priceless blood of the Lamb, as assuredly as if they had been of the highest rank. Of this the Fathers made great account, regarding it as the first-fruits of their newly planted vine, not doubting that He who had given it beginning would cause it to flourish ever more and more.

CHAPTER VIII[1]

On Tour with the King

Although on the one hand the King seemed to entertain a high opinion of the Christian religion, as is plain from what has already been said, and that in many ways he gave it preference above all others, arousing thereby great hopes of his embracing it, yet, on the other hand, so strongly was he attached to his mad ambition to be esteemed as some great Prophet, or demi-god on earth, that there was no means of winning him to submission to the law of Christ. It is quite true that he held the law of Mahomet of no account; but he was much addicted to the worship of the sun, to which he made prayer four times a day, namely, in the morning when he arose, at noon, on retiring to bed, and again at midnight. On each occasion he repeated as many as a thousand and fifty names of the luminary, which he counted by means of small balls threaded like our paternosters, but consisting of beautiful precious-stones.[2] One often saw him doing reverence to the pictures of our Saviour and our Lady, and even wearing suspended from his neck by a gold chain, a reliquary, which had on one side of it an Agnus Dei, and on the other an image of our Lady. But one saw him also place himself daily at a window of his palace where he could be seen by large numbers of people, who, as soon as he appeared, prostrated themselves, and worshipped him with a certain ceremonial that the Gentiles use when praying to their false gods.[3] We have already spoken of his willing acceptance of the vows paid to him.

These things, so contrary to one another, perplexed the minds of his subjects to such an extent that they knew not to what sect or religion their King belonged. There were some who thought that he meant to invent a new religion, and to that end had summoned many learned men, well versed in all sorts of laws, to take from each that which seemed to him good. For seeing that, if he embraced the faith of Jesus-Christ, he would have to abandon many vices to which he had long been addicted, he wished, or so it was believed, to make a mixture of laws, or to try them all, until he found one which would allay the pangs of conscience, without necessitating a change in his mode of life.[4] But since it is impossible to find true repose outside the true faith, his labours were fruitless.

Now in order to drive from his mind these illusions of the devil, and arouse him from his sleep of obstinacy, it pleased the good God, who desireth not the death of a sinner, but rather that he should be converted and saved, that he should undergo certain punishments. The first was the defeat of his second son, the Soldan Morad, who, as narrated above, had been sent with a big army to Guzarate,[5] to make war on Melique, king of the Decan, to whom belonged the town of Chaul, which the Portuguese now hold, on the sea-coast some fifty or sixty leagues to the north of Goa. This son was slain in the war; and with him the King lost the bravest Captains that he had.[6] He received this news when he was celebrating the feast which they call New Year's Day, which takes place when the sun enters the sign of Belier [Aries]; so that we may believe that God purposed, by this means, to make him understand that he was being chastised for his foolish worship of the sun. Echebar, however, did not profit by this lesson. He soon afterwards sent another of his sons to continue the war, giving him his own sword, and four hundred thousand crowns for his journey; while he himself continued to follow the same superstition. Our Lord, therefore, visited him with a second chastisement, sending it this time on the day of the Passover, in the year 1597, about the same time that a similar punishment befell the king of China, as will be narrated in its proper place.[7] Whilst he was on the terrace of his palace, making, so it is said, a great feast in honour of the sun, in the presence of the Prince his eldest son, and many great lords and gentlemen of his court, behold, fire fell from heaven, and catching first the sumptuous pavilion of the Prince, burnt it to ashes before anyone dared to go near to extinguish it; for all were so amazed, that none had the courage to approach it. The fire spread thence to other tents on the same terrace, enveloping them likewise, with the thrones, seats, and other valuable things which they contained. Amongst these was a massive throne of gold, estimated to be worth a hundred thousand crowns, which was either melted or lost. But this was not all; for the flames reached even to the King's palace, the greater part of which was reduced to

PLATE V

THE *BARGAH-NAUROZ* OR NEW YEAR'S DAY DARBAR
Probably of the year 1589

[*face p. 74*

cinders. The latter, it is true, was built only of wood. That which grieved the King most was the loss of all his treasures, both those which he had inherited from his ancestors, and those he had amassed during his own reign, and which were worth many millions in gold; for the fire consumed everything, including large quantities of draperies of cloth of gold and silk. It is said that the gold, silver, and other metals melted in this conflagration ran down the streets like streams of water.

In consequence of this disaster, the King at once left Lahor, though it was said that he had decided to do so before it happened, and went to spend the summer in the kingdom of Caximir [Kashmir], or as others call it, Cascimir, which he had recently conquered.[8] Thither he was accompanied, at his own request, by Father Hierosme Xauier and Benoist de Gois, Father Emmanuel Pignero being left at Lahor to complete the building of the church and the house, which had already been commenced. The kingdom of Caximir is one of the pleasantest and most beautiful countries to be found in the whole of India, we may even say in the East. It is completely surrounded by very high mountains, which for the greater part of the year are covered with snow, and all the rest of the kingdom is a beautiful plain clothed in verdure, diversified with groves, orchards, gardens, and well watered by springs and rivers: a very pleasant land for those who dwell therein. Owing to the mountains, the climate of the country is somewhat cold, though it is more temperate than that of the kingdom of Rebat,[9] which joins Caximir on the east. In the month of May, great numbers of wild-duck come from the mountains of Rebat and settle in huge flocks on the streams which flow near to the town of Caximir,[10] the capital of the kingdom, because of the warmer climate. About three leagues from the town there is a lake of sweet water which, though not more than two leagues in circuit and half a league broad, is so deep that large vessels can float upon it. In the middle there is an artificial island on which the King has a palace, where he refreshes himself when he goes to shoot the duck which abound on this lake. On the banks of a river, the waters of which flow through the lake, there is a species of very large tree, the trunk and leaves of which resemble those of the chestnut, though it is quite a different tree.[11] The wood is very dry, and has a grain like rippling water; it is much used for making small caskets and similar articles. The country abounds in wheat, rice, and other food grains. They plant vines at the roots of the mulberry trees, so that grapes and mulberries are seen hanging from the same branches. People say that this kingdom was one of the most formidable in these parts, and that the Great Mogor would never have been able to subdue it but for the factions which existed amongst the inhabitants. Knowing that it was a kingdom divided against itself, he invaded it with a large army, and easily made himself master of it. Formerly all the people of this country were Gentiles; but about three hundred years ago they joined the sect of Mahomet, and the majority of them are now Saracens.

When the Great Mogor retired to this kingdom of Caximir, with all his household and family, Father Hierosme Xauier, observing that he had now more leisure, resolved to speak to him on the subject of his conversion, intending, when the opportunity offered, to remind him, on the one hand, of the great blessings he had received from God, and on the other hand, of the chastisements which the same Seigneur had sent for his admonition, hoping that thereby he might induce him to hear with attention, and not at odd moments as hitherto, the things relating to the salvation of his soul, and that in the end he would find himself able to accept and follow the holy law. But when they reached Caximir, the Father was attacked by a severe illness, which lasted for the space of two months. During this time, the King showed him much kindness, giving orders for the liberal supply of all his wants, and sending his own physician to attend him; he even went in person to see him, which was a very special favour; for it is his custom never to visit anyone. Towards the end of the summer, when the Father began to recover, the King himself fell sick. On several occasions during his illness, he sent for the Father, and had him brought to the chamber where he lay, which even the greatest lords of his court were seldom permitted to enter. Owing to these illnesses, the Father had no opportunity, before the return to Lahor, of speaking to the King as he had intended on the subject of his conversion.

Whilst they were in the kingdom of Caximir there was so grievous a famine[12] that many mothers were rendered destitute, and having no means of nourishing their children, exposed them for sale in the public places of the city. Moved to compassion by this pitiable sight, the Father bought many of these little ones, who, soon after receiving baptism, yielded up their spirits to their Creator. A certain Saracen, seeing the charity of the Father towards these children, brought him one of his own; but the Father gave it back to the mother, together with a certain sum of money for its support; for he was unwilling to baptise it, seeing that, if it survived, there was little prospect of its being able to live a Christian life in that country. At daybreak the next morning, however, the mother knocked at the door of his lodging, and begged him to come to her house and baptise the child, as it was about to die. Accompanied by some Portuguese, he went with her to the house and baptised the child, having first obtained the consent of its father. The latter, after it was dead, wished to circumcise it; but this the Father would not permit, but buried it with Christian rites. There was another mother, a Mahometan woman, who brought to him, under similar circumstances, her infant son to be baptised; and in this case, too, as soon as the rite had been performed, the spirit of the little sufferer ascended to heaven.

When the summer had come to an end, the King set out on his return journey to Lahor. He had desired Father Xauier and his companion to travel with him; but the latter, anxious to avoid the commotion of the court, asked and obtained permission to go on before. On their journey they suffered much from cold and hunger, as well as from the badness of the road; for they had to go by rough paths which were often so narrow that there was room for only a single horseman. They were obliged, therefore, to travel very slowly and to stop frequently. Moreover, the elephant which carried their goods had great difficulty in climbing the mountains. Sometimes, feeling insecure on its feet, owing to the load which it carried, it supported itself with its trunk, making it serve the purpose of a staff.

At length, on the 13th of November, after many hardships, they arrived at Lahor, from whence they had set out on the 15th of May of the same year, 1597. The people of the town exhibited towards the Father and his companion a more friendly attitude than was their wont. It had previously been their practice to throw stones at them, and offer them other insults; but on this occasion they displayed neither incivility nor disrespect. The King and the Prince arrived some days later, having lost on their way many horses and elephants, and several of their attendants. The Prince, too, had been in great danger of his life. One day, mounted on a female elephant without tusks, he went in pursuit of lions, and in the course of the chase, fell in with some lion whelps. As these were but half grown, the elephant had no difficulty in killing them with her trunk. The next moment, however, the lioness their mother appeared, and in her rage would have hurled herself upon the Prince, had he not pierced her with an arrow as she was in the act of springing. But the wound was not mortal, and the infuriated animal still strove to reach him who had struck her, to rend him with her claws and teeth. Again the Prince discharged his arquebus, piercing her through and through a second time; but the savage beast was not vanquished; and goaded to even greater fury, she sprang upon the elephant, and so nearly reached the Prince that he was splashed with the foam from her mouth. Seeing himself in such danger, he grasped his arquebus like a club, and with the butt dealt the lioness so severe a blow on the head, that she fell to the ground stunned. A soldier then came up and killed her with his sword; but not before she had avenged herself on her last assailant, whom she tore severely with her claws. Perhaps it was our Saviour's will to save the Prince from this danger in order that the Church might increase, and many souls win salvation, when he came to the throne.

We must now return to the Fathers. It was at the festival of Noel, at the close of this same year, that the companion of Father Xauier, Benoist de Goïs, adorned the altar of the newly built church with a small *creche*, representing the birth of the Son of God. This he designed with such skill, and decorated it so beautifully, that not only the Christians, but Pagans and Saracens came in large numbers to see it, in so much that, to satisfy all, it was necessary to keep the altar thus garnished until the octave of the Three Kings. On Christmas night, they played a pastorale in the Persian language, illustrating the mystery of the Nativity of our Saviour, introducing into it various Industani[13] phrases and sayings. This was greatly

PLATE VI

PRINCE SALIM ATTACKED BY A LIONESS

[*face p. 80*

appreciated by the people of the country, and also by some of the Saracens, and gave to many a new idea of the Christians and their law. Several prostrated themselves before the image of Jesus-Christ, worshipping Him as though He were actually lying in the manger. The Gentiles manifested greater approval of these things than the Saracens. Some of them even paid vows to our Lady, and brought her offerings according to their means. Amongst these was a woman who, on being asked the reason for her gift, replied, "I besought the Bili [*bibi*, 'lady'] Mariam to grant me a son; and having obtained my desire, I bring this as a thank-offering to her for her goodness."

But it was not only the humble people who displayed affection for the things of our faith. One day, a Prince came and presented two beautiful candles, each four feet long, and so large round that it required two hands to grasp them. The Prince took one of these, and with closed eyes, as if engaged in meditation or in prayer to God, charged the Father to burn it in honour (as he said) of the Seigneur Jesus-Christ. He then presented the other to be burnt in honour of the Lady Mary. After this, he gave as alms the equivalent of thirty crowns, which sum was, by order of the Father, distributed amongst the poorest of the Christians. The King's eldest son was likewise very favourably disposed towards the Christian faith, and lost no opportunity of defending it. He publicly expressed his devotion to our Lord and our Lady, and placed their pictures, on which he delighted to gaze, in his own chamber. Whenever the Portuguese, or other Christians at the court, obtained good copies of such pictures from India or Portugal, they used to present them to the Prince, knowing that this would greatly please him. That which more than anything else prevented him from embracing our faith was his incontinency. He once said that if the law of the Evangelists permitted several wives, many would accept it; "for all else that it teaches is," he said, "both good and reasonable." It is not to be wondered at that he found such difficulty in overcoming his carnal desires; for though he was not yet thirty-six years old, he had already married a score of wives.

About this time, the Father Provincial of India wrote a letter to the King, which he requested Father Xauier to deliver. As it is the custom in this country never to appear before princes empty-handed, the Father took with him, and presented in the name of the Father Provincial, two beautiful pictures which had come from Iappon, one representing our Saviour, and the other the blessed Father Ignace Loyola.[14] These greatly pleased the King, especially the latter, which he had not seen before. He asked whose portrait it was, and the Father then told him the story of the blessed Father Ignace, to which he listened with much interest, and at its conclusion begged the Father to set it down in writing in the Persian language. At this moment they were joined by the Prince, who, on seeing the portrait, requested his father to lend it to him, that he might have another painted like it. A day or two later, when the Father was again visiting the King, his Majesty handed him the letter he had received from the Father Provincial, requesting him to read it aloud before his courtiers. This he did, reading it first in Portuguese, and afterwards explaining it in Persian. While listening, the King showed by signs his approval of what the Father Provincial had written to him: how that he felt under a deep obligation to his Majesty for the many favours and the kind treatment which those of the Company had received at his royal hands, and how he had caused him to be commended to our Lord Jesus by all his flock. In pronouncing this holy name the Father uncovered and bowed his head with great reverence; whereon the King, wishing to explain the meaning of this act of homage, took his hand, and turning to his courtiers said, "The Christians have a great respect for this holy name, Jesus, and that is the reason why the Father uncovered his head as he uttered it." He then asked the Father if this was not so, who replied that his Majesty had said rightly.

After the letter of the Father Provincial, another was read which had been written to the King by Father Monserrat, who had been at his court the first time with Father Rodolfe, and who, after having been six years in captivity, as has been related above, had returned to Goa.[15] The King wished to know the reason why he had been captured and so badly treated by the Turcs. Father Xauier said that the Saracens and Turcs were sworn enemies of the Christians, and especially of the Fathers of the Order, whom they ill-treated in every way possible because of their opposition to the law of Mahomet; although, he added, they ought to love them because of their desire to show them the true road to salvation. He then went on to narrate how, on a previous occasion, the Father Abraham George,[16] who had gone to Ethiopie, had been killed because he had refused to deny his faith, and embrace Mahometanism. Many Mahometans who were with the King were offended at his discourse. One of them, out of the friendship which he had for the Father, advised him to be more guarded in his language when speaking of the law of Mahomet; " For," said he, " there are none but Mahometans present; and when you speak evil of their law, they thirst for your blood; and even I, who am your sincere and firm friend, when I hear you speak ill of our Prophet, am so angered that I could plunge my dagger into your body."

As for the King, though willing to listen to discourses on the Christian faith, he showed no signs of abandoning his superstitious worship of the sun, which he adored every day at sunrise, and an image of which he kept constantly near him. He was, otherwise, still in a state of irresolution, not knowing where to fix his faith. He told Father Xauier that some twenty years previously he had caused thirty little infants to be shut up before they had learnt to talk, and had had them strictly watched, to prevent the nurses that fed them from teaching them the language of the country, desiring to know by this experiment what language they would speak when they grew up; for he had intended, he said, to follow the law of that nation whose language they spoke. But he found when he released them, that none of these children could utter distinctly or intelligibly a single word; and on this account he decided not to change his law.[17]

Although, as we have shown, the Fathers enjoyed the good-will of this great monarch, they were called upon to face many violent storms. I shall describe one of these, which arose in the following manner. There was in the town of Lahor a certain Armenian, a member of the Christian community, though in his manner of life he resembled a Saracen, or Turc, rather than a Christian, who, having lost his wife, desired to marry her niece; and when the Fathers refused to permit this incestuous union, he contrived to induce the King to ask, or order them, if not to consent, at any rate to shut their eyes to the transaction. His Majesty accordingly summoned them to appear before him. The Fathers, suspecting the reason of this summons, hastily committed themselves to God, and putting on the armour of steadfastness and prayer, a surer defence than a panoply of steel, made their way to the palace, resolved to die rather than countenance so evil a deed. Their companion, Benoist de Goïs, remained in the house during their absence. The latter, though he avoided the court as much as he could, was anxious to accompany them on this evening, that he might share with them the crown of martyrdom, if they were called upon to die in the cause of righteousness. As they would not permit this, he assembled in the house as many of the little Christian children and catechumens as he could collect, and, whilst the Fathers were at the palace, made them a long exhortation, encouraging them to die firmly for the Christian faith; this was followed by the discipline,[18] and a devout prayer that it would please God to give the Fathers courage to resist the enemies, at whose instigation the King was pressing them to consent to the incest of the Armenian. But the affair passed off more quietly than they had anticipated; for the King, though he urged them strongly to consent to the marriage, seeing that they were resolved to die rather than approve of such a sin, ceased to press them further.[19] He was, however, moved to anger by the outspoken reply of Father Xauier to his question: " What harm is there if a man marries two sisters, or a daughter of one of them, and adopts my religion ? " (For the Armenian, seeing that that which he desired would not be permitted under the Christian law, had abandoned it, and joined that of the King.) The harm, Father Xauier told him, was that he was abandoning the road to paradise for the road to hell; for the Armenian, he said, and every one else who became a follower of that law, and died in the same, would assuredly be damned. This answer, as I have said, displeased the King, in as much as it condemned before all his courtiers the law which he had framed. He, nevertheless, controlled his resentment, and looked at the Fathers without anger.

But if the King was displeased, there were many among those present on this occasion who marvelled greatly to see the Christians willing and prepared to shed their blood in defence of their law, whilst the Saracens were unwilling to endure the smallest inconvenience to uphold their Alcoran. The Prince, when he heard that the Armenian had abandoned his faith, was very angry, and had a great desire to punish him, but was restrained by fear of his father.

The Armenian's desertion of the faith of our Saviour was more than counterbalanced by the many unbelievers who, in the same year 1598, were converted and baptised at Lahor, though these were all people whose lives were despaired of; for the Fathers did not, at first, baptise those likely to live long, for fear that they might afterwards renounce their faith; for they are a fickle and inconstant people. There were, however, two cases in which the rite not only saved the soul, but cured the body. On the other hand, some Saracen children, whom their parents had brought to Lahor to be baptised, died almost as soon as the rite had been performed, and went to dwell in heaven. In another case, a nobleman of the country, whose wife had given birth to a child at the same hour in which our Lord was born, brought the infant to the church, and placing it beside the *creche* which adorned the altar, permitted it to be baptised, after which both he and his wife were enrolled as catechumens, and commenced to learn the Christian doctrine, so that, when sufficiently instructed, they too might receive baptism.

The lot of another woman was less happy, though that of her child was in a special degree blessed. This was a certain Mahometan woman who, having given birth to a child on the eve of Easter, brought it, three weeks later, to the Fathers, and earnestly begged them to baptise it. After her wish had been granted, her neighbours and relatives taunted her so bitterly and unceasingly with the shame of having a Christian child, that at last, unable to endure their reproaches, she resolved to put an end to them by putting an end to the life of her child; and on the eve of the Ascension of our Lord (in the year 1598), which was eighteen days after its baptism, and forty days after its birth, she caused its death by mixing poison with its milk. For seventeen hours the child endured violent convulsions of the stomach, its sufferings being but too plainly indicated by its cries and moans, and the writhings of its little body. It died on the altar of the chapel where it had been baptised, confessing the faith of Jesus-Christ, not by words, but by dying for it. Father Pignero wrote that, after this little infant had yielded up its spirit, its face remained so beautiful and resplendent, that it seemed as if God wished to show in its countenance the glory which its thrice-happy soul was enjoying in paradise.

About this time, the Great Mogor, having returned from Caximir to Lahor, and having already sent one of his sons to continue the war against Melique, king of the Decan, who had slain his second son, the Soldan Morad, resolved to proceed to the war in person, at the head of a large army. He accordingly set out from Lahor in the direction of Agra, the capital of a kingdom of the same name which he had conquered a short time before.[20] This town of Agra is distant about a hundred leagues from Lahor, and in a southerly direction, the kingdom of the Decan lying still further to the south. The King marched in such grand array, that eight hundred elephants and seven thousand camels scarcely sufficed to carry his tents and pavilions; which is not to be accounted strange, seeing that his Secretary took with him seven hundred camels and seventy elephants. Finding that the King was setting out for these regions, Father Xauier offered to accompany him, if it should be his pleasure. This he did for sundry reasons; but chiefly that he might maintain him in his good opinion of the Christian religion, and his affection for the Company. The Father's proposal greatly pleased the King, who embraced him very kindly, and told him he gladly consented to it. He at once gave orders that he should be supplied with money, horses, elephants, camels, and all else that he needed. The Father said that one camel for his companion and himself would suffice; but he was not allowed to take less than four.

This expedition of the Great Mogor caused much alarm amongst all the kings of these regions; and indeed they had reason to fear a monarch so powerful, and who approached their territories with so great an army. Nevertheless, having arrived at Agra, he remained there more than a year.[21] During this time the Father Xauier was not idle. He obtained permission from the King to send for some more Fathers of the Society to be the companions of Father Pignero, who had remained at Lahor to keep the new Christians steadfast in their faith and piety; and we may here recount a conversation which the Father had with the King in the town of Agra, on the 16th of the month of July in the year 1599. On that day, finding his Majesty in a favourable humour, he told him that he had something to say which he desired to communicate to him privately, so that none should overhear, if he would be pleased to listen to him. The King, thereupon, withdrew from those who stood around him, and, taking the Father aside, asked what it was that he wished to tell him. Following the instructions he had received from the Provincial, the Father said, "Sire, we have received letters from our Superior, who writes thus: 'Since you have now been five years with the King, and have acquired the language of the country, I have no doubt that he is now able to understand you well. Therefore you will humbly beg him, since he has called you to hear the declaration of the Gospel, now to say what he requires of you, so that I may decide how I ought to employ you.'" After reading the letter, the Father continued: "It is a great trial and grief to us to remain at your court without being able to accomplish anything. We therefore beg your Majesty to be pleased to listen to us, in accordance with the promise made to us on the day that we arrived at your court, so that you may hear what concerns your salvation, and that you may discover the truth, which you have assured us it is your desire to know." The King, having listened to the Father's complaint, answered in these terms: "I acknowledge that I have summoned you in order to understand and know the truth, so that I may embrace and follow the law which I find most in conformity with reason. But I am now proceeding to the Decan, where I shall halt very close to Goa. I shall then be less occupied with other affairs, and shall have leisure to attend to you. It is," he went on to say, "because of my special desire to speak with and listen to you, that you have been sent to me. But how can you say that the time you have spent with me has been profitless, seeing that formerly the Saracens had so much credit in my land that, if any had dared to say that Jesus-Christ was the true God, he would straightway have been put to death; whereas you are now able to say this, and to preach the same in all security?" The Father acknowledged that this was so, and expressed his gratitude, again begging his Majesty to hear at his leisure the explanation of the Christian law, both for his own salvation (which was his chief concern), and that of many others, as well as to afford him and his companions some consolation for their labours. This the King promised he would do; and with that the interview came to an end.[22]

We must now, for a brief space, return to Lahor. There, since the departure of Father Xauier, who had followed the King to Agra, Father Pignero had baptised thirty-eight catechumens. Three of these, who were citizens of Lahor, and had previously belonged to a Pagan sect, exhibited great courage in overcoming the obstacles placed in the way of their conversion by their relatives and friends, who used to meet in secret to conspire against them, lest by their public profession of Christianity they should bring disgrace and dishonour on their law. But these brave proselytes displayed such constant resolution that they triumphed over Satan and his band, and on the day of the Pentecost of the year 1599, they, in company with others, were cleansed in the water of holy baptism. The ceremony was performed publicly, and with great magnificence.

The street down which this holy company passed was decorated with green foliage, and shaded with palm branches. The candidates left the house in which the Fathers lodged in an orderly procession, each one carrying a palm leaf in his hand, while those who were already Christians walked two and two on either side of the street, which was strewn with flowers. Musicians marched in front of them with drums, trumpets, clarions, flutes, and other musical instruments, on which they played till the procession reached the church. There Father Pignero awaited them, robed in a surplice and cope, or pluvial. He received them at the entrance to the church, where was assembled so great a multitude of Pagans and Saracens that he knew not on which side to turn, nor how to conduct the service, because of the noise and tumult; for as nothing like this had ever before been seen in the town, the people came in dense crowds, so that it was with difficulty that anything could be done. But at last, having completed the sacred rites which it is customary to perform at the church door, the Father led them inside, and baptised them, deriving therefrom as great comfort as those who received the divine sacrament. Many remarkable incidents happened on this occasion; but, for the sake of brevity, I shall speak only of one, namely the baptism of a young girl who had not yet passed her fifteenth year. She had come there to see the ceremony; but, as water was being sprinkled on the heads of the candidates, she placed herself among them, and asked that she too might be baptised. As she had not been enrolled in the number of the catechumens, the Father told her that she must wait until she had received the necessary instruction, and when she understood the Christian doctrine, her wish would be granted. " But what more have I to learn ? " she asked. " I have heard the explanation of the catechism, and know all that a Christian ought to know. I want to be baptised with these others, and I will not leave the church till my wish has been granted." Seeing her resolution, the Father asked her where she had learnt about Christianity. She replied that she had listened while instruction was being given to others; and, indeed, when the Father then and there put her to the test, he found that she knew the catechism well. For this reason, and because of her prayers and importunity, he baptised her with the rest, and gave her the name Grace. Now when this young girl returned to her home, her parents, enraged at what she had done, heaped every kind of abuse upon her, and finally, without providing her with any means of support, drove her from their house, threatening to have her severely beaten if she went again to the church, or made any complaint to the Fathers. At the same time, a certain Saracen, at the instigation of some evil spirit that she might be tempted the more, told her that he wished to marry her, thinking that in her destitute condition she would willingly consent. But she replied with great firmness that she was a Christian, and according to the divine law she could not marry him. When this came to the ears of Father Pignero, he at once sent for the girl, that he might encourage her in her resolution, and strengthen her if she should waver. But she courageously protested before him her readiness to die rather than quit the faith she had accepted at her baptism. Seeing that her determination was unshaken, the Father sent her to the house of a certain Christian who was married. This greatly enraged the Saracen who wished to have her to wife; and the outcry he raised would have astounded anyone unused to the ways of the Industans. At the same time her father and mother, finding that their threats were of no avail, and that all they said of the authority of the King and the indignation of their false prophet was wasted, carried their complaint to the Governor of the town, before whom they accused the Father of baptising the girl without their knowledge or consent. The Governor, thereupon, sent someone to the Father to enquire into the matter, and at the same time ordered the girl to be brought before him to be examined. When the Saracen became aware of the orders of the Governor, he hastened, accompanied by a crowd of people, to the house where the girl was, thinking that he already had his prey in his grasp. But he found there were others more cunning than himself; for the Father, aware of what was going on, and lest she should be entrapped on the road, sent her to the Governor well protected, and by another route, to the great mortification of the Saracen. Moreover, Father Pignero, learning that many charges were to be made against her, and that it was to be feared the judges would be won over by her adversaries, who would argue that her conduct was contrary to their Alcoran and to the ordinances of the King, immediately went himself to the house of the Governor, and by God's grace, arrived while the latter was questioning her. She showed her courage by the answers she gave, in one of which she said, "I am a Christian, and I do not recognise this man as my husband." Then approaching the Father, and taking hold of his cloak, she added, "This is he whom I regard as my father." On being again asked why she had quitted the law of Mahomet, she replied that it was because she had come to know that it was a worthless law and full of untruths, and because, on the other hand, she was convinced that Jesus-Christ was the true God, and Saviour of the world. The Saracens who were present could be seen now clenching their teeth, now blushing for shame, and now pale with anger; for their countenances changed every moment as they listened to the answers of this young girl, whose firmness and spirit filled them with amazement. Indeed, from the way in which she spoke of, and gave the reasons for her faith, it might have been supposed that she had imbibed it with her mother's milk; whereas it was only forty days before that she had commenced to learn the catechism. In short, she vanquished Satan and his band, to the great glory of God and the confusion of his enemies. For the Governor, perceiving her resolution, permitted her to follow the law which she had embraced; and the Father took her to the English church, where she was married to a very honest Christian. The Saracen tried to stop the marriage by a further outcry; but his attempt failed, and thus the affair ended happily. Such then was the state of Christianity in the territories of the Great Mogor at the close of the year 1599. Since then, others have continued the work of the Mission, and many have joined the church in the town of Lahor, where the Fathers of the Company usually reside.

But they were unable to accomplish their primary object, which was the conversion of King Echebar, who died at the end of the month of October in the year 1605, in the state of mind we have described, and without, so far as is known, having formed any definite intention of embracing Christianity. The Fathers had earnestly considered whether they should speak to him once more on the subject; and when they learnt the fatal nature of his malady, they hastened to the palace. On their arrival, however, finding that his condition was not so critical that his death was to be feared, they decided to defer their purpose till another occasion. But they never saw him again; for, a day or two later, the poison, from which it was believed he was suffering, suddenly attacked the heart.[23] Remedies proved unavailing, and the Fathers had no further opportunity for speech with him. Thus God often forsakes at the hour of death those who forsake him in their lives, and pay no heed to his divine inspirations.

CHAPTER IX[1]

At the Seat of War

We have told, in the fourth book of this History, how the King of Mogor, named Achebar, having determined to conquer the kingdoms of the Decan, and others in India further to the south, set out from the city of Lahor, and having marched with his army to Agra, proceeded thence to the Decan. During this expedition, Father Hierosme Xauier, and his companion Benoist de Goës, kept themselves constantly by the King's side, in order to maintain him in the good affection he appeared to have for the Christian faith, and the Fathers of the Company. That his time might not be spent idly, Father Xauier wrote a book to which he gave the title, *The Fountain of Life*, in which, by many forcible arguments, he established the truth of the Christian faith, and refuted the doctrines of the infidel sects, and particularly of those who follow Mahomet. This book he dedicated to the King, whom he introduced into it in the character of a philosopher in search of the truth. Having completed it, the Father set himself to translate it into Persian, being assisted by certain persons learned in that language, though he himself had made such progress therein, that the Persians themselves confessed that they had learnt from him many new phrases and figures of speech.[2]

The King continued his southward march with an army, horse and foot, of a hundred thousand men, and more than a thousand war-elephants. The mountains of Gaté[3] were crossed by passes so rough and difficult that it sometimes took a whole day to cover a distance equal to the range of an arquebus; for they had, it seems, to cut their way through the rock. One of the great captains,[4] who had been sent in advance with fifty thousand men, captured by force the chief stronghold of King Melique,[5] after which the Great Mogor had little difficulty in making himself master of his other forts. It was thought that he would now march forward to the conquest of Idalcan[6]; but, unwilling to leave any fortress of the enemy in his rear, he proceeded towards the city of Breampur,[7] which, as we shall narrate later, he found deserted.

In the confusion, worse than Babylon, of this great camp, Father Xauier and his companion performed their devotional exercises as earnestly and calmly as though they had been in some Christian town, celebrating the holy mass in their portable church, and fulfilling all the other duties of their calling. But Father Pignero, who had remained at Lahor to take care of the small band of Christians that had been won for our Lord, was feeling the loneliness of his position, being separated nearly two hundred leagues from Father Hierosme (for the distance from Lahor to Breampur was no less). On this account, Father Nicolas Pimenta, who was then Visitor, decided that a priest should be sent as companion to him, not only to comfort and encourage him in his labours, but in order that, if God should call one of them from the world, the rich harvest that had been gathered in might not be abandoned. The priest selected for this purpose was Father François Corsi,[8] who, after reaching Daman, proceeded to Cambaya, from whence it was his intention to visit Father Xauier, and consult with him touching his journey to Lahor. He reached Cambaya at the beginning of the month of March of the year 1600. Here he was obliged to await a favourable opportunity for making his way to the King's camp. But his time was not wasted; for he greatly comforted the Christians who were there by his discourses and instruction, as well as by celebrating the divine service of the holy mass, and administering the sacraments, particularly the confession and the communion, of all which privileges the people there were deprived, being without a Christian priest. Here, too, the Baneanes[9] (who are certain Gentile merchants of India, living after the manner of the Pythagoreans) brought him the letters-patent of the King of Mogor, which had been sent by Father Xauier, containing permission for those of the Company to travel to Agra, Lahor, and Catai [Cathay], with orders to the various governors to supply funds for their journeys, and provide them with trustworthy guards.

The Governor of Cambaya, on seeing these letters, offered to take Father Corsi with him, for he was on the point of setting out for the court; but the Father, thanking him for his kindness, said that in accordance with the orders of his Superior, he must first make known his arrival to Father Xauier. The

Governor then offered him as much money as he needed for his journey. This likewise the Father declined; whereon the Governor commanded his son, who was to administer the province during his absence, to see that he was provided with everything that he needed.

Some time afterwards, the Father left Cambaya, and reached the King's camp a month later, on the 4th of June. His journey had not been without danger. Soon after leaving Cambaya, he and those with him fell in with a band of five hundred robbers, from whom, by the will of God, they were delivered by none other than the captain of the band, which happened in the following amusing manner. The said captain, having entered the town of Cambaya (doubtless to ascertain the time at which the Father and his companions were to set out), the Governor, and Coge-Soldan Hamet,[10] who went to Goa as ambassador of the King, sent for him, and charged him to conduct the Father, and those who travelled with him, in safety to Sambussar [Jambusir], which is two stages from Cambaya. This duty he faithfully accomplished, escorting them with a large body of horsemen. On the way, he pointed out to them the band of robbers, to whom, at the same time, he sent orders not to advance.

From Sambussar they were escorted for a distance of three leagues by the captain of the town with a hundred horse and some elephants, after which they were sent on with forty soldiers, twenty mounted and twenty on foot, and all arquebusiers, who took them as far as Baroche. Here they were met by a messenger with letters from Father Xauier; and they were also warned that there were robbers on the road they were to follow. They discovered, however, that these had been put to rout by the Governor of Cambaya, who had encountered them on his way back from the court, slaying five hundred of them, and capturing ten of their elephants. This we learn from a letter written by Father Corsi on the 12th of May.

In a letter describing the last portion of the journey, Father Corsi states that they were accompanied by more than a thousand soldiers, mostly mounted, who had been sent by the King of Mogor to escort Meira Mustaphar,[11] the son of the King of Guzaraté, who, on account of a certain affront he had received, had left the twenty companies of which he was the chief, and, out of spite, had become a Iogue. They were also joined by about four thousand merchants and other travellers. Nevertheless, about three stages from Breampur, they were attacked by a hostile force of more than four thousand horse; and a fierce conflict ensued, in which a hundred of the enemy were killed, and many wounded. Of the King's troops, only twenty were killed. The lives of the others were saved by an elephant which rushed furiously against the enemy's horse and threw them into such disorder that they were speedily put to rout. At last, Father Corsi reached the King's camp. He was received with great affection by Father Xauier and his companion; and the same day he went to pay his respects to the Great Mogor. From Breampur he continued his journey to Lahor to join Father Pignero. We shall refer to what he did there, after we have told the story of the war of which we have spoken.

It must be stated at the outset that it had long been the intention of this King of Mogor, called Achebar, to seize the whole of this region which is properly called India, and which lies between the two rivers, the Indus and the Ganges; and being already in peaceful possession of the greater portion of it, he wished to make himself master of the remainder, taking first of all the kingdoms of the Decan, and afterwards those of Goa, Malabar, and Bisnaga. When some years before he had gone to conquer the kingdom of Decan, the queen who then ruled, a woman of great spirit and courage, aided by the Portuguese and her own great lords, resisted him with such vigour that she slew many of his people at the entrance to the kingdom of Barara, where is a passage through the mountains forming an approach to this kingdom.[12] But after her death, the Decanins divided themselves into various parties, which led to the complete ruin of their kingdom; for some were gained by money, while others were deceived by promises (each party seeking its own advantage), so that, as ordinarily happens in a kingdom divided against itself, the road was left open to the enemy, with the result that the Great Mogor made himself master of the kingdom of Melique, in which he left a large force, and one of his sons to govern it.

Passing from thence, he came to the kingdom and city of Breampur, which was at once abandoned by its King, named Miram,[13] who retired to the fortress of Syr [Asirgarh], his chief stronghold, which on account of its site, and as possessing every other feature that could render a fortress strong, appeared to be impregnable, being placed on a high mountain five leagues in circuit, and surrounded by three concentric lines of fortifications, so cunningly constructed that the holders of each line could assist in the defence of the other two. Besides water from a living well, there was within the fort sufficient wood, vegetables, and other provisions to support for many years the seventy thousand soldiers who defended it. It was fortified with three thousand pieces of artillery, most of which were so large that the noise of their discharge was like terrific thunder.[14] There were in the fort, in addition to King Miram, seven other princes, each bearing the title of king, who, following the custom of the kingdom, remained shut up there with their families throughout their lives, unless the King died without issue, when the next in succession succeeded him.[15] The Governor of the kingdom, who was an Abyssinian and a very brave captain, was also there, and with him were seven other captains who, though of the sect of the Saracens, were of Portuguese descent. These eight captains were as active as they were courageous in their defence of this stronghold; so that although the Great Mogor invested it with as many as two hundred thousand men, he could achieve nothing; for the situation of the fort, its artillery, and the bravery of the captains within, prevented him from approaching close enough to take it by storm. But money and presents, the most effective engines for bombarding forts or capturing kingdoms, brought about its downfall, as we shall now relate.[16]

His inability to approach the fort greatly vexed the Mogor, who, finding the lion's skin ineffective, changed it for that of the fox, making use of the arts of cunning and deceit, of which he was a master. He sent a message to King Miran, saying that he had a great desire to speak with him, and swearing by the head of the Prince (an oath which a king, in these parts, regards as inviolable, as when he swears by the head of his father) that he should return at once to his fortress without let or hindrance. The unhappy King deliberated whether or not he should go. The Abyssinian governor and the other seven captains were firmly opposed to his leaving the fortress; but certain others, who had already (as we may suppose) been won over by money, expressed the contrary opinion. Following the advice of the latter, the King set forth,[17] wearing about his neck a chapperon, which is made after the manner of a stole, and which reached to his knees, as a sign of subjection. As soon as he came within sight of the Great Mogor, he made three obeisances, to which the other paid no heed, remaining motionless as a statue. King Miran then came close up to him; and as he was in the act of making another obeisance, one of the captains laid hands on him, and pulling him downwards by means of his chapperon, forced him to touch the ground with his nose.[18] It cannot be supposed that he would have dared to act thus without the consent of the Mogor, albeit the latter pretended that the incivility displeased him; for he rebuked the captain, though by no means severely. Having addressed some polite words to King Miran, he then and there made him write a letter [*il lui feit escrire tout aussy tost une lettre . . .*][19] to those who held the first line of defence, giving them orders that, on receipt of his letter, they should at once give entrance to the lord who was approaching, and whose coming was free from evil intent. But afterwards, when he wished to return, the Great Mogor, either forgetting or disregarding his oath, caused him to be arrested. On learning this, the Abyssinian governor immediately sent one of his sons to the Mogor with a letter in which he said that he was detaining his King, who had come forth under his Majesty's parole, and that it was unreasonable that he should hinder his return to his own people, since he had sworn to let him depart whenever he wished. He, therefore, prayed his Majesty to allow him to return, after which he could carry on the war in any way he pleased.

The King, knowing that the Abyssinian was, as it were, the key of the fortress, and that if he could be gained over, the place would be surrendered forthwith, asked his son whether his father would come to him, if invited to do so. The young man boldly replied that since his father had sent him to deliver this message, it was plain that he was not a man to surrender his fort in such a fashion, or to come there to parley; and his Majesty, he said, might rest assured that, as long as his father lived, he would never enter the fort. He added that if King Miran was not allowed to return, there was no lack of other kings in the fortress to succeed him.

This reply so enraged the Mogor that he straightway caused the young man to be put to death. When the Abyssinian was informed of this, he sent word to the Great Mogor that he prayed God he might never behold the face of a king so perfidious. Then, placing a chapperon about his neck, he addressed those who were in the fortress, reminding them that, as winter was at hand, the Great Mogor would be obliged to raise the siege and retire, so as not to risk the loss of all his troops. As for the fortress, he told them that there was no living soul who could gain possession of it, save God alone, or he to whom God or they themselves should be willing to deliver it; that there was no better or more honourable lot than that of those who fought for justice, and that they must, therefore, defend themselves with valour. For himself, he said, he preferred to die rather than live to look upon the face of so wicked a man. So saying, he tightened the knot of his chapperon, and strangled himself.[20]

To put an end to his life because he was unable to endure the look of his enemy, much less the torment he might inflict on him, was an act of cowardice unworthy of so brave a man. Though amongst the Pagans there are some who would esteem this a laudable act and one indicating great courage, yet, according to natural reason, it is rather to be esteemed an act of cowardice and worthy of our censure. For violence is a virtue when used to vanquish and surmount the evils and difficulties which stand in the way of our duty, not when it enables us to choose a small evil in order to avoid facing one that is greater.

But to return to our story. On the death of the Abyssinian, those in the fortress continued for some time longer to defend themselves, putting the Mogor to great difficulty, so that at last, finding that all his plans for the capture of the place were of no avail, he decided to bombard it with artillery; and having brought no guns with him for the purpose, he sent for Father Xauier and his companion, who were in his camp, and told them that they must write to the Portuguese at Chaul (a seaport of their country distant about a hundred leagues), and that he himself would also write, stating that he had not the necessary artillery and munitions to bombard this fortress, and requesting them, as they were now his friends, to send him both as soon as possible. The Father replied [*le Pere luy respond*][21] that his Majesty had commanded him a thing which he could not perform; for it was not lawful for him to ask this of the Portuguese, or to counsel them to such a step, for to do so would be a direct violation of the Christian law.[22] This was, in my belief, because the Portuguese had a short time previously made an alliance with King Miran. The barbarian was so displeased at the Father's refusal that he grew mad with rage, and ordered him and his companion to quit his court without delay, and return to Goa. They left his presence with the intention of departing; but a gentleman of the court, with whom they were on friendly terms, advised them not to stir; for they might be quite sure that if they set out, the

King would cause them to be killed before they had gone many leagues. He recommended them rather to keep out of sight until the storm had blown over.[23] They followed his advice, and in a short time the King's wrath subsided, and they were completely restored to his favour.

At last the King began to bombard this fortress with guns more powerful than those which are made of iron, and with shot more effective than cannon-balls. In other words, he bombarded it with great sums of money, acting on the principle of Philip of Macedon, who guaranteed to capture with ease the strongest fortress provided that a mule laden with gold could enter it. Large quantities of gold and silver were sent secretly to those who conducted the defence, which was so weakened thereby that none of the seven kings who were there to maintain the succession would accept the throne; for seeing that the captains and soldiers showed so little spirit, and so little resolution to defend themselves, they knew that their royalty would be of short duration. And they were not mistaken; for a few days later, the fortress, and consequently the whole kingdom, was surrendered to the Mogor,[24] who thus became master of it, and of the inestimable treasures and wealth which it contained. The Mogor pardoned all except the King, who was already in his hands, and the seven princes who would have succeeded him. These he sent as prisoners to his own country, giving King Miran a pension of four thousand crowns, and two thousand to each of the others. When the captains of the fortress were brought before him, he asked them to what religion they belonged; and when they replied that they were Saracens, he ordered them to be cruelly treated [*il comande qu'on les maltraictast*]. But Father Xauier begged that they might be handed over to him; to which the King replied that, by the Portuguese law, they deserved death, seeing that, though the descendants of Christians, they had turned Saracens; but as the Father had asked this favour of him, he willingly granted it. Father Xauier straightway applied himself to the saving of their souls, and it pleased our Saviour to vouchsafe to him the happiness of winning all the seven captains to the Christian faith. But this was not all that the Fathers accomplished through this expedition; for the sons and daughters of many Portuguese came into their hands, all of whom Benoist de Goës took with him to Goa, as will presently be narrated. In addition to these, more than seventy persons received baptism, many of whom were straightway received into the glory of heaven. Amongst these the happy lot of a female infant was noteworthy. A servant of Father Xauier having found this child lying like carrion on a dunghill, reported the matter to the Father, who thereupon had it brought to him and baptised it. The child survived for one day, and then went to join the company of the blessed in paradise. Thus was fulfilled to the letter that which is written, *De stercore erigeas pauperem, ut collocet eum cum principibus*, &c.

CHAPTER X[1]

An Embassy to Goa

About this time, Father Emmanuel Pigneiro, who had remained at Lahor, came to the camp, partly for the comfort of seeing Father Hierosme Xauier, for it was nearly three years since they had met, and partly to visit the King. The latter had been apprised of his departure from Lahor, and was the first to inform Father Xauier of his coming. On his arrival, the two Fathers went to pay their respects to his Majesty; and as it was not customary to appear before him empty handed, they took with them as their present a picture of our Lady very beautifully executed on paper. The King was seated at a window, listening, as was his custom, to those who sought speech with him. As soon as he saw Father Pigneiro, he invited him to approach, receiving him with much kindness, and bidding him uncover his head, and show him the present he had brought. On seeing the picture of our Lady, he bowed his head and raised his hands to his face, which, amongst these people, is a sign of great reverence. He then ordered the picture to be taken away and placed in his lodging; for he was seated upon his throne, and he deemed it unseemly that the picture of the Lady Mary should be below him. As he had ordered it to be removed so soon, the Fathers feared that it had not greatly pleased him, for the picture was on paper only, and, being drawn in ink, was uncoloured. Accordingly, they went on the following evening to his lodging, where he sat in less state, and where those who spoke to him could come nearer to his person. Here none but the most favoured persons were received. The Fathers, nevertheless, obtained entrance, and presented to him, besides some smaller gifts, another picture, this time of our Lady of Lorete,[2] painted on gilded calaim. Calaim is a metal which comes from China. Though it resembles tin, it is a different metal, and contains a large proportion of copper.[3] Nevertheless, it is white, and in India they make it into money. It can also be gilded, like silver. But to resume. Father Xauier addressing the King said that Father Pigneiro had come from Lahor to kiss his Majesty's feet, and begged that he might be permitted to approach. "By all means let him do so," replied the King; whereon the Father advanced and, bending down, embraced his feet. The King looked kindly on him, and in token of his good will laid his hands upon his shoulders, a mark of favour which he bestowed only on his chief captains and favourites. On seeing the picture of our Lady, he bowed low, and taking it into his hands, placed it on his head. Then boldly, in the presence of the assembled captains and lords, he did reverence to it with clasped hands, paying it outwardly as much honour as though he had been a Christian, except that he did not go down on his knees, for this is not their custom even in their mosques and places of prayer. When the

Father said that this Lady ought to be the guardian of his realm, he replied that he knew well that the Lady Mary was worthy of great veneration, and that it was for this reason that he had ordered the removal of the picture they had brought to him the previous day, for it did not seem fitting that he should be on a high seat, and the picture of our Lady below him. He then placed the cover on the picture with his own hands, and gave it in charge to one of his personal attendants. After this, he asked various questions about the Pope, desiring to know, amongst other things, what ceremonial was observed when he was visited by the Emperor; and on being told that the Emperor kissed the Pope's foot, he exclaimed, "Yes! That is because the Christians regard the Pope as the Vicar of the Lord Jesus." The Father then explained that the Pope, to show that he does not regard such homage as due to himself, except in so far as he is our Lord's Vicar, wears a small cross on his foot, and that it is this cross that is kissed.[4] On hearing this, the King and those with him marvelled greatly. While they were still discussing the cross, and the reverence in which we hold it, a young noble who had been a disciple of Father Pigneiro, and who happened to be present, made the sign of the cross. The King asked if he had done it correctly; and the Father replied that he had. He then asked why it was made on the forehead, the mouth, and the breast, all of which was explained to him.

So greatly did this powerful monarch desire to make himself master of Goa and the Portuguese possessions in India, with the regions adjacent thereto, that he constantly referred to the subject when conversing with his friends. On one occasion, while speaking of these things to the nobles assembled in his palace, he told them with bold assurance that, having conquered the kingdom of Decan, he would have little difficulty in overcoming Idalcan, after which he would soon have Goa, and all the Portuguese possessions in those parts. Now a certain Portuguese soldier, who on account of some misconduct had been obliged to quit India, happened to be present at this conversation, and hearing the King's remark, begged permission to speak. When this was granted, he said in the Persian language, "Your Majesty appears to be very confident of accomplishing these designs; but, as we say in my country, there is such a thing as reckoning without one's host. If your Majesty's opinion of the valour of the Portuguese is as high as people say, how can you expect to get the better of them so easily? Even though you regard them as so many chicken, yet chicken will peck before they allow themselves to be caught." "I have no intention," said the King, "of engaging them hand to hand. I shall overcome them by hunger." "Excellent! Sire," said the soldier. "You are of much the same mind as they are; for they intend to overcome your Majesty by thirst." (This was, I conclude, in allusion to the dryness of the Mogor's territories.) The King was delighted with this repartee, and made much of the Portuguese soldier. Nevertheless, the conquest of the Portuguese was at the root of all his designs. With this end in view, he frequently sent his agents to Goa, ostensibly as ambassadors, but whose real business was to keep an eye on what the Portuguese were doing, and to ascertain their military strength. He always sent his agents at times when ships were said to be due from Portugal, so that they might take note of what came in them, whether in the way of merchandise, or men.[5]

It was in pursuance of this object that he despatched an ambassador who reached Goa at the end of the month of May, of the year 1601. The ambassador sent on this occasion was from the kingdom of Cambaya, a person of great wealth and influence, a Guzarate by birth, and of the sect of the Saracens.[6] The alleged object of the mission was to establish a permanent peace by land and by sea with the Portuguese. The ambassador was also to make inquiry as to the most suitable present that his Majesty could make to the King of Portugal, to whom he contemplated sending an ambassador in order to confirm and strengthen their alliance.

The mission was received at Goa with great magnificence. It was met and escorted through the town by an imposing company of Portuguese nobles, and the ambassador was accorded all the honours usually paid to the representative of a great monarch. But the chief feature of his reception was a terrific salute of artillery which was continued throughout the day, both from the guns in the city and from those in other parts of the island; for the Portuguese had a great store of artillery of high quality. The ambassador fully appreciated the significance of this music. The gifts which he presented to the Viceroy on behalf of the Prince were some rich carpets, a panther which had been trained to the chase, another smaller panther, and a very valuable horse.

But far more valuable were the gifts which Benoist de Goës, the companion of Father Xauier (who accompanied the ambassador by the King's command), presented to our Saviour and the Church; for he brought with him to Goa many half-casts of both sexes, the children of Portuguese, born amongst the thorny paths of Paganism and Mahometanism, who, upon the reduction of the fortress, became the slaves of the Great Mogor, who handed them over to the said Benoist de Goës. These, after receiving some instruction in the Christian faith, were all baptised. The Viceroy showed them much kindness, and signified his desire to stand godfather to them. Amongst them was a Portuguese Jew who was ninety years of age. For more than forty years he had publicly professed Judaism; but God at last shed the light of heaven upon him, and he was converted to Christianity, and baptised. The letter which the ambassador carried to the Viceroy, setting forth the object of his mission, was to the following effect:—

'The message of the great Lord of the law of Mahomet, high and mighty King, slayer of hostile Kings, to whom the Great pay homage, whose dignity is unsurpassed, who is exalted above other kings, and whose government is renowned throughout the world, to Ayres de Saldagna Viceroy:—

'Meeting with favour and grace at the hands of the King of Kings, honoured and privileged by him, know that, by the grace of God, all the ports of Indostan, from Cinde to Chatigan and Pegu, are under our high prosperity; and it is always in our royal heart, and before our eyes, that the rich merchants and those who traffic may be able to go and come with all assurance and safety, so that they may continually pray to God for the increase of our prosperity, and especially the inhabitants of the kingdoms of the Portuguese, who, outside this kingdom, cannot go and come freely, and who are accustomed to navigate the sea of Indostan. [For this reason our royal honour has willed and arranged that one of our servants and courtiers has been sent as ambassador to confirm once again the basis of the alliance, so that there may henceforth be no occasion to doubt it. On this occasion the Father Benoist de Goës has been sent together with our trusted servant Cogetqui Soldan Hama to your parts, where, after informing themselves with all diligence of things as they pass, they may accurately advise us, so that conformably to the status of each one, our good fortune may make provision for the going and the sending.][7] And if there are any skilled craftsmen who desire to visit our royal court, which is like the mansions of the blest, he shall give them all that they need in food and apparel, and bring them with him to this our court, the fulcrum of the world, on the understanding that, having been in our service, they shall have leave to return to their country whenever it shall be their will to do so. It is fitting that they should be given good expectations, so that they may desire, of their own accord, to kiss the buttress of our throne. And as to whatsoever our ambassador may wish to purchase in the way of precious stones, fabrics, and other things of a like valuable nature, our desire is that he may be given all assistance therein, so that he may do his business and return speedily, since he is in our royal service. As to other matters, he will make them known to you by word of mouth. The 9th day of Fauardi of God,[8] of the forty-sixth year of the era.'

Such was the style in which this Prince wrote. They regard the period of his reign as an era, and the month of Fauardi [*Faridun*] is the first of the year, which they commence on the day of the Spring equinox, and which in this year was the 20th of March.[9] Let us now see what was taking place at Lahor at this time.

CHAPTER XI[1]

Father Pigneiro at Lahore, 1600–1

Whilst Father Hierosme Xauier and Benoist de Goës accompanied the Great Mogor on this expedition, Father Emmanuel Pigneiro remained at Lahore to look after the few Christians who were there, and to endeavour to lead others to our Saviour. Both Mahometans and Gentiles used to seek speech with him, going frequently to his house to question him on divers subjects. Many came away with a lower opinion than before of their own sects; while many were left doubtful and wavering. But there were others who laughed at the idea that there could be a better law than the law of Mahomet; and when strong reasons were put before them, they said that their minds could not grasp such matters, and that it was enough for them to believe what Mahomet had told them. That which, more than all, they could neither understand nor believe was that God could have a son. For so carnal-minded are they that the purity of this mystery is beyond their conception. To convince them, the Father bade them say if God could see and hear; and on their answering in the affirmative, he continued, " If God has neither eyes nor ears, how is it possible for him to see and hear ? " They answered that it was by some means which none could understand. " And likewise," said the Father, defeating them with their own weapons, "in some wonderful manner which none can understand, God had a son."

The Gentiles were more easily persuaded; for, in the end, they were ready to admit that there was only one God, and that those which were sold to them as such, were not Gods. Whatever aversion they had to the Fathers, was due to the Brachmanes, who instilled into them the belief that the Christians were a barbarous and ignorant people, who ate rats, cats, and such like animals, and practised other absurdities. Notwithstanding, the Fathers lived in their midst at this time with as much assurance, and spoke as freely against the sect of Mahomet, as though they had been amongst Christians.

The Viceroy and Governors, or magistrates of the city, treated them with much respect, especially the Viceroy, who spoke of them in terms so high that modesty forbids their repetition. He often offered Father Pigneiro money for his daily expenses, and the Father used to thank him and say, that if at any time his need should be urgent, he would have recourse to him as to a father. Nevertheless, not to seem uncivil, and to avoid giving offence, he accepted from him gifts of melons, grapes, and other fruits. The Viceroy used frequently to visit him, and attend the Christian festivals, by which he drew upon himself the wrath of the Saracens. The Governors of the town likewise held the Fathers in high esteem, granting them concessions which they might have found difficulty in obtaining even from Christians, such as the pardon of two persons who had committed manslaughter, and other considerable favours. Once, when a violent quarrel arose between the chief judge [*Iuge-mage*][2] and the King's treasurer, and a conflict between their armed partisans was imminent, the Father succeeded in bringing about a reconciliation, thus preventing much bloodshed and loss of life. In making a report of this affair to the Viceroy, one of the parties said, in support of his story, that the Father knew how it all took place; upon which the Viceroy said, "If the Father knows, that is sufficient for me; for I place more reliance on him than on a thousand witnesses."

Not very long afterwards, this good Viceroy died, whereat the Fathers were greatly grieved, and the more so because, in return for his many kind actions, they had been unable to help him in that which concerned him most, namely, the salvation of his soul, by leading him to our Saviour. He left behind him thirteen hundred thousand crowns in gold coin, and a large store of gold and silver ware, precious gems, and other valuable things, besides many horses and elephants; for the splendour of his retinue surpassed that of the greatest lords of Spain. So wrote the Father Pigneiro. But when he quitted the world, hell was all his heritage, and his riches passed to the King, who, according to the usage of Indostan, succeeds to all the property of his vassals. He was succeeded in his office by his brother, whose children had been pupils of Father Pigneiro. The new Viceroy told the Father, when he went to visit him, that he would continue towards them the favours which his brother had shown them; and that his appointment need cause them no apprehensions.[3] This he soon made apparent. For the enemies of the Fathers, thinking that, as the former Viceroy was dead, they could now attack them with impunity and do them any ill they chose, were constantly watching for an opportunity to satisfy their malice. Accordingly, on a certain day, one of their number, seeing a great crowd collected outside the church, went to the Catual (one of the Governors of the town, who has charge of the guard), and urged him to destroy the building, and drive the Fathers away. The Catual replied that he could not do this, in as much as it was the will of the King that the Fathers should stay there, and that their church should remain standing. "If," he added, "you want the Fathers driven away because you see yourself held in less repute than they, Father Pigneiro is still there; why do you not go and vanquish him in dispute?" To this the other rejoined that the Father would not dare to come forth and dispute with him. "But it is you," said the Catual, "who do not dare to open your mouth before him. For the King, and every one else, knows that the Father's knowledge is very great, and that yours is very small." When the Viceroy heard of this man's designs, he had him placed in a dungeon, and it was only at the request of Father Pigneiro that he was released.

CHAPTER XII[1]

THE CONFIDENCE TRICK

ALTHOUGH the Viceroys and Governors of the town displayed both respect and regard for the Fathers, there were certain Gentiles living near them who constantly sought to do them some ill turn. Once, because some of their relatives had been won over to the faith, they circulated a number of malicious and slanderous reports about them, in which they accused them, amongst other outrageous charges, of eating human flesh. Speaking generally, however, the Gentiles, and indeed most of the Infidels, treated the Fathers with much respect, sometimes even with affection; for the latter often interceded for them with the King and the Governors of the town, recommending their petitions for consideration, or allowing those guilty of misdemeanour to take refuge in their church, where the officers of justice dared not enter to search for them; for by the King's decree the building had been declared a sanctuary.

But the lives of the Fathers were not free from adversity. Here, for example, is an account of a piece of roguery of which Father Pigneiro was the victim. To make the story clear, it must be premised that it was the custom of the Fathers to distribute daily, at the door of their house, relief to more than a hundred poor people, without counting those whose cases were exceptional. Now, amongst the latter, there appeared one day a young man about twenty years of age, who was a native of Fuximir [Kashmir?], though his features resembled those of a Portuguese, and who appeared to be well-to-do. He said that he was of noble birth, but that he was forced to fly from place to place to escape from certain persons to whom he had given offence; and with tears in his eyes he begged the Father to shelter him. Thinking that he might be able to convert this young man to Christianity, Father Pigneiro acceded to his request, and allowed him to take refuge in his house. Two or three days later he brought in another young man, whom he described as his brother, but who was in reality a confederate, who had been instructed in the part he was to play in this evil enterprise, which was to murder the Father and those who were with him, and, unless God prevented them, to carry off everything of value in the house. A favourable opportunity arrived; for the guard of the house, which had not yet been properly enclosed or secured, absented himself, leaving the coast clear for the two thieves. One of these rascals then went into the kitchen, and threw into the cooking-pot, and into the drinking water, a certain seed called *doturo*,[2] a poison which, though not deadly in its effects, is sufficiently powerful to render those who take it insensible. At the customary hour, the Father commenced his supper; but after taking one or two mouthfuls, he noticed something unusual in the food, and suspecting what it was, retired to his chamber and lay down, which is a sovereign remedy against this kind of poisoning. The servants ate the remainder of the food, and were soon so dazed that they knew not where they were. The Father forced himself to vomit, which is also beneficial in such cases; but having drunk some of the poisoned water, he suddenly fell to the ground senseless. In short, all happened just as these rascally thieves desired; for the Father was completely overcome, and knew nothing; and the servants were in a similar condition. One of the watchers, the most faithful of all the servants, was given the *doturo* in a melon, while the other stayed away the whole of that evening.

There were twenty armed men in the street ready to defend the two in the house. The latter went upstairs, and finding the Father lying unconscious, carried him into one of the rooms and locked him in. They then went to another room in which, because it was locked, and the key in the Father's keeping, they expected to find the valuables they were in search of.

The noise they made in breaking open the door of this room aroused the Father, who tried to cry out, but could not; and in any case there was none to hear him, for all in the house were in the same plight as himself. He then went to the window, which he threw down into the street,[3] in the hope of bringing the neighbours to his assistance. After that, he again tried to cry out; but the poison had affected his throat, and as sometimes happens to persons who are oppressed in the night, he was unable to utter a sound. At last, the thieves made off, taking with them whatever they could lay their hands upon. Though the articles stolen were not of great value, they were worth much to the Fathers; for amongst other things they carried off a small cabinet containing some relics and some beautiful images, as well as a model of the sepulchre of our Saviour, which Father Hierosme Rodrigues had brought from Hierusalem.

In the mean time, it was reported, and the rumour soon spread through the town, that the Father was dead; and the neighbours flocked to the door of the house to mourn for him. He had, however, by this time, recovered, and showing himself at the window inquired why they wept. His appearance filled them with amazement, and they rejoiced greatly to behold alive him whom they were lamenting as dead. Leaving the chamber in which he had been confined, the Father proceeded to the one which he usually occupied. This the thieves had ransacked, and the extent of their depredations was evident. But, by the grace of God, there yet remained wherewith to repair the loss; for the Father found under his bed the small chest in which his limited funds were kept. The Catual, of whom we have spoken above, was greatly concerned on hearing what had taken place. He at once sent his son to inquire into the affair, and soon afterwards came to the house himself. The Viceroy, who was ill at the time, sent a message expressing his indignation at the outrage, and assuring the Father, that if the property stolen from him was not recovered, he would make good the loss himself. Shortly afterwards, when Father Pigneiro made his appearance in the town, the people plainly showed that they were pleased to see him alive and well. Some said, "It is the holy Father; but he is now penniless; for the thieves took from him all that he had." Others said, "This is the Father who was robbed of seventy thousand crowns; but who holds more account of one small book than of all the money in the world." Thus the affair terminated. Let us now pass on to other matters.

CHAPTER XIII[1]

Some Notable Conversions

As the outward forms and symbols of Christianity, and, in a special degree, the holy ceremonies of the Church, exercised a powerful influence on the Infidels, leading many of them to abandon their worthless sects, and embrace our faith, those who laboured for their conversion made use of these as a means of drawing souls to our Saviour; and, to this end, they celebrated the principal feasts of the Church, in which we commemorate the most solemn mysteries of our faith, with great pomp, particularly those of Noel and the Passover.

At the festival of Noel of the year 1600, the Father Pigneiro fashioned on the altar of the church a manger in which lay the image of the infant Jesus-Christ, together with other scenes illustrating the stories and mysteries of holy scripture. He also made figures of some of the better known of the prophets, of whom these people had heard, inscribing beside them in Persian their prophecies of the birth of our Saviour. The adoration of Jesus-Christ, God and Man, by the three wise Kings was also represented. It greatly astonished the Saracens to learn that the holy writings of the Old Testament spoke so clearly of the birth of the Son of God into this world.

On the first day of the octave, the Viceroy,[2] accompanied by all the nobles of Lahor, came to see these things, and listened to everything he was told concerning them. But that which pleased him most was a pastorale which was fortunately being acted on that day, dealing with the evils and afflictions which had befallen mankind through the sin of our first parent Adam, who was represented on the stage bemoaning his miseries, while the aged Simeon sought to console him with the certain hope of the coming of the Messiah, who will heal all our infirmities. Next appeared a philosopher, reviling his senses for making him adore things created instead of his creator, though this was contrary to his philosophy, to whom came Adam, telling him of original sin, from which had proceeded ignorance and all the other defects of human nature, which was perfect when man was first created. They then entered into a dispute about the divine essence, and the trinity of the Persons, in which Adam, by many arguments, demonstrated that God, though perfect in purity, nevertheless had a son, to which in the end the philosopher assented. In the next scene a discussion took place between Mercy and Divine Justice touching the sin of Adam; and in the next, an angel appeared, and announced to some Brachmanes the birth in the world of the Son of God. This filled the Brachmanes with dismay; but a shepherd, who said that he had come from Bethlehem, allayed their fears, telling them that the little child who was born, though he was indeed God, was not come, like their own false gods, to destroy men, but to save them and give them eternal life. Such was the theme of this drama, which was very well received by the infidels, and from that day forward they regarded our faith in a new light. So great was the number of people, both from the town and from a distance, who came to witness the festival, that for the forty days during which it lasted, the church was always full. Amongst the number were several Rayas (who are the princes and great lords of the country) who listened very gladly to all that was told them of the mysteries of our faith. It was a great consolation to the Christians, and especially to the Father, to see these infidels prostrate themselves before the altar as devoutly as though they had been the best Christians in the world. But their prayers were, after all, for children and riches; and it was with the same end in view that they made offerings to the representation of our Saviour on the altar.

The Catual, though a narrow-minded Mahometan, came to the festival accompanied by many people. A small Brachmane lad explained to him all that he wished to know; and when the Catual asked him whose son he was, he replied that he was the son of a Brachmane, and that he was preparing to become a Christian. "For what reason do you wish to become a Christian?" asked the Catual. "Because," said the lad, "it is only in the law of the Christians that salvation is to be found; for by the law of the Saracens, or that of the Gentiles, none can be saved." The numbers who came to the services during Holy Week and Easter were equally large. The Viceroy again attended, to the great vexation of the Saracens, who urged him not to countenance these Christian feasts; but their opposition was of no avail.

As to the primary purpose of the Fathers, which was the conversion of the infidels, things go on from day to day in such a manner that they are unable to tell what may be God's purpose in regard to this country. For when, on the one hand, they contemplate so vast a wilderness of Mahometanism and Paganism, they despair of ever attaining their goal, and feel that the time and labour spent in preparing a soil so barren might be employed to more profit elsewhere. On the other hand, when from time to time blossoms appear, and souls are won for our Saviour, they are filled with renewed courage, and a renewed hope that this land, which is now so unfruitful, may one day yield an abundant harvest.

In the course of this year, the Fathers baptised on one occasion thirty-nine persons, on another twenty, and on a third occasion, forty-seven. The last of these services was conducted with great solemnity on the octave of the Assumption of our Lady, and was largely attended both by Christians and infidels. Amongst those who were baptised on one of the former occasions were the two infant sons of a certain infidel who himself brought them to the church to be cleansed in the water of holy baptism. It seemed as though our Lord had chosen them that He might make haste to bestow upon them the crown of glory; for a few days later He called them to Himself. Their father and mother remained Mahometans. A case which followed equally deserves notice. A woman of noble family, who had for some years associated with Christians, though obstinately adhering to her superstitious beliefs, finding herself approaching the gates of death, summoned to her side Father Pigneiro, and said that she desired to die in the faith of the Lord Jesus, that she might be saved. The Father, having given her such instruction as the shortness of the time permitted, for she was grievously sick, baptised her, and within a short while her soul went to enjoy eternal felicity.

Another woman while contemplating the manger felt God's touch so strongly that she did not dare to return to her village until she had become a Christian. As she did not know what steps to take for this purpose, she inquired of a Pagan woman who lived near the Fathers, and, by her advice, she enrolled herself, together with one of her servants, amongst the catechumens. In another case, a woman who had been frequently to the church, was so impressed by the modest behaviour of the children who were being taught there, that she was prompted to become a Christian; and both she and her husband, together with their children and daughter-in-law, were baptised. Learning what she had done, her relations, of whom she had many, rushed into her house and beat her without mercy; but this brave woman answered every blow with the same words: "You are welcome to kill me, since God, in His mercy, has taken me for His own."

A young man of the race of the Xaques [Shaikhs][3] (who in this country are regarded as holy men) who had formerly been an inveterate enemy of the Christians, and had bitterly persecuted his own brother for receiving baptism, was converted to the faith in the following circumstances. He had gone, out of devotion, or rather superstition, bare-footed to Meque, there to improve his knowledge of the law of Mahomet, and in this study had spent twelve years. On returning to his country, a graduate as it were in this same law, he sought out and entered into dispute with Father Pigneiro. In the end, he was obliged to acknowledge defeat, and at the same time God so touched his heart that he resolved to reject the law of Mahomet, and to embrace that of Jesus-Christ. When he had taken this resolution, he told the Father that never whilst at Meque had he enjoyed happiness or peace of mind, but that now he had found both peace and consolation, while God had manifested to him many things that for years he had been longing to understand. After he had been catechised and baptised, Father Pigneiro sent him to Father Xauier, that he might be of service to him in the conversion of others.

A woman of Chacata [Chaghatai], who was of royal blood, following the example of her mother who had already become a Christian, was converted to the faith, in spite of the strong opposition of her relations. A gentleman who had heard the Christian religion much spoken of, decided to embrace it, which he did, together with his wife and five children. A Brachmane, on seeing the holy manger of which we have spoken, made up his mind to abandon his Pagodes, and straightway brought to the Father the best of those which he had. It was made of black stone, and was very finely carved. Many Gentiles were in the habit of attending the sermons which were preached in the church, and from these they appeared to derive much satisfaction.

The catechumens serve a long probation before they are baptised; for it is well to proceed thus in a country where, as we shall see in the next chapter, there is so much opposition; yet there are not a few, even among young children, who firmly adhere to the faith they have chosen. One lad, for example, during a certain feast of the Gentiles at which (following the custom of the Persians) they worship the sun, fled to the house of the Fathers, because his mother insisted on his observance of this superstitious rite. On this account he had suffered much; but he avenged himself on those who pursued him by saying a thousand evil things of their Pagodes. Another lad came and asked the Fathers if it was a sin to worship idols, and, on being told that it was, said, " Then I promise you that I will never again worship them, even though my father kills me for it." Father Pigneiro asked him why he did not bring to him his father's Pagode.[4] " That," said the youth, " would be an easy thing to do; but it would only make matters worse; because my father would say that his Pagode had gone to heaven, as another Gentile said, who had lost his." His father was, in fact, so superstitious that one evening, on returning to his house and finding his Pagode warm, he said that it must be angry. But his son laughed, and said, " It is not to be wondered at that it is warm, since it has been all day in the sun. I should be warm too, under similar circumstances." The father was much disconcerted by this remark, and blushed for shame to find himself being taught by one whom it was his duty to teach. Another case was that of a young Brachmane who, because he had become a Christian, suffered much ill-usage at his father's hands, for which, however, he cared nothing. One day, his father being away, his mother told him to give food to the Pagode, for, being a woman, she could not do this herself. "Mother," said the youth, "do you eat that which you wish given to the Pagode; for stones do not eat." Not long afterwards, when the father was on his way to a certain village, a whirlwind arose which raised so much dust that he lost his way. As he was wandering over the hills not knowing whither he was going, a person of venerable and majestic aspect appeared before him, and inquired who he was, and, on learning that he was a Brachmane, said, "For the time being you are pardoned, because you allow your son to go to the church." All this the Brachmane told to his neighbours, who thenceforward were much more ready to let their children attend the church, and commenced to show a greater respect for the Christian religion.

It was through one of these children that Father Pigneiro became acquainted with a personage of authority, and the head of the town in which he lived, to whom he paid a visit at a time when there was great need of rain. Now it chanced that rain fell heavily during the time that the Father was there; and as these people are very superstitious, both the chief himself and all the inhabitants of the town made much of the Father, and displayed so great a regard for the law that he preached that they openly declared it to be the true law, and told him that he was welcome to take possession of their mosque and turn it into a church.

The same Father persuaded several Armenians to join the catholic church. Some of these abandoned their Mahometan and Gentile concubines, while others married in the church those whom they had before misused. The Armenians of this country, as a whole, are less ready than formerly to scorn and insult the Church; for it is known that the Fathers enjoy the favour and support of the Viceroy, and that the officers of justice have orders to banish from the town any whom they name to them. The behaviour of the Armenians was also influenced by the fact that their Archbishop, on whose advent they had been counting, died on his way to India. Having reached Ormuz, he had been prevented from continuing his journey by sea and set out for Lahor by way of Persia. He perished on the road, unsuccoured by God or man. His books and all else he possessed were stolen. The former fell eventually into the hands of Father Pigneiro, which greatly annoyed the Armenians, who had desired to present them to the King. They thought that this prelate was coming to India to be Archbishop of Serre,[5] that is of the Christians of St. Thomas in Malabar; but that office was filled in a different manner, as will appear later.

For the rest, the Gentiles continue to pursue their foolish superstitions. On the 10th of July in the year

1600, there was an eclipse of the sun at noon. This was a great source of profit to the Brachmanes on account of the offerings they extracted from poor and ignorant people, persuading them that the sun and moon were fighting against each other, and that there would not be peace between these luminaries until vast offerings had been made to them. The people also went to bathe in the river, thinking thereby to cleanse themselves of their sins; for these they said were the cause of the discord between the heavenly torches which, as soon as they came out from the water, would cease their strife and shine as before.[6]

CHAPTER XIV[1]

A Brave Champion

The Gentiles, and especially the Brachmanes, who are, more than all others given to idolatry, exhibited the greatest resentment when any of their children became Christians; and their hostility on this account was the most formidable obstacle which the Fathers encountered in their efforts to extend the boundaries of the kingdom of Jesus-Christ in the territories of the Mogor. Whenever a young man showed a disposition to abandon the sect of perdition to which he belonged, and to embrace our faith, he was subjected to continuous persecution by his parents and other relations. It would be possible to describe many such cases; but, that my story may not be too long, I shall confine myself to one noteworthy example.

A young married man called Polada[2] (from the name of one of the false gods of the Gentiles), a Brachmane by birth, and a Pandito by profession, that is to say a doctor, and the son of one of the leading citizens of Lahor, became a catechumen, and not only proclaimed the same on all sides, but openly held up to ridicule the faith of the Gentiles. His father and mother, taking this as a great affront, determined with the assistance of their relatives and friends, to prevent him from carrying out his good intention. The young man courageously resisted their evil efforts until, finding that his mother continued night and day to torment him in order to turn him from his purpose, he resolved to abandon father, mother, wife, brothers, and friends, in short, all that he had in the world, and to come to the Church and serve our Saviour who called him. He lost no time in carrying out his resolution, while his wife declared her intention of becoming a Christian with her husband. His father and mother thereupon seized their daughter-in-law, and carried her away to the mountains, where they kept her in a cave, trying to make her swear that she would never embrace Christianity, and that if her husband did so, she would refuse to see him again, and would burn herself alive, by doing which, they told her, she would be held a saint by all the world. For the Gentiles have this senseless idea that the wife who burns herself for love of her husband goes straight to Paradise; and not only she, but all her relations to the fourth generation.

But their daughter-in-law had no desire either to become a saint herself, or to sanctify her relatives, by any such method; and to all their importunities she replied with firm resolution, that she was a Christian, and had no wish to go to hell. They then took her to, and kept her in a certain village, where she continued to answer them in the same way; and her relatives mourned her as one dead. By keeping her in seclusion they thought to get her husband into their power, believing that he would come in search of her, and thus give them an opportunity of seizing him;

but she contrived to escape from their hands, and took refuge with her husband in the church, declaring that she wished to live and die in its service. The mother of the young man, seeing that forcible methods had failed, had recourse to cunning. She went several times to the church to see her son, and told him that she was well content that he should be baptised, provided that this did not take place publicly on the night of Noel, as he had intended. She also said that she and her husband, and her other children, likewise desired to become Christians; and Father Pigneiro, believing her words, allowed her to take her son to her house. But this wicked mother, unable to reason him out of his determination, tried by means of some magic powders, which she mixed with his food and his drink, to make him lose his desire to become a Christian. Her enchantments were, however, of no avail. For a time, indeed, the catechumen's mind was deranged: he could not bear his mother out of his sight, and was unable to remember anything, or to do anything but cry out continuously, "Mother! Mother!" But, in a short time, our Saviour delivered him from the power of the spell, and restored him to his senses. After that, he no longer trusted his mother, and would take nothing to eat or drink from her hands. Nevertheless, she did not relinquish her evil efforts. Five times she tried to poison him; but God saved him, even when he had the poison in his mouth.

Father Pigneiro knowing the danger to which he was exposed, withdrew him to his house. To this his parents at first pretended to consent; but, aware of his constancy, for he remained as firm as a rock, they assembled all their relations, and went with them to the door of the Father's house, where they made a great clamour, crying out that the Father had kidnapped their son in order to force him against his will to become a Christian. Hearing this, Father Pigneiro bade the catechumen go forth, and tell them himself why he was there. As soon as he was outside the door, they fell upon him like so many tigers, with the intention of seizing him and carrying him out of the town. With great vigour and courage, the young man defended himself against his assailants, amongst whom was his mother who had seized him by his legs. He succeeded, however, in freeing himself from her grasp, and also from the hands of his father and his relations. In short, he went beyond the counsel which S. Hierosme gave to Heliodore, when he said, *per calatum perge patrem, per calatam perge matrem, & ad vexillum crucis euola*; for he had seized a sword and had already raised it above the head of his father, who had a firmer hold on him than the others, when, at the same moment, Father Pigneiro arrived on the scene, and took the weapon from his hands, though he was very unwilling to give it up. This was by the providence of God, as he would assuredly have inflicted some grievous hurt on his father, if the sword had not been taken from him; for he was as yet new to the teaching of our Saviour, and thought himself at liberty to kill any one who attempted to shut him out from salvation; and in the heat of his anger he cried out, "Leave me alone! Let me kill these idolaters who worship wood and stone, and who wish to keep me from being saved, and to take me to hell with them!"

The mother, seeing that they had not accomplished what they had designed, which was that the catechumen should be captured, or, at any rate, that one of their number should be wounded, so that they might have a complaint to lay before the Justice, picked up her little grandson, a child of one and a half years, and, as though it had been a piece of wood, flung it with all her force upon the steps of the doorway, intending either to kill it, or cause it serious injury. Believing the child to be dead, the Gentiles renewed their uproar, crying out that the Father had killed it. But when the Father lifted the little creature up, it seemed to be asleep, and was without injury, or sign of any. This brought the disturbance to an end, and the Gentiles withdrew, confused and humiliated.

A few days later they returned, accompanied by some of the leading members of their community. The young man, however, soon dispelled any doubts they may have entertained regarding him. He told them that, as long as he had life, he would never abandon the law of Jesus-Christ; and in proof of his determination, he severed in their presence the thread which he wore round his neck (amongst these people no act signifies so completely as this the renunciation of their sect), and having broken it into four pieces, he threw them on to his mother's head. That done, he took some scissors, and, with his own hand, cut off his *sendi*,[3] which is the long lock of hair they let grow on the top of the head, as a mark of Gentilism. This filled the Pagans with consternation; for they had never seen any one do such a thing before. Some of them were so shocked and bewildered that they hastily departed. Others, and these were the persons of quality whose support had been solicited, begged pardon of the Fathers, saying that they had come there out of kindness to the father of this young man, whom, they had been given to understand, had been subjected to coercion; but having themselves witnessed his resolution, they had nothing more to say in the matter.

The relatives of the catechumen next induced certain Pagans of position, who were the assistants of the Nauabo, or *Iuge-Mage*,[4] to whom, and also to the Viceroy, they acted as counsellors, to bring a number of defamatory charges against Father Pigneiro. In these he was accused of the most heinous crimes, the least of which were that he ate human flesh, that he stole children and sent them to Goa to be sold, that he was an accomplished sorcerer and magician, that he had killed a young man and cut off his head, which he used, together with the teeth of a bird unknown in that country, in making drugs and potions, and that with the latter he cast spells upon people, so that he could do with them whatsoever he willed. The said Pagans, actuated more by their zeal for their sect, which they deemed would be disgraced if the catechumen quitted it in this fashion, than by any belief they had in the truth of these charges, carried the indictment to the Nauabo, and read it through to him from beginning to end, causing great astonishment. By a fortunate chance, Father Pigneiro, ignorant of the plot against him, went, at the same time, to see the Nauabo, whom he was in the habit of visiting. The Nauabo said nothing about the charges; nor did he show any sign of having seen them, but spoke of other things. On his way back to his house, the Father met the Catual, who told him what was going on, and that the Nauabo was anxious to see the young catechumen. The Father at once sent him, together with his wife (both of whom had now been baptised) to the Nauabo's house, where he found his father and mother awaiting an opportunity to seize him.

The Nauabo allowed no one to be present at the investigation except the Catual and certain intimate friends of his own. He first asked the young man if these were his father and mother. "Formerly," replied the young man, "when I was an idolater, I acknowledged them as such; but now that I am a Christian, whilst they are Pagans, I no longer regard them in this light." His father and mother thereupon cried out, that the Father was a wicked man, and had taken their son from them by force. But the Nauabo bade them hold their tongues, and not only upbraided them, calling them slanderers and liars, but gave them blows with his fists, saying that he was well acquainted with the Fathers, and knew them to be good people, and not such as they described them. After that, he continued his questions, asking the young man if he was a Christian. "Yes," he replied, "through the mercy of God." "Are you willing to abandon this law?" was the next question. "I would more willingly," he said, "give up my life than the law of the Lord Jesus, into which, through His grace, I have already been received." His wife, on the same question being put to her, replied with equal firmness, and far greater courage than one would expect to find in one of the weaker sex. The Nauabo said "*Thama Theogoda*,"[5] 'May the benediction of God be on this woman'; then turning to the father and mother of the husband, he said, "What more do you want? This young man is no longer an infant; but has reached years of discretion. He and his wife have chosen to follow the law of the Christians. This is a good law; and they regard it as such, and do not wish to follow your law. Go home, and leave them in peace." After that he privately instructed the Catual to guard the young man, and see that no harm was done to him. The Catual accordingly took him to his own house, where he kept him for two or three days, treating him as though he belonged to him, and permitting none but Christians to speak with him.

About this time, the Father went to visit the Nauabo, whom he found in conversation with his assistants, or advisers. The latter, being of the same sect as the parents of the catechumen, gave vent to their indignation against the Father, and spoke to him in very violent language. But he had no need to defend himself; for this the Nauabo did very effectively, praising the law of the Christians as ardently as though he himself followed it. The Gentiles, he said, possessed neither law, nor scriptures, nor prophets; they were *Bidins*,[6] that is, people who had no law; while the Christians possessed the law of the Lord Jesus, which was good and holy, and had likewise their scriptures and their prophets; and the young man, he added, had done well to forsake idols of wood and stone for so holy a faith. When the Gentiles said that the Neophyte was a minor, the other rejoined, "Why do you say that? I have seen him, and his wife also. They are quite old enough to take this step; and they are both so constant to the faith they have embraced that they told me they would rather sacrifice their lives than be deprived of it."

The Nauabo was so favourably inclined towards the Christian faith that he defended it not only against the Gentiles, but against the Saracens, though outwardly he appeared to be a Mahometan. The Fathers were on one occasion at a gathering at which the Nauabo and many of the King's captains were present, as well as a certain Mulla, or doctor of the law of Mahomet, who had done little to further their interests with the King; and on a discussion taking place as to the truth or otherwise of the Christian law, the Nauabo so strongly supported the arguments of the Fathers, the soundness of which he said that there was no gainsaying, that at last the Mulla, in great anger, said, "If your Lordship takes the side of the Fathers and defends the Christian law, who will dare to disagree, or to defend the law of the Lord, that is, of Mahomet, whom they call absolute Lord?" This made no impression on the Nauabo; for he held little account of the law of Mahomet, neither fasting during the Ramadan, nor troubling himself about its other superstitions. He was, however, fast entangled by the hundred wives he kept in his seraglio.

But let us return to our brave champion. The Nauabo, in order to show that he was impartial, and had no desire to favour the Fathers at the expense of justice, and being weary of the complaints with which the Gentiles incessantly besieged his ears, referred the case to the *Cateris*,[7] who are certain Pagan judges of great authority, before whom the Brachmanes, and the Panditos who were with them, maintained that never, since the beginning of the world, had such a case been known in Indostan, and that when the King heard of it, his anger would be great; for once, when the son of a Brachmane (whom they named) had wished to turn Saracen, his Majesty had refused his consent, and rebuked the man so severely that he abandoned his intention. The Nauabo, on hearing them say this, told them that they were fools; and going away, he gave instructions to the Catual that he was to summon the Panditos, and that, in their presence, the young man was again to be asked by the judges whether, or not, he wished to return to the law of the Gentiles[8]; that if he did, he was to be handed over to his relations; and that if he persevered in his resolution, he was to be placed in the charge of the Fathers. Before carrying out this order, the Catual, without the knowledge of the Father Pigneiro, had the young man conducted to the house of the Coxi, who may be described as the Vicar-General of the supreme Prelat of the Gentiles (*qu' eſt comme le Vicaire general du Prelat souverain des Gentiles*),[9] whither he was accompanied by his parents, and a crowd of four or five thousand Gentiles. The ſtreets through which he passed were thronged with people, and numbers more were to be seen at the windows and on the roofs of the houses; for they came from every quarter of the city, many having shut up their shops that they might come and see what was taking place.

This one poor lamb in the midſt of so many wolves endured a thousand insults, in addition to kicks and blows, from which, because the crowd was so great, the Catual's people were unable to protect him. From every side abuse was heaped upon him; whilſt many cursed him for blackening their faith by an act such as none of his race had ever before committed. The young man boldly answered, "You speak these things because you do not know what you are saying." But in his heart he said (as he afterwards told the Fathers), "Lord Jesus, for love of Thee, I joyfully suffer these trials; and though more come upon me, I will never abandon Thy law." He assured the Fathers that never in his life had he experienced such comfort of mind as during this ordeal, and particularly when he confessed and avowed himself a Chriſtian in the presence of the judges.

Amidſt an indescribable tumult, he arrived at the house of the Coxi. His parents, thinking he was already in their power, held him so firmly that, though he ſtruggled manfully, plying both feet and elbows with great vigour, he was unable to free himself from them; and at last the judge himself had to order them to fall back. He then addressed the young man, admonishing him for the wrong he had done the Gentiles, and the sorrow he had brought upon his parents and relations by embracing a worthless law. He next told him that he had collected from the Gentiles two thousand rupees (which is the name of a coin used in this country, of the value of twenty-six *sols tournois*[10] of our country), and that he himself would contribute two hundred more, in order that he might go and wash in the Ganges. For these Gentiles (as has been said previously) have a foolish idea about this river, believing that all who wash in it are cleansed of their sins, for which they obtain a kind of plenary indulgence.

In this river, then, the Pagan judge wished the Neophyte to go and bathe, that he might be purged of the foul sin which, in his opinion, he had committed by embracing Christianity; and to persuade him thereto, he added to the money already mentioned, many other tempting baits. When he had finished, the young man said, "For the torments of hell, and the loss of my soul, both of which I should suffer by following your advice, your two thousand rupees would console me no better than this spittle"; and he spat upon the ground. "I would rather," he continued, "in my need, receive in alms from the Fathers a single *damaris*[11] (which is a coin of very trifling value), than a hundred thousand rupees from you. And, if the Fathers are willing to give me shelter in their house, as they have done up till now, I shall count it happiness to sit on the lowest step of their doorway, and to eat what is left by those who serve them." With a fierce and angry countenance, the Pagan judge told him that he should be put to death if he did not instantly abandon this Christian madness, and listen to better counsels. "You delay too long!" answered the Neophyte. "Do your will! I am quite ready to die; for it has long been my greatest desire. It is a very strange thing that when any Gentile wishes to become a Iogue, or a Mahometan, there is none to stand in his way; but when he wishes to become a Christian, it seems that the Devil and hell are leagued against him, to turn him from his purpose. From this I perceive the difference between your sects and the law which I follow; for your sects, since they are all of the Devil, do not oppose one another; but my law, being the law of the true God, is assailed by you and by all the powers of hell." On hearing him speak thus, the judge turned to his father and mother: "Your child," he said, "is lost. He is not worth any further thought or trouble." And with these words he concluded his inquiry, and sent the young man away.

As he returned through the streets after leaving the tribunal, the Neophyte was subjected to even worse insults and ill-usage than he had suffered on his way thither. The Catual, on being informed of what was happening, was in great anger, and sent a large number of people to escort and defend him; but so dense was the multitude of the Gentiles, that they could afford him little protection.

But this was not all. From the house of the Catual, he was taken before the King's Cazique,[12] who is a kind of Mahometan bishop; and in his presence, after answering with invincible firmness all the questions that were put to him, he made, like St. François, a public renunciation, which his relatives had demanded, of all that he possessed, or was heir to. When this had been done, the Cazique instructed the judge to hand the deed to the father and mother, and to have the young man taken to the church and placed in the charge of Father Pigneiro, as ordered by the Nauabo. This happy issue filled the Christians with incredible joy and satisfaction; for they had seen the champion of their faith return victorious from battle, the Gentiles shamed, the Mahometans put to confusion, hell and the Devil balked of their prey, and Jesus-Christ triumphant over unbelief.

The next day, Father Pigneiro took the Neophyte to visit the Nauabo, who received him very kindly, and warmly commended his constancy to the Christian faith. He then asked him where his cross was, seeing that he was a Christian. The other showed him a reliquary which he carried; but the Nauabo was not satisfied. "That," said he, "is not a cross." The Neophyte then took from his neck a chain with a cross attached to it, and showed it to him. On seeing it, the Nauabo turned to some Gentiles who were present, and said: "This young man has done well to abandon worthless things, and embrace the law of the Lord Jesus." In short, he took a great fancy to the young man, and often invited him to his house. Sometimes he would give him a present of some rupees. If he gave him ten rupees, the Gentiles spread the report that he had given him a hundred; if he gave him a hundred, they reported it as a thousand, which increased the ill-will of the Pagans. Thus terminated the most noteworthy episode in the lives of the Christians during the year 1602.

CHAPTER XV[1]

AN IMPERIAL FARMAN

HAVING taken, as we have seen, the fortress of Syr, and made himself master of the kingdom of Breampur, Echebar, finding that his affairs were not in a satisfactory state,[2] decided to return to his country, though it was still his intention to carry on the war, and to conquer all the kingdoms of Melique and Idalcan, for which purpose he left several of his captains in the lands he had conquered. He himself withdrew to the city of Agra, and thither the Fathers, who usually travelled in his suite, accompanied him. These were Father Hierosme Xauier and Father Emmanuel Pigneiro, who had come from the city of Lahor, where François Corsi, of whom we have spoken above, was at that time residing.

It was at this juncture that Father Antoine Machado and Benoist de Goës (who was to go to Catai) were on their way to meet the King and join the Fathers who followed the court.[3] It took them seven months to travel from Goa to Agra. The Fathers were informed of their approach by the King, to whom information of their movements had been sent; and Father Pigneiro at once proceeded to a spot some leagues distant from the city to welcome them. This was the sweetest refreshment which the travellers had known during their journey through the fierce heat, which at this season burns like fire throughout the country.

Having arrived at Agra, and having paid their respects to the King, who received them with great cordiality, they set themselves to renew their spiritual fellowship, and, during the month that they were together, they formed themselves into something like a small college, maintaining, as far as was practicable, monastic discipline. They also at this time had some important conversations with the King, the chief result of which was the issue by his Majesty of a general permission to his subjects to become Christians. This came about in the following way. Father François Corsi, who was at this time in charge of the church at Lahor, which is the capital of the estates of the Mogor, was much depressed, partly because he was without a companion, and partly because he saw that Christian affairs were not prospering. For after the deaths of the two Viceroys who had displayed so much goodwill towards the Fathers and their Church, a third had succeeded, who was of an opposite disposition[4]; for besides being a Saracen and strongly opposed to Christianity, he was a sworn enemy of the Portuguese, whom he had fought against some years previously, when governor of Guzarate, and whose courage he had experienced in several encounters, in one of which he had been wounded. Moreover, the Portuguese had seized a ship loaded with merchandise, which he was sending to Meque, without having obtained from them any safe-conduct.[5] As soon as he was installed as Viceroy, he began to annoy the Fathers in many ways, and also to persecute the Christians, seizing their wives, and endeavouring by force to make them renounce the faith of our Saviour. But, thanks to God, they all remained constant, and he was never able to achieve his purpose.

The Fathers who were at the court of the King, on learning of these things, made their way to his Majesty. And because it is a recognised custom, as we have before stated, that those who go to speak with him should tender some gift, they took with them and presented to him two portraits drawn from life, one of the great Albuquerque, and the other of the Viceroy of India, Ayres de Saldagna. These the King expressed great pleasure at receiving.

At the time the Fathers entered the palace, his Majesty was counting a huge quantity of gold pieces of different values which he had had made. He was surrounded by some hundred and fifty dishes full of these, besides a great number of bags likewise full, which had either been counted, or were waiting to be counted. All of these were examined by him, as well as by others. He used every day to spend a portion of his time in this way; for it was thus that he diverted himself when he returned weary to his palace after the public audiences, which, three times daily, he held for those who desired to speak with him. All the money having been counted and tied up in bags, was deposited amongst his treasures, which were very great.

When the Fathers entered, the King bade them approach, and welcomed them with his accustomed cordiality. They then told him of the lonely state of

Father Corsi at Lahor, and of the hindrances and annoyances to which he was subjected, and begged that Father Pigneiro might be permitted to return to Lahor. To this his Majesty readily agreed, saying that he thought it a wise measure. The Fathers regarded his consent as a great favour; for they had anticipated a refusal, in as much he had shown a special liking for Father Pigneiro, and greatly desired his presence at his court. In regard to the second point, he asked them if it was the Viceroy who thus troubled the Fathers and the Christians. They replied that such was the case; and, as a protection against such treatment in the future, they begged his Majesty graciously to grant them letters-patent, in the form of an edict, signed by his own hand, proclaiming his goodwill, not only towards themselves, but towards the Church and the Christians, so that all in his Empire might know that they enjoyed his favour, and that he regarded them as his own.

The King granted all that they asked without demur, ordering one of his eunuchs, a person of great authority who managed everything for him, to draw up the patents. The eunuch asked the Fathers for a draft of what they wished the letters to contain, which they accordingly gave him, including in it what most of all they desired, namely, that all the subjects of his Majesty should know that they were free to become Christians if they so wished, without any person being able to hinder them. Now since, up to this time, no such dispensation had been obtained, at any rate in letters-patent signed by the King, but had only been granted by word of mouth and as a special favour, the eunuch, when he came to this clause, stopped short, and refused to include it, without first consulting the King. When he did so a few days later, the King told him to get the letters prepared in the manner the Fathers desired; for, having given them his promise, he could not revoke it; and, further, that it was his intention that the letters should go forth in that form.

On learning the King's decision, the eunuch included this article with the others in the patents, and then took them to the *maistre d'hostel*,[6] who is a great captain, and through whose hands all letters-patent and edicts pass. The *maistre d'hostel* was full of promises; but when he came to this same clause he, too, paused, and delayed the affair from day to day. When the Fathers went to him and begged him to pass their letters as soon as possible, he told them that his delay was due to the clause in which the King gives leave to all his vassals to become Christians if they wish, without any being able to prevent them; for this clause was full of difficulty, in as much as it threatened to deprive the Mahometan law of all its credit, and would, moreover, give grave offence to the Viceroy of Lahor[7] (who was his father-in-law). It was, therefore, necessary, he said, for him to speak to the King before proceeding further; and this he promised to do in their presence, if they would be at the palace when the King came forth. The Fathers were there punctually at the hour arranged; but when the King appeared, the other made no attempt to speak to him, excusing himself to the Fathers by saying that it was not the time, nor the place, for bringing the matter forward. It was better, he said, to wait till the King was alone; and he promised to approach him as soon as a favourable opportunity occurred. This was only a pretext for further delay; for the *maistre d'hostel* had no intention of speaking to the King at all; and the fair words he addressed to the Fathers were merely to keep their beaks to the water, as we say, whilst he devised means for shelving the business permanently.

The matter was already in the mouths of the great ones of the court, who, being for the most part Mahometans, looked upon these patents as prejudicial to their law. Some of them said that the clause should be deleted, and others that the Fathers had no business to demand such an edict, and that it was sufficient for them to be able to make converts in the manner they had done hitherto. In short, so many difficulties were raised by these officers, that the Fathers had almost despaired of attaining their end, when their cause was taken up by one who enjoyed the special favour of the King. This was a young gentleman who had been one of Father Pigneiro's pupils during the latter's first year in the country. Though he had studied for a brief period only, he still retained a strong regard and respect for the Fathers; and he now found an opportunity of speaking to the King on the question that was being so much discussed, and of telling him all that had taken place in connection therewith. The King again confirmed what he had already said and decreed, after which the other, by using all his influence, was able to carry the affair through. For although the signing of the letters was vigorously opposed by the Saracens, and in particular by the captain Agiscoa, who was as it were the grand chancellor,[8] and whose business it was to seal them and present them to the King for signature, nevertheless, this young gentleman was able, after one or two more interviews with his Majesty, to hand to the Fathers their patents duly completed, sealed, and signed by the King's own hand. In return for his assistance, he asked the Fathers to give him a certain very sacred image of our Saviour which they possessed. Though very reluctant to part with it, the Fathers could not do otherwise than grant his request, since it was for our Saviour, and the increase of His glory, that he had rendered them this service. They made up their minds, however, to redeem it as soon as they could obtain an image which pleased him more.

The Saracens strongly resented the passing of these letters, and for some days little else was talked of at the court. For never before had such a dispensation been granted in a Saracen country; so that many were confirmed in their belief that the King was no longer of their law, and that he had bestowed his affections on the Fathers, as, indeed, he had clearly shown, by standing his ground and according them this favour.

Having obtained the object of their desires, the Fathers returned thanks first of all to God, the centre and fountain of all good, who holds the hearts of kings in His hand, and moulds them to His will, and then to the King and others to whose help they were beholden. Shortly afterwards, Father Pigneiro went to take leave of the King prior to his departure for Lahor. His Majesty dismissed him with much kindness, and gave him a horse from his own stables for his journey, which was more than a hundred leagues. This was highly appreciated by the Fathers; for such favours did much to enhance their credit in the eyes of the Saracens and Gentiles.

CHAPTER XVI[1]

A Miraculous Picture

While Father Pigneiro was ſtill in the city of Agra, Father Xauier, who was also there, presented to the King a treatise in the Persian language on the life, miracles, and teaching of our Saviour Jesus-Chriſt,[2] which his Majeſty had himself asked for, having a great desire to see the same. He showed, too, that he valued it very highly, and often he made his great captain Agiscoa[3] read it aloud to him, in doing which the latter found so much pleasure that he asked the Father for a copy of it for himself. Indeed the book was so much spoken of amongſt the great ones of the court, as to arouse the hope that it was God's purpose to make known by its means His only Son, our Saviour, to these infidels and misbelievers. The King afterwards asked the Father to write another book on the lives of the Apoſtles.

But that which more than anything else impressed the inhabitants of the town of Agra was a picture of our Lady, copied from that at Rome called *di Populo*,[4] which the Fathers had obtained two years previously from Portugal, but which, until now, they had not dared to exhibit, for fear that the King might ask them for it. However, at the feaſt of Noel of the year 1601, and at that of the Circumcision of our

Saviour in the year 1602, they decided that it should be placed in the church,[5] which, on this occasion, they decorated as splendidly as possible, having no other motive beyond their own devotion and that of the Christians.

One day during the octave, some poor women who lived near the church, having asked and received permission to enter the building, were so deeply moved by the beauty of the picture that they went out and proclaimed on all sides its wonders and perfection, so that the tidings passed from mouth to mouth until they were spread throughout the city. In consequence, a huge crowd collected at the church, the people leaving their shops and their work to come and see this marvel. That same evening, more than two thousand people came to the church from the streets in the neighbourhood.

Early next morning, when the door of the church was opened, many were waiting to enter. The Fathers made haste to say their masses; and, lest any disorder should arise, they placed guards at the doors of their house, while each of them took his place at one of the doors of the church, to receive the people and speak to them. The picture of the Holy Virgin was placed on the altar of the chapel, between lighted candles, and was covered by two curtains, one thin and transparent, the other of silk taffeta. As soon as the church was full of people, the coverings were removed; and beside the two boys who always stood by the altar when the picture was shown, was one who explained in the language of the country who this Lady was whose likeness they beheld, and that her Son was none other than our Saviour and Redeemer Jesus-Christ, who became incarnate in the womb of this same blessed Virgin Mary, and came into the world that He might teach mankind the true law, and the path which leads to salvation. The opportunity was also used to explain to them the principal mysteries and the foundations of our belief, all which things filled them with astonishment. The picture affected them in a manner that was wholly miraculous; for it aroused in them not only wonder, but remorse for their sins, while at the same time it brought exceeding consolation to their hearts. In short, as they went away, the Fathers were amazed at the change that had come over them. For afterwards, when they spoke (as they were in the habit of doing to the gentlemen and others of position) of the wonderful works and virtues of our Saviour and of His thrice holy Mother, exposing at the same time the deceptions and vices of Mahomet, their hearers listened attentive and abashed, and without denying anything that was told them. And this was no small thing where Mahometans were concerned, who cannot endure that anyone should speak evil in their presence of their false Prophet, and seeing that they hold pictures of all kinds in great abhorrence; notwithstanding which they went away full of veneration for the Virgin, and deeply impressed by her sanctity.

That all might be done in an orderly manner, only as many people as the church could conveniently hold were admitted at one time, others passing in as these came out. The men were separated from the women, an arrangement which was generally appreciated. Those who came on the first two days belonged for the most part to the lower orders; but on the third and following days men of learning, who are called Mullas, began to come, as well as nobles and others of rank, who had before deemed it discreditable to enter a Christian church. The example of these great ones was followed by people of every sort and quality. By counting those who entered the church on a particular day, it was shown that the daily attendance exceeded ten thousand persons. The Fathers had so much to do to maintain order in so great a concourse of people that they were unable to spare even a quarter of an hour for their repast, which they were obliged to postpone till night.

Amongst the gentlemen and grandees who came was a great captain, accompanied by more than sixty men on horseback and many others on foot, who, as soon as he saw the picture, stood as one in a trance, so overcome was he with admiration. After him came others, and others again after them, all of whom returned to their houses so full of wonder that they could talk of nothing but the picture, and sent all the members of their families, even their wives, to see it. Many of the latter were grand dames, whom the Fathers received with great honour and respect, allowing none to enter the church with them except their own attendants. One of the King's officers, a person high in authority, and of the sect of the Saracens, whose duties prevented him from visiting the church except in the early morning, was conducted thither by one of the Fathers. When the picture was shown to him, he gazed on it for a long time in silent wonder. Presently, tears filled his eyes and began, one by one, to roll down his cheeks. The Father made him sit down and, not to lose so favourable an opportunity, commenced to speak to him of divine things; but he continued to weep, without withdrawing his eyes from the picture. After a time, the Father said to him: "What evil can Mahomet and his followers find in the use and veneration of pictures, seeing that by their means our hearts may be changed and comforted?" He answered that this was something which the Saracens did not understand; after which he spoke so ill of Mahomet, and so highly of Jesus-Christ, that the most pious of Christians could not have said more. Having remained in the church until the Father was obliged to open the doors, because of the great crowd of people awaiting admission, he departed, greatly comforted in spirit, and expressing on all sides his unbounded admiration of our holy faith.

The church was also visited by a brother and a nephew of the King of Xhander [Khandesh],[6] with some cousins and other relations of the same King, and by the son of the King of Candaçar who came two or three times, accompanied by a big retinue. Some of the gentlemen and grandees of the court, after seeing the picture, told the Fathers that they could not, without incurring the royal displeasure, refrain from making known to the King a thing so marvellous, and so worthy to be seen. Accordingly, on leaving the church, they went to the palace, and told his Majesty all about it. The King said that he had already heard of the picture, which he, too, had a great desire to see, and that he would be very glad if it could be brought to him. When the Fathers intimated that it was a great pity his Majesty should not see it in its proper place on the altar, he said that he would go to the church; but his courtiers told him that he could not do this without great inconvenience, because it was a long distance to where the Fathers lived (and in fact though their lodging was in the city, it was distant a good half league from the palace), and that it would be better if the Fathers had it brought to the palace. This they did the next day, but after nightfall, so that the people should know nothing of it. When the King was told that it had arrived, he expressed his satisfaction, and ordered it to be brought to his chamber. While Father Pigneiro was fetching it, he had a black *gaban*,[7] or rain-cloak, brought, which for some days he had been intending to present to the Fathers; and addressing Father Xauier, he asked him if he considered it a useful and suitable garment for them. "Yes, Sire," said the Father, "it will serve to protect us from the rain when we go into the country with your Majesty; but these tassels and silken cords (for it was fastened by lacing) are not suitable for us." "That is nothing," said the King; "cut them off, if you do not like them." And descending some steps of the throne on which he had been seated, he placed the cloak with his own hands on the Father's shoulders. At the same moment, Father Pigneiro entered with the picture, which was of the height of a man, suitably draped, and veiled in the manner described above. As soon as it was uncovered, the King descended from his throne, on which he had resumed his seat, and, partially baring his head, approached it and made a deep reverence. His pleasure at seeing the picture was very great. Out of respect for him, the nobles who were in attendance did not venture to approach; but he called them to him one by one that they might see it, and all alike showed their astonishment, and vied with one another in praising our Lord and the holy Virgin, thereby filling the hearts of the Fathers with joy. The King was greatly impressed by the picture, and said how much it would have been appreciated by his father, who, he added, had he been presented with such a thing, would have granted the giver of it the highest favours he could ask. The drift of this remark was not lost on the Fathers, though they pretended not to understand it, and with a few complimentary words sought to turn the conversation. "For this night," said the King, "you must let me have it in my sleeping apartment." And thither he immediately conducted the Fathers, saying that it should be put in the place they considered most suitable. When this had been done, he again did homage to the picture, this time almost completely removing his head-dress, a thing which it was never his custom to do. His reason for wishing to keep the picture that night was, as the Fathers knew, that he might show it to his wives and daughters. This he did, telling them of the excellence and holiness of the Virgin Mary. They came again to see it in the morning, and all of them, though they were Mahometans, paid it great honour and veneration. One of them who had previously been strongly opposed to our faith, came away in an altogether different frame of mind, and with her opinion of the Christian religion completely changed.

The Fathers returned to the palace the next day, in great anxiety lest the King should wish to keep the picture; but, by the grace of God, he restored it to them; and with joy in their hearts, they made haste to carry it back to their house.

When the people knew that the picture had gone to the palace, they were very sorrowful, fearing that they would never see it again; and no sooner did they hear that it had been restored to its place, than they again flocked to see it. It was not long, however, before their devotion was a second time interrupted; for the King's mother, who was very advanced in age, on hearing of the wonders of the picture, greatly desired to see it, which she had not been able to do whilst it was at the palace, and begged her son to ask the Fathers to send it to her. In excuse for his request, the King said that, although his mother was a very old lady, she expected, not unnaturally, all the indulgence and attention which was due to her position. The Fathers at once had it taken to her residence[8]; and on its arrival, the King himself, allowing no one to help him, took it in his arms and carried it into her chamber, placing it in a high position, which had been prepared for it beforehand, where it could be seen, not only by his mother, but by his wives and children, who, though they had already seen it, again contemplated it with admiration and delight. The King stood all the time by the picture, allowing no one to touch it, and finally sent it by one of his eunuchs to the Fathers who were waiting without.

As a great crowd of people had assembled in the palace yard in the hope of being able to see the picture, some of the captains and nobles begged the Fathers to show it to them. As they could not with courtesy decline this request, and seeing that they would be able to satisfy so large a number of persons at one time, they placed it where all could see it and publicly uncovered it. The moment it was exposed to view, the noise and clamour of the crowded courtyard was hushed as if by magic, and the people gazed on the picture in unbroken silence. As the Fathers carried it back to their house, those in the streets through which they passed congratulated them on having recovered it; for when they had seen it being taken to the palace, they thought that the King intended to keep it for himself. They began once more to flock to the church; but this was only for a few days; for many of the King's friends had persuaded him to have the picture copied, though he had assured them that none of his painters could equal its perfection. However, to put the matter to the test, he summoned to the palace all the best painters of the town,[9] at the same time requesting the Fathers to send him the picture. They, accordingly, took it to the palace, and themselves placed it in position, while the King, who was also there, himself arranged that a good light should fall on it; he also gave strict injunctions to his pages to allow no one to approach it. As many gentlemen, both Saracen and Gentile, as well as a nephew of the King, came there, the Fathers, not to let slip so good an opportunity, discoursed throughout the day, with great boldness, of the mysteries of our holy faith, and the marvellous virtues of our Lady and her holy Son. The Saracens were willing listeners, and seemed to be pleased at what they heard, and to derive therefrom an idea of our religion very different from that which they had previously held. And this cannot but be esteemed a very noteworthy circumstance, since they are accustomed to regard with great contempt all that relates to our law.

This time, the picture remained some days at the palace. But though the painters put forth their utmost skill, they were fain at last to lay down their implements, acknowledging that such perfection of portraiture was beyond their skill, and that they were unable to compete with the Portuguese in this art. Upon this, many tried to persuade the Fathers to present the picture to the King; but they courteously excused themselves, and on the plea that the feast of the resurrection of our Saviour was approaching, begged his Majesty that it might be returned to them.

When the picture was once more in their possession, the Fathers were very unwilling to part with it again; and though many great Lords asked for it, that they might show it to their wives, they declined, except on two occasions when refusal seemed impossible, to comply with their requests. One of those to whom it was sent was Agiscoa,[10] the greatest captain of the court, and foster-brother to the King, in whose favour he stood very high. Each was the father-in-law of the other's children; for one of the King's sons was married to a daughter of Agiscoa, and a son of the latter to a daughter of the King. The goodwill of this powerful noble was a matter of importance to the Fathers, and they, accordingly, took the picture to his house, where he had assembled his wives, his daughters, his daughters-in-law, and numerous other relations. Agiscoa received them with many compliments and courtesies, and taking the picture from them, carried it, with the assistance of one of his eunuchs, into the house, afterwards restoring it to them in the same manner. The happy result of this event was that this noble, though an influential Saracen, remained from that time forward much more kindly disposed towards the Fathers than he had formerly been. The following morning, he sent one of the chief members of his household to thank them on his behalf for the favour they had done him, and to assure them that his services were at all times at their disposal. He also expressed a desire to understand the mystery of this Lady, and offered, in the event of the Fathers being willing to part with the picture, to give them whatever price they asked for it; if this was impossible, he begged them to procure him another like it, promising to defray all the expenditure incurred.

The other, whose request it was found impossible

to refuse, was the King of Candaçar,[11] who had for some years resided at the court of King Echebar, to whom he had ceded his kingdom, being unable to defend it against Abduxam, King of Husbech.[12] When he asked that the picture might be sent to him, one of the Fathers took it to his house, a number of people accompanying him. While the King exhibited it to his wives, the Father remained outside, talking with his son, who asked him, amongst other things, what opinion the Christians held of Mahomet. The Father told him that we regard him as one of the greatest imposters that ever entered the world. The other was much astonished to find that people such as we do not hold him in the same esteem as the Mahometans; for he belonged to an Eastern country, where the law of Mahomet has taken firm root; and hence he thought that all the world followed it. The King returned the picture with profuse thanks and acknowledgments, sending some crowns for the boys who had come with the Father, and a larger sum of money for the Father himself. But neither the Father nor the boys would accept anything from him, at which the servants of the King, as well as the King himself, marvelled much; for the idea of refusing money when it was offered, was something altogether strange to them. Now that the picture was once more in their safe keeping, the Fathers refused, despite all entreaties, to send it away gain.

Thus was God glorified, and the Christian faith announced and exalted amongst the Saracens and Gentiles, by means of this picture of the holy Virgin,

Mother of our Saviour. And we may believe that, in as much as through her we have received the eternal Word, clad in our own nature, so, through her intercession, the infidel peoples will receive the light of truth, and the knowledge of the same Word. Let us now turn our attention to what has been taking place in the territories of the Mogor.

CHAPTER XVII[1]

Events of the Year 1602

Although in the conversion of souls there was not so much progress in this land of the Saracens, who are as hard as diamonds to work upon, as in other lands where this sect has not taken root, yet God did not withhold his mercies from his sheep scattered in this vast forest of unbelief.

In the year 1602, there were at Rantambur some forty persons, for the most part children or grandchildren of Portuguese, with their wives and relatives, who had been taken by the Great Mogor at the capture of the fortress of Syr, and had been enslaved. For though the King had led some of his prisoners to Agra, where he afterwards set them at liberty, trusting that they would not run away, he left the majority of them in the fortress of Rantambur, where they would have been completely forgotten, if the Fathers had not borne them in mind. Deeming the season of Lent, which was then approaching, a suitable time for visiting them, the Fathers went to the King and begged that, in as much as Christians are bound at this season to fulfil the principal obligations of their law, namely to confess and to communicate, his Majesty would be pleased to permit one of them to visit these Portuguese prisoners in order to instruct them, and enable them to do their duty as good Christians. The visit, they said, would not occupy more than twenty days. In reply, the King told them that the prisoners might be brought to Agra, which was what the Fathers most desired. They were straightway sent for; and with them came five Turcs, that is to say, Turcs of Europe; for two kinds of Turkish soldiers are found in India, those of Asia, to whom the name Turc is given, and those of Europe, who are mostly from Constantinople, which has been called the New Rome, on which account they are called Rumes both by Indians and Portuguese, who have corrupted the Greek name Ρωμαιος into Rumes.[2]

These five Turcs, then, being also prisoners, were, through the interposition of the Fathers, brought to Agra, for which they showed themselves very grateful; for if they had not found this means of liberation, they could have hoped for no other. The prisoners were all brought in chains; but these were taken off at the solicitation of the Fathers, who also obtained the King's consent to their being employed in his service, and receiving food and clothing. In granting this petition, the King told the prisoners publicly that though they deserved death, because they had killed many of his people in the war, yet because of his love for the Fathers, he gave them not only life but liberty. It was the wish of one of the King's *maistres d'hostel* to place them in the service of an Armenian, who was the lord of certain villages; but the Fathers begged the King that they might remain near them, so that they might instruct them in the faith; since, if they were separated from them, they would soon become more uncivilised than they had been before. The King granted their request, and the prisoners were lodged close to them; and after they had instructed them in their faith, of which they knew little or nothing, they baptised all who had not been baptised before, which included the greater portion of them.

Now since these, and certain others who had come before, had been captured in Breampur and taken to places further south, their wives, daughters, and other relations had been left behind, and were in great need and peril. Accordingly, the Fathers, being unable as yet to withdraw these, despatched letters of credit to them, to provide them with a means of livelihood until they could be sent for. This could not be done for some time, owing to the debts which they and their husbands had incurred; for it was necessary to wait until these had all been paid. Subsequently, by the will of God, a young Armenian, of a very honourable disposition, whom the Fathers had commissioned to assist these poor people, brought them all back with him, trusting to the Fathers to repay him what he had spent, which they did very willingly, thanking him for having done so good a work. After they had arrived, and baptism had been administered to those who had not received it, they were re-married, according to the laws of the Church, to those who had also been baptised. Finally, they were all lodged near the house of the Fathers, and at their expense, which was a great blessing to these poor people; and they regarded it as a sign of God's special providence that in their captivity and misery He raised up the Fathers to succour them, who not only taught them the way of salvation, but ministered to their temporal needs with true paternal charity. Who can help marvelling at God's wisdom in using these means to make Himself known to these poor men and women, sprung from the Portuguese race, who, but yesterday, were dwelling amongst infidels, known only as Franks (for so they call Christians in these parts), without baptism, and without any knowledge of God; and who, to-day, are living like honest men, keeping the commandments of God and the Church, and recognising very clearly the truth of the Christian faith, and the grace which God has shown them in receiving them into His fold?

Here is a noteworthy case in which we see very clearly the wonderful effect of divine interposition and predestination. A certain woman, the slave of a Christian, fled from her master, and, returning after a long time, came to the Fathers and begged for aid and sustenance. Now while the Fathers were investigating her case, the devil tempted her, so that she fled a second time, and, though she was married to a Christian, abandoned herself body and soul to a Saracen. On her again returning at the end of a month, the Fathers lodged her with a very honest Christian, where she straightway fell sick in giving birth to a daughter, and lay at the point of death. One of the Fathers, though he saw nothing alarming in the condition of the child, except that it was weak, nevertheless baptised it, and on the following night, contrary to the expectations of all, its spirit returned to God. But the slave, though she appeared to be dying, and twice confessed her sins, did not merit so blessed a fate; for, having recovered from her sickness, she fled a third time, and was never seen again. From this, we very plainly see that all her comings and goings, and the illness which God sent to her, were designed to save this little one, whom he had predestined to glory.

In another case, a Mahometan woman, noticing a small infant lying on a heap of refuse by the wayside, and moved with compassion at the sight, lifted it up and took it to the Catual, asking his permission to take it to the church, and place it in the care of the Fathers, which, on her request being granted, she did forthwith. The Fathers immediately baptised it, and soon afterwards this fair soul, newly cleansed in the blood of Jesus-Christ, went to partake of the joys of heaven. The Fathers arranged a very beautiful funeral. Swathing the body in a seemly fashion, they exposed it, with its face uncovered, in the church, where so many came to see it that one would have thought that some solemn festival was being held. Later, accompanied by a large number of people, it was carried through the middle of the city, the bier decorated as if for a fête, and the body covered with flowers. This greatly raised our faith in the esteem of the Saracens and Gentiles, who spoke loudly in praise of the Christians for the respect which they showed towards their dead.

Father Pigneiro baptised at Lahor the two sons of the Persian ambassador, named Manuquer, who after four years' residence in this country was about to return to Persia.[3] He was a Georgian Christian, and wore a cross on his arm, though it was concealed from view. During his sojourn in Lahor, he had made the acquaintance of the Fathers and had showed them much kindness and affection. It was his intention, he said, to persuade the King of Persia to invite other Fathers to come and preach the Christian faith and build churches in his kingdom.

There came also certain Turcs, who had been sent by a Baxa [Pasha] to ask permission of the King to trade in his country. With them was a young man, a native of Hungary, of the town of Bude [Buda Pesth], whom they had enslaved. When this became known to the Fathers, they managed to withdraw the young man from their hands, and sent him to Goa, that he might receive instruction in the faith, and be able to lead a Christian life.[4]

A young Christian woman, who was married to a Christian of the Greek nation, happened, while travelling with her husband from Lahor, to pass through the town of her birth. Her husband did not know that this was her native place; for he had obtained her from a Saracen who had stolen her from her parents when she was very young, and who had told him that she was a Gentile, and belonged to another part of the country. The Greek had her carefully brought up in the house of some honest people, and eventually, following the counsel of the Fathers, made her his wife. On reaching this town, the woman, having a desire to see her mother and relatives, told the circumstances of her birth to her husband, and asked his permission to visit them. The latter, suspecting no evil, sought out his wife's mother, and allowed her to see her daughter. The next day, the woman made a complaint to the judge, saying that she had discovered her daughter and the man who had stolen her. The judge immediately sent twelve men on horseback and thirty on foot to seize the two of them. When they had been taken, the husband was led before the judge, who questioned him on the matter, and at the same time sent some officers to his wife to ascertain how she came to be in this man's power. In answer to their inquiries, the woman said that a certain Mogor had seized her when she was very small, and had given her to him to whom she now belonged. She told them that she was married after having become a Christian, and added that she recognised her mother quite well, and would acknowledge her provided that she became a Christian, but not otherwise. The Saracens tried hard to induce her to quit the faith of Jesus-Christ; but with great firmness she replied, "I have not accepted this law in order to abandon it; I would rather lose my life than do so"; and when they sought by force to place her in her mother's charge, she told them that if they did so, she would kill herself, pretending that she would do this willingly, though it was very far from her desire. On this account, and partly because they found that her husband was known to the King, for he had shown them the letters-patent which he carried, they allowed her to go free. In the end, her many relatives were pacified, while all the town marvelled at her firmness. But what was more extraordinary than all else was that her mother followed her, and throwing herself at the husband's feet, begged his forgiveness; after which she went with them to Lahor, and herself became a Christian.

In the same year 1602, two ships of the Portuguese navy, while sailing northwards in the gulf of Cambaya, were wrecked on a portion of the coast which was under the sway of the King of Mogor. Some fifty Portuguese and fifteen servants contrived to reach land, but were instantly made prisoners by the captain who governed that country in the name of the King. The latter, to whom the circumstance was at once reported, ordered the prisoners to be sent to him. In the course of their journey, the poor fellows endured so many hardships that when they reached Lahor[5] their plight was pitiful to behold. The King gave orders that they were to be imprisoned; but Father Xauier, who happened to be there, begged that they might be placed in his charge, promising to deliver them up to his Majesty's officers whenever so ordered. His request was granted, and the Fathers accordingly took the prisoners to their house where they sheltered them, and later transferred them to another house which the King placed at their disposal. They were supported throughout at the expense of the Fathers, but for whom, they would have perished miserably from hunger and other afflictions. That they found such a refuge was a manifestation of the providence of God. Their captains were Louys d'Antas Lobo and George de Castillo. The Fathers strove to secure their freedom, but for a long time their efforts were fruitless, since they lacked the wherewithal to make rich presents; for where avarice and disloyalty reign, nothing can be obtained except by money. The King, however, sent them four hundred *xerafins* for the purchase of clothing, and consented, at the instance of the Fathers, to grant the two captains an audience. A substantial donation was also received from the Prince, the eldest son of the King, who, so soon as he heard of the misery of these poor people, sent the Fathers a thousand crowns to relieve their necessities. Eventually, having been detained for more than a year, they were set at liberty. This they owed to the intercession of the Fathers in their behalf, as was stated in the letter which the King gave them when they were released, in which he wrote that he sent them back free men to please the Fathers. In consequence, these good Portuguese and the two captains in particular, knew not how to praise God sufficiently for His mercies, or how to thank the Fathers for their charity, without which they would one and all have died in captivity.

CHAPTER XVIII[1]

PRINCE SALIM

THROUGHOUT almost the whole of the year 1602 there was serious discord between the King and the Prince, his son and heir to his estates, of which the cause was this. The King being at the war in the Decan, the Prince, impatient to take the reins of government into his hands, and chafing at the long life of his father, which kept him from the enjoyment of the dignities he so much desired, resolved to usurp the same, and on his own authority began to assume the name and to exercise the prerogatives of a king. On learning this, Echebar at once abandoned his project of conquering in person the kingdoms of the Decan, and leaving, as has been said, some of his captains to carry on the war, returned to Agra, whither he summoned his son to appear before him. The latter was unwilling to obey the summons; and it was not until message after message had reached him as he moved from place to place, that he resolved to go to meet his father; but this he did with a large army at his back, bringing under subjection all the country through which he passed.[2]

Learning that he was approaching in such array, and with so powerful a force, his father's suspicions were aroused, and fearing that his son's designs were evil, he assembled his great captains and men-at-arms, and made preparations for war. At the same time, he sent many messages to his son, in some of which he attempted to soothe him with kind words, while in others he used threats to intimidate him. Alarmed at these messages, and yet more by his father's warlike preparations, the Prince thought better of his intentions, and returned to Alahabech [Allahabad] whence he had established his court, still continuing, however, to use every means of furthering his designs.

It was at this juncture that the King summoned to Agra an eminent and very astute captain, who was then in the neighbourhood of his son, and in whom, by reason of his prudence and courage, he had great confidence. On becoming aware of this, the Prince, knowing how valuable the advice of this captain would be to the King, caused him to be followed on his march by certain people in his pay, who assassinated him, and carried his head to the Prince.[3] This greatly enraged the King, and filled the whole court with consternation. Nevertheless, after repeated negotiations, a reconciliation between father and son was brought about, though they continued to live apart, and to hold separate courts.

The Prince exhibited far greater regard for the Fathers, and the Christian religion, than the King. He had already secretly opened his heart to Father Xauier, and had given such proofs of his devotion to our Saviour and His thrice-holy Mother, as to justify the hope that God would one day work in him a great miracle. He directed a servant of his household, whom he was sending to Goa on business, to go to the Father Provincial of the Company, and ask him to allow some Fathers to come to him and reside at his court in the same manner as those who were with his father. The request was accompanied by a present consisting of three handsome and costly carpets, and some smaller articles of less value. The Provincial, however, did not think it prudent to send Fathers to him at that time, in as much as he was in revolt against his father, to whom he (the Provincial) was much indebted; but to please him as far as possible, he sent him a letter in which he wrote that the Fathers who were in those parts would serve him as willingly as they served the King.

The Prince was as intimate with the Fathers at the King's court as though they had been at his own. He used to write letters to them in his own hand, and in such terms that any one seeing them might have supposed them to be the letters of a Christian prince to his confessor. He used to subscribe them, as we do, with a cross. In one of his letters to Father Xauier, he reproached the Father for sending him no news of himself, and with it he sent him a short black cloak. He was well aware, he wrote, that to such men as the Fathers, the most acceptable gifts were love and affection of the heart, and it was as a token of these sentiments that he sent this cloak, which he had more than once worn himself. Now since, at this time, the Prince was setting the King's authority at defiance, and, in consequence, anyone at the court who was in correspondence with him was held to be suspect, the Fathers, on receiving the letter and cloak, took them at once to his Majesty, and told him what the Prince had written. The King took up the cloak and looked at it, then handed it back to the Father. The courtiers, who saw the letter, and recognised the Prince's handwriting, were much astonished, regarding it as a sign of great favour. Father Xauier replied to it in Portuguese, so that it might not be understood by the Saracens; for they knew that the Prince had a certain Italian at his court, who could read it to him. This was one, Iacques Philippe, who had come from Goa with the Fathers. The latter had sent him to the Prince, who kept him in close attendance, and showed him much favour. It was through him that the Fathers had received the Prince's letters, and the Prince theirs.

At the time when he was marching with his army to meet his father at Agra, the Prince instructed the Italian, who had obtained his permission to go on before him to the city, to visit the Fathers on his behalf, and to present to them, with every expression of his regard, certain gifts which he was sending to them. He also bade him assure Father Xauier that he had not forgotten him, and that he was in no way changed from what he had before been (words which both understood); that he had a great love for Jesus-Christ, and that he begged the Fathers to remember him in their orisons; and finally that he greatly desired to have one of them with him, and that if they did not dare to come to him without his father's permission, he would himself obtain it for them; to which they replied that in this way and in no other could they come to him.

One evening, while in conversation with the said Iacques Philippe, the Prince, observing that one of his servants was dressed as a Christian, called him up and asked him whether he was free or a slave, a Christian or a Saracen. The young man replied that he was a native of a free country, a Christian, and the servant of Iaques Philippe. The Prince then inquired why he had become a Christian; was it by compulsion, or because he had been paid for it? "Not so, Monseigneur," replied the other. "It was of my own free will that I embraced this law, because of the great satisfaction I found in it, and because there is no other by which a man can be saved. I was also influenced by the holy lives of the Fathers, whom I served for many years, before they came to the Decan to find the King." He was next asked if he knew the Christian prayers, and how to make the sign of the Cross. "Yes, Monseigneur," he said, "I know all these things." And on being told to say some of the prayers, he made the sign of the Cross, and repeated the Paternoster, the Ave Maria, and the Credo. When he had finished, the Prince said, "You have done well to embrace so good a law." Then, still addressing the Italian, he added these words: "I have a very great affection for the Lord Jesus"; and to show that these were not mere words, but that he spoke from his heart, he drew aside his robe, and showed him a cross of gold, which it was his habit to wear suspended from his neck.

In another letter to Father Xauier, written by his own hand, the Prince, after many expressions of respect and goodwill, declared that he was in the same frame of mind as when he had spoken at Lahor of becoming a Christian; and in proof of this, he sent for the church an image *en bosse* of the infant Jesus; it was of silver, well made and massive, weighing twenty-seven *marcs*.[4] For the Father himself, he sent a small ornament made in the form of a reliquary attached to a golden chain, and having on one side of it the image of our Saviour in enamel, and on the other side that of our Lady; this, he wrote, he had worn on his breast, or rather on his heart. Once, when he was with his captains, he asked them on whom they would call for aid if they found themselves in great danger. Some answered in one way, and some in another. "As for myself," the Prince said, " I should call on none other but the Lord Jesus; for it is He alone who can succour us in all our perils and adversities."

Now after the Prince and the King his father had been estranged for a long time, each holding his court in a separate town, and each styling himself king (for the Prince so styled himself, though he called his father the great King), they were at last reconciled in the following manner.

The King, in great indignation with his son for assuming the title and style of a sovereign during his own lifetime, ordered him to his presence. But the Prince, fearing that his father would deprive him of his royalty, if not of his life, and put his grandson (that is, the Prince's son) in his place, for it was rumoured that such was his intention, turned a deaf ear to the summons; and learning that his father had assembled a large army, and was marching against him, he proceeded to surround himself with a no less powerful force; for many had adopted his cause, preferring, as men are wont to do, to worship the rising, rather than the setting sun. The mother of the King, who was ninety years of age,[5] was sorely distressed at this discord. She was devoted to the young Prince; and fearing that he would be vanquished in an encounter with a veteran warrior like the King, she tried her utmost to turn the latter from his purpose. But her efforts were of no avail; and on this account, so heavy was her sorrow that she became dangerously ill. The King was already on the march; but being informed of his mother's condition, and desiring to show her obedience, he retraced his steps, and went to visit her.[6] By the time he arrived she had become worse, and a few days later she died. In a single day and a night, her body was taken to a place forty leagues away, where it was laid in the tomb of her husband. As a sign of mourning, the King shaved his head, his beard, and his eyebrows,[7] and put on a dress of a blue colour, for such, in this country, is the custom when mourning the dead. His example was followed by the whole court, but only for a period of three days, at the expiry of which both the King and his courtiers attired themselves as usual. The Queen-mother left in the house where she died a large store of wealth, and a will directing that the same should be distributed amongst her sons and grandsons. The King, however, chose to keep the whole of this treasure for himself.

After this, negotiations were renewed, and the King sent so many agents, letters, and messages to the Prince, that the latter was induced to approach his father, unaccompanied by a military force. The King received him in a certain gallery at Agra with many signs of affection; then drawing him apart, he conducted him to a separate lodging where he confined him, treating him very leniently[8]; but three days afterwards he set him at liberty, and provided him with a house and retinue. In short, he behaved towards him, at this time, as though there had never been any differences between them. The Prince contented himself with the kingdom of Cambaya or Guzarate, which his father made over to him, until, little more than two months later, he found himself King of the entire realm; for the death of his father, which he had so much desired, placed it in his hands, as we shall narrate, after recording certain events which happened previously, and after referring again to the signs which the Prince at this time displayed of his devotion to the faith of our Saviour.

A Christian Armenian had, through the influence of the Fathers, placed his son in the service of the Prince, who gave him the charge of three horses. One day, the Prince asked his soldier what law he followed; whereon the other, thinking to please him, said that he was a Saracen. On receiving this reply, the Prince, who knew that he was a Christian, was so indignant that he dismissed him there and then from his service, to which he was never again admitted. He afterwards said that he had been on the point of ordering the man's tongue to be cut out because, seeking to gain favour by saying that he was a Saracen, he had denied his faith.

While residing at Agra after his reconciliation with the King, the Prince showed the Fathers, with whom he was on very intimate terms, many proofs of his devotion to our Saviour and His holy Mother, whose images he held in the highest veneration. Indeed, the Fathers could make him no more acceptable present than a well-executed representation of either; though he employed the most skilled painters and craftsmen in his father's kingdom in making him the like. He also had engraved on an emerald, the size of a man's thumb, the image of our Saviour crucified, and this he was in the habit of carrying about with him, attached to a gold chain.

One day, Father Xauier presented him with a book containing the life of our Saviour Jesus-Christ, which he had composed himself, and translated into the Persian tongue, and to which the King had given the title, *The Mirror of Purity.*[9] The Prince read it from beginning to end, whereby his love for our Saviour was greatly increased. He also had painted in a book pictures illustrating the mysteries of His life, death, and passion; and because at the beginning of the book there was a cross illuminated in gold with the superscription, *Sicut exaltauit Moyses serpentum in deserto*, &c., he ordered the artist to paint thereon the figure of Jesus-Christ crucified; and on another page on which

PLATE VII

THE MAGDALEN
Copied from an Italian picture by one of Prince Salim's painters

[face p. 190

was the name Jesus, encircled with rays, he had painted in the midst a picture of our Lady and her infant Son with His arms about her neck.

Lastly, seeing that there was no church at Agra, as there was at Lahor, in which divine service could be held, he conceived the desire to build one as his father had done in the latter city. He, accordingly, asked his Majesty to permit a church to be built, and to grant a site for the same; and on his requests being granted, he gave a thousand crowns for the commencement of the work. But enough of the Prince. Let us now turn to other happenings which preceded the death of the King.

CHAPTER XIX[1]

Persecution of the Fathers

Although the work of spreading Christianity seems to make little progress in this land of the Mogor, where Mahometanism and Paganism are so strongly established, nevertheless, through the few Christians dwelling there, our Saviour is often glorified, both by the constancy with which they hold to their faith, and by their earnest devotion, which is seen not only amongst the older Christians at Lahor, but amongst those more recently converted at Agra; for in both these places there are churches, and a goodly number of Christians, whose devotion is being stimulated by every means possible. Moreover, the infidels are often deeply impressed when they see the adornment of our churches, and the vestments which are used at the divine services; for, by these outward demonstrations, our faith gains much credit amongst these people, who, notwithstanding that they are infidels, frequently, and of their own accord, come to the church, bringing with them offerings, sometimes for our Saviour, and sometimes for his glorious Mother, to whom, in their need, they have recourse as their advocate with God, that, through her intercession, their prayers may be heard.

Amongst others, the wife of the Viceroy of Lahor, a very high-born lady, but of the sect of the Saracens, came to salute the Lady Mary (for thus they call our Lady), to whom she made a rich offering, and with great devotion vowed to come again to pay her homage, if she would reclaim for her one of her sons, who was leading a life of debauchery.[2] Another great lady, having heard of the miracles that God had worked at the intercession of the Virgin, became her devotee, and vowed that she would go to the church to salute her image, and would make her an offering, if she would obtain for her from God a son, which was the desire of her heart. Our Lady heard her prayer, and she was blessed with a son. When the child was born, she came with it to the church in fulfilment of her vow, and with her heart overflowing with gratitude to the glorious Virgin for the blessing she had received.

A Saracen, a man of note, and one of the chief officers of the Prince, approached the Father one day when he was at the palace, and said, "I am greatly beholden to the Lord Jesus because He has granted me the boon I craved of Him, namely, a son, which I have long been desiring. Having made my supplication to Him, it seemed to me that one night I saw Him in a dream. His face was shining and wonderful, and in His hand He had an apple, which He divided, and gave a portion to me to eat; then suddenly He vanished. I thought that this was a good omen, and that my petition had been heard. And so it was; for, twenty or thirty days afterwards, my wife became pregnant. I, for my part, do not doubt that the Lord Jesus has given us this child; and as soon as it is born, I shall take it and offer it to Him for His own." When the child was born, he came to tell the Father, and asked him what he should do with it. The Father answered that he should bring it to the church, and present it to Him whose gift it was; and this he did very willingly. The Father, however, did not think it desirable to baptise the child at once, being uncertain whether, left to the care of its father and mother, it would persevere in the faith.

Amongst those who were baptised was a certain learned Saracen, who was a captain, and physician to the Prince. After many discussions with the Fathers, he finally agreed to listen, without speaking, to the explanation of the mysteries of our faith. Of these he acquired so good an understanding (even of those that are hardest to believe), that he determined to accept the whole Christian law, and to be baptised forthwith. He begged the Fathers, however, to keep his conversion a secret; for he was about to go to his country to see his relatives, who ruled there; and that he might the more easily lead them to our Saviour, he thought it better not to declare himself to them until he had prepared their minds for knowledge of the truth. The Fathers yielded to his wish, and also gave him advice how to proceed in the task he had set himself. At his baptism he was given the name, Paul, with which he was well pleased. The next day, he brought to the Fathers one of his intimate friends, to whom he had disclosed the precious jewel of the faith, urging him to accept it and be baptised. His friend, who commanded a hundred horse, after converse with the Fathers, in which he showed a clear comprehension of all that was told him of our law, asked that he too might be baptised; but this was deferred till he had ridded himself of his four wives.

Meanwhile, though the Fathers were so beloved by the King and by the Prince (as has already been said), yet they did not escape either opposition or persecution; while at times it seemed that they might even be called upon to endure martyrdom, as the following shows. A Saracen of high position and authority, a native of the kingdom of Husbech, and grandson of Abdulaxa,[3] governor of the kingdom, which had formerly belonged to the great Tamburlan, came one day to the church. At the time of his visit, the Father was speaking of the mysteries of our faith, and, amongst other things, said that our Saviour was the true Son of God. On hearing these words, which always rouse the Mahometans to fury, one of the Saracen's retainers sprang to his feet, and drawing his sword, was twice in the act of cutting off the Father's head, when he was restrained by those who were near him.

On another occasion, the Viceroy of Lahor,[4] who had hitherto shown himself to be the friend and protector of the Fathers and, outwardly at any rate, of the Christian religion, asked them how they regarded Jesus-Christ. They replied that they believed Him to be, beyond all question of doubt, the true Son of God. The Viceroy, hearing this, sought to prevent them from pursuing the subject, by speaking of other things; but they continued to reiterate their statement, confirming it with weighty arguments. He then gave them to understand that, unless they desisted, he would have their heads cut off; to which the Fathers replied that if such were his will, they would gladly offer him their heads; for it was their intention to confess their faith not only before him, but before all the world, and that if they had a thousand lives, they were ready to sacrifice them all in doing so. Now this Viceroy was an extremely ardent supporter of the law of Mahomet, on which he considered himself a greater authority than any man then living, or who had lived before him, a claim which, by way of flattery, or to gain his favour, was admitted by many learned men, including even the Caziques. Hence, the freedom and boldness with which the Fathers encountered him, confessing and clearly establishing the divinity of Jesus-Christ, threw him into so furious a passion that he heaped a thousand abuses upon them, calling them vagabonds, and seducers, who roamed about the world to cheat mankind. Finally he warned them to keep to their own house, where they were welcome to expound their doctrines to any who were sufficiently depraved to seek them out; but he bade them take good care never again to speak ill of Mahomet in his presence. The Fathers answered that not only in their house with closed doors, but in the centre of the city, in its streets and open places, nay, on every side, far and near, would they preach the truth of the Christian law, for it was for that purpose that they had been sent there. To this the Viceroy had nothing to reply, knowing full well that the Fathers had the King's leave to preach the faith of Jesus-Christ, and to baptise all who desired to embrace it. He, therefore, altered his demeanour, and spoke to them with more courtesy.[5] But so strongly was he attached to his Mahomet, that it was not long before he manifested anew the ill-will he bore them. The occasion was as follows.

Certain Gentiles, who were bitterly hostile to the Christian religion and to the Fathers who preached it, desiring to find some means of driving the latter out of the country, and knowing that the Viceroy had a grudge against them in his heart, resolved, after taking counsel together on the subject, to secure his alliance and co-operation. They, accordingly, entertained him, in the house of one of their number, who happened to stand high in his favour, at a sumptuous banquet, at which, after making him a rich present, they placed in his hands a scandalous indictment of the Fathers, in which some of the least crimes imputed to them were that they ate human flesh, stole children and sent them to be sold in Portuguese countries, committed murders, and used spells to make people abandon their law and embrace Christianity. This last they had done (so they said) in the case of a certain Gentile whom they named, and also in the case of many Saracens, the latter being specially mentioned to kindle the indignation of the Viceroy, and increase his resentment against the Fathers. Finally, they begged him to sell them a large house which the King had given to the Fathers, and in which a number of Christians were lodged, offering him for the same a large sum of money, and other valuable things.

Impelled by these accusations, and still more by the animosity which he already harboured against the

Fathers, the Viceroy determined to put into execution the schemes he had long been meditating. He, accordingly, ordered the Fathers to vacate their house; and when they produced papers to show that it had been given to them by the King, he merely repeated his order, which, they were told, was to be complied with within five days. Seeing him behave in this manner, the Fathers vacated the house even before the date fixed, informing him that they had no desire to contend with him for the things of this world, but only for the things of heaven, should he seek to deprive them of these, or for the law of God which they had come to proclaim.

The Gentiles, thinking that victory was within their grasp, and eager to follow up their advantage, were already devising plans for the banishment of the Fathers, and for forcing the Christians to renounce their faith. The Viceroy encouraged their hopes; but as he delayed from day to day taking any further steps, the Gentiles, in order to bring pressure to bear upon him, prepared for him another great feast, close to the church and the house of the Fathers, presenting to him, on this occasion, a large sum of money, some horses, and other costly gifts, all which things he readily accepted.

The plan devised by the Viceroy for making the Christians renounce their faith was to seize their wives and young children. Of this, the Fathers received warning from the Catual, who had always been a friend to them. He advised them to conceal the small children, and those who were weak, in certain houses of his own, which he offered secretly to place at their disposal; and this the Fathers did, as soon as they knew the day on which the Viceroy was expected.

On this occasion, the older Christians displayed great courage. All were eager to enter the field of battle against the enemies of the faith which they had adopted, and to show their loyalty to the same, and how they were ready and eager to die in its defence. The catechumens were equally steadfast. One of them, a young man, fell in with and was seized by some Gentiles who, because he intended to become a Christian, threatened to take him before the Viceroy. The catechumen said very calmly, "I am content to go before the Viceroy; for I have nothing to fear from him; nor can he hinder me from adopting the faith that pleases me; because that is according to the law which the King has made, and which he intends shall be observed in his realm." Seeing him thus determined, the Gentiles let him go; for, as many of them had written to their friends and relatives, they expected soon to see every Christian expelled from the country.

But God, who never neglects the needs of His faithful servants, confounded the designs of the Viceroy and the Gentiles, and turned their joy to lamentation. On the very day they had appointed for their raid on the Christians (which was the 15th of September in the year 1605[6]), the son of the Viceroy, who had been sent on a campaign by his father, entered the town, a solitary fugitive, having been defeated in battle, with the loss of four hundred horse and a great number of infantry.[7] The Gentiles, to their great mortification, saw all the schemes they had devised against the Christians fall to pieces; for the Viceroy was now too much occupied with his own disordered affairs to think about the ruin of the Fathers. Without delay, he set out to collect his scattered soldiers, who were wandering here and there like sheep without a shepherd, and at the mercy of the enemy.

Thus were the Christians of Lahor delivered from the snares of the Gentiles and Saracens, and other enemies of their faith, and suffered once more to live their lives in tranquillity. It only remained to recover the houses of which they had been deprived. To this end the Fathers at Lahor wrote to those at Agra, where the court was then located, telling them all that had passed. With the help of the Prince, letters-patent, such as the Fathers desired, were obtained from the King. These were in the form of an edict, and were handed to the Viceroy with the seal and approbation of the Prince (a very unusual procedure[8]). The Viceroy, having read them over two or three times, lifted his eyes from the paper, and fixed them on the Fathers, appearing greatly astonished at the course they had taken, and to find that they had so much credit at court; and, after again reading the letters, he gave orders that their houses, and all else that had been taken from them and the Christians, should at once be restored.

It was not long before divine justice overtook the Viceroy, and others who had instigated this persecution. The former suffered more than the defeat of his army, which his son had commanded; for soon afterwards the enemy captured one of the King's cities, which was in the district of which he had charge, pillaging it, and laying it in ruins. He then heard that the Prince was coming to punish him, and that he was to be put to death.[9] At first he prepared for resistance, and placed the city of Lahor in a state of defence. Then he had misgivings, and began to distrust everyone, even his own people, fearing that they would deliver him into the hands of the Prince. At the same time he received repeated summonses from the King to appear before him, which reduced him to such a state of perplexity that he knew not what to do. At length, seeing no other remedy, he ventured into the presence of the King, with the fear of death before his eyes. Though he escaped with his life, he suffered innumerable indignities, notwithstanding the immense presents he made to the King.

As for the Gentiles, who were at the bottom of all the mischief, one of them was soon afterwards imprisoned by the new Viceroy; moreover, having attempted to resist justice, he was wounded, and dragged a long distance along the road by the hair of his head. While in prison he was flogged many times, and, in addition, was made to pull down a fine house he had built on a piece of land which, with the connivance of the late Viceroy, he had taken from some poor folk, to whom he was now forced to restore it. Another lost his only son, whose body was eaten by dogs. A third was taken and condemned for theft. The ringleader and organizer of the plot did not escape. He had been drawing a large pension from the King, and had made the Viceroy a present of more than fifty thousand rupees, worth twenty thousand crowns of our money. When the said Viceroy went away, the King took from him his pension, and gave it to another. Deprived of his income, the miserable fellow went to the son of this Viceroy, to whom he had presented so large a sum, and begged him to return at least a portion of it; but for answer he received only blows. During his absence, his son and brother were seized and thrown into prison, where they were so closely immured that it was only after giving large presents to the guards that he was permitted to convey food to them. They were confined, and subjected to much ill-usage, until they had paid the whole sum which the other owed to the King. That was how these unhappy wretches were rewarded for persecuting the Christians. Let us now speak of the death of the King.

CHAPTER XX[1]

The Death of Akbar

The death of this great and powerful monarch took place on the 27th of October,[2] in the year 1605. He died as he had lived; for, as none knew what law he followed in his lifetime, so none knew that in which he died. This was the just judgement of God; for when he had the means of learning and recognising the truth, he refused to make use of them. Hence he was unworthy of God's grace; so that, at this hour, none was at hand to take the bandage of unbelief from his eyes, or to offer him the means of dying in the law of Jesus-Christ, the holiness of which he had so often admitted and extolled.

The Fathers, who had full information of the King's sickness, went on a Saturday to see him, in the hope that he would hear the words which, after long thought, and having commended the matter to God, they had prepared for this hour. But they found him amongst his captains, and in so cheerful and merry a mood, that they deemed the time unsuitable for speaking to him of the end of his life, and decided to await another opportunity. They came away fully persuaded that he was making good progress, and that rumour, as ordinarily happens when kings are sick, had exaggerated the seriousness of his malady. On the Monday following, however, it was reported on all sides that the poison which had been administered was taking effect, and that his Majesty was dying. On hearing this, the Fathers went to the palace; but they could find no one who would make their arrival known to the King, or dare to speak to him of them; for already such matters were more in the hands of the great nobles than of the King himself; and hence, every means by which the Fathers tried to gain entrance was ineffectual.[3]

Up to this time, the Prince had not ventured to appear before his father. Some said that this was because his father suspected him of having given him the poison. Others said the Prince feared to come to the palace lest the great nobles should seize him, and, taking the kingdom from him, give it to his son, to whom the King had shown himself well inclined. Such fears and forebodings did, in fact, weigh heavily upon him, so that one night he seemed like a fugitive, not knowing whom he could trust. Soon, however, as groups of the common people joined him, he regained his courage; while the nobles, after turning the matter over in their minds, judged it better that the kingdom should be given to him to whom by right it belonged. Accordingly, the leading noble,[4] having been sent by the others as their representative, came to the Prince and promised, in all their names, to place the kingdom in his hands, provided that he would swear to defend the law of Mahomet, and to do no ill or offence either to his son, to whom the King wished to leave the kingdom, or to those who had sought to secure his son's succession. All these conditions he swore to fulfil, and, accompanied by a strong guard, went to see his father. The latter had already lost the power

PLATE VIII

JAHANGIR
Shortly after his Accession

[*face p. 204*

of speech, but retained sufficient consciousness to direct his son by signs to place the royal *toque* on his head; then, indicating his sword, which lay at the foot of his bed, he signified in a like manner that he should gird it on. The Prince made the *iorda*,[5] that is, the adoration, touching the ground with his head, then rising, after which the King signed to him with his hand to withdraw. This he did with alacrity, and assured of his kingdom, returned to his quarters, followed by the acclamations of the people. Meanwhile, the King suffered the last agonies attended only by a few of his most faithful retainers, who remained constantly near him. They sought to put him in mind of their Mahomet; but he made no sign of assent; only it seemed that, from time to time, he tried to utter the name of God.[6]

Thus died Echebar, or Aquebar, but now the terror of the East. And indeed he was a great King; for he knew that the good ruler is he who can command, simultaneously, the obedience, the respect, the love, and the fear of his subjects. He was a prince beloved of all, firm with the great, kind to those of low estate, and just to all men, high and low, neighbour or stranger, Christian, Saracen, or Gentile; so that every man believed that the King was on his side. He lived in the fear of God, to whom he never failed to pray four times daily, at sunrise, at sunset, at midday, and at midnight, and, despite his many duties, his prayers on these four occasions, which were of considerable duration, were never curtailed. Towards his fellowmen he was kind and forbearing, averse from taking life, and quick to show mercy. Hence it was that he decreed that if he condemned any one to death, the sentence was not to be carried into effect until the receipt of his third order. He was always glad to pardon an offender if just grounds for doing so could be shown.

Amongst his great nobles he was so predominant that none dared lift his head too high; but with the humbler classes he was benevolent and debonair, willingly giving them audience and hearing their petitions. He was pleased to accept their presents, taking them into his hands and holding them to his breast (which he never did with the rich gifts brought to him by his nobles), though often with prudent dissimulation he pretended not to see them. At one time he would be deeply emersed in state affairs, or giving audience to his subjects, and the next moment he would be seen shearing camels, hewing stones, cutting wood, or hammering iron, and doing all with as much diligence as though engaged in his own particular vocation. He ate sparingly, taking flesh only during three or four months of the year, his diet at other times consisting of milk, rice, and sweetmeats.[7] With great difficulty he spared three hours of the night for sleep. Twice at least in each day he gave audience to his subjects, showing himself at a window, from which he listened to all who sought speech with him. He had a wonderful memory. He knew the names of all his elephants, though he had many thousands of them, of his pigeons, his deer, and the other wild animals which he kept in his parks, and of all his horses to which names had been given. Each day, a certain number of these animals were brought before him for his inspection. He watched these from his window; and as each animal passed him, its name and that of the person responsible for feeding it was read out to him. He noticed if it had grown fat, or become thin, and increased or decreased the salary of its keeper accordingly. Though he could neither read nor write, he knew everything that took place in his kingdom; for from every quarter his captains wrote to him monthly, informing him of anything new they had seen or heard of. These letters were read to him after he had finished his other business, or before he retired to sleep. After the lights had been lit, he used to sit in a great hall, surrounded by numerous people whose duty it was to read books to him, or narrate stories. Here, too, he received strangers, who came for the first time to his court, questioning them concerning their King or Prince, the nature of their country, customs, trade, and similar matters, and remembering all that they told him. Amongst other books which he had read to him was the life of our Saviour, which Father Xauier had composed in Persian; for he had a great admiration for Jesus-Christ, of whom he always spoke with reverence, and whose images he treated with profound respect. But he would sometimes say that he believed our Saviour performed His miracles, giving sight to the blind, raising the dead, &c., by human means, since He was a great and wonderful physician. This idea was put into his mind by the Saracens.[8]

Echebar was one of the most fortunate monarchs of his time. Everything came to him that he wished for. He greatly extended the territories which his father had bequeathed to him; for he conquered the new kingdoms of Caxemir, Sinde, Guzaraté, Xischande,[9] a great part of the Decan, and the whole of the country of Bengala. Scarcely ever did he engage in an enterprise which he did not bring to a successful conclusion; so that "as fortunate as Echebar" became a common saying throughout the East. But he missed the greatest thing of all: the knowledge of the true God and His only Son Jesus-Christ, who came to save mankind; so that, in spite of all his worldly prosperity, he was unable to escape everlasting torment.

He was some sixty-three years old when he died, having reigned for about fifty years.[10] When all was over, his son and successor arrived, and the body was at once wrapped in a winding-sheet. Some wished to pray for him in the Saracen manner; others did not dare to; and in the end neither Saracens, nor Gentiles, nor Christians would claim him as theirs, so that he had the prayers of none. His body, having been placed on a bier, was carried on the shoulders of the King and his son without the fortress in which he died, a new exit having been made, as is the custom, by breaking down a portion of the wall. It was then conveyed to a garden about a league away, where it was buried. Of the small company that followed, a few only wore mourning; for neither the King nor his courtiers were in mourning dress, but only his son and some of those with him, who wore it for that evening alone. Thus does the world treat those from whom no good is to be hoped, nor evil feared.[11]

So ended the life and reign of King Achebar.

NOTES TO CHAPTER I

AKBAR, THE GREAT MOGUL

(N.B. The major portion of this chapter has already appeared in my *Scenes and Characters from Indian History* (Oxford Univ. Press, 1925). My thanks are due to the Publishers for permission to reproduce it.)

[1] Du Jarric's description of the emperor Akbar and his court is derived almost exclusively from Battista Peruschi's *Informatione del Regno e Stato del gran Rè di Mogor;* and Peruschi's description is, in its turn, a reproduction, practically *in extenso*, of that given by Father Anthony Monserrate in his *Relaçam do Equebar, Rei dos Mogores*. The latter work, which has served as the basis of all subsequent accounts of the person and court of Akbar, was written at Goa after the author's return from the first Mission to the Mogul court, and was completed on the 26th November, 1582. Monserrate acted as historian of the first Mission, and the *Relaçam* is a compilation from his daily notes. Its contents were subsequently incorporated in his larger work, entitled *Mongolicæ Legationis Commentarius*. The complete Portuguese text of the *Relaçam*, together with an English translation and many valuable notes by the Rev. Father Hosten, S.J., is contained in the *Journal and Proceedings of the A.S.B.* for 1912.

The fact that du Jarric studiously reproduces Peruschi's misspellings of proper names is, as Father Hosten observes, a sufficient proof that he took his account from the *Informatione*, and not from the *Relaçam* itself. It is, I think, equally clear from his statement (see p. 15) that he was unable to discover the name of the priest who visited Akbar's court in 1578, that he never saw a complete copy of either work; for, in both, the name of the priest in question is clearly stated. It follows, therefore, either that du Jarric used a mutilated copy of the *Informatione*, which would explain his inaccurate description of the Indian rivers (p. 5), or that he depended on extracts only, which may not have been made with scrupulous accuracy.

The original Italian edition of the *Informatione* was published in 1597 at Rome, and also at Brescia. A French translation was published at Paris in the same year, and German and Latin translations followed at Maintz in 1598. There are copies of the Italian (Brescia) and Latin editions in the library of the British Museum. The same library has a copy of John Hay of Dalgetty's collection of Jesuit writings, in which Peruschi's work is included. My references are to the Brescia edition.

Peruschi's account of Akbar is briefly summarised by Guzman (*Historia*, Bk. III, chs. XXVI and XXVII). Count von Noer had a copy of the *Relaçam* itself, though he was unaware of the author's identity, and made considerable use of it in his account of the Kabul campaign of 1581 (see *The Emperor Akbar*, tr. Mrs. Beveridge, Bk. II, ch. 1).

The remaining portion of the *Informatione* (utilised by du Jarric in the two succeeding chapters) contains an account of the first Mission, based on other letters written in 1582. This is followed by three letters relating to the third Mission, which will be noticed later. Peruschi makes no reference to the second Mission beyond stating that certain Fathers were sent to Akbar's court in 1591, and that they returned to Goa with their object unattained.

[2] 'Mogor,' a corruption of the Persian *mughal*, was the name given by the Portuguese not only to the Great Mogul himself, but also to his dominions. The word 'India' they used to designate only their own possessions on the West Coast. The latter word was used in a similarly restricted sense by other European nations who possessed settlements in the East, including the English.

[3] Bajazed's cage has long since been relegated to the realm of myths. Catrou refers to the story as "an ornament I would not deprive my history of, did I believe it sufficiently warranted: but besides that the best historians make no mention of it, the silence of the Mogul Chronicle in that particular makes me think that the cage was an agreeable fiction invented by the Greeks, inveterate enemies of Bajazet. They took a pleasure it seems in representing the confinement of the unhappy Prince under circumstances which flattered their hatred of him" (*History*, ed. 1709, p. 24). See also Gibbon's *Decline and Fall*, ch. lxv.

[4] In the *Relaçam* of Monserrate he is called *sexto neto*. The Portuguese word *neto* signifies a grandson, or descendant in the second generation. *Bisneto* is a great-grandson, or a descendant in the third generation. *Terceiro neto* is a great-great-grandson, and so on. By 'eighth king after him' du Jarric presumably means, eighth king of his line. The names of the ancestors of the Mogul emperors are often to be found at the heads of royal farmans. Akbar's farmans frequently commenced thus: Jalal-ud-din Muhammad Akbar, Padshah, Ghazi, son of Humayun Padshah, son of Babur Padshah, son of Umar Shaikh

Mirza, son of Sultan Abu Said, son of Sultan Muhammad Mirza, son of Miran Shah, son of Timur Mirza Sahib Qiran.

[5] So also Peruschi: *Nacque Echebar nella Prouincia chiamata Chaquata* (*Informatione*, p. 5). In the *Relaçam* we find, *a sua nacam e patria he Chaquata*, which Hosten renders, "By nationality and country he belongs to Chaquata." Amarkot, where Akbar was born, is in Sind. Chaquata, or Chagatai, was the name given to the territories, or Khanate, inherited by Chagatai Khan, the second son of Chinghiz Khan. It included the whole of Transoxiana, Afghanistan, and Baluchistan, but did not, at that date, extend eastwards beyond the Indus.

[6] Mirza Muhammad Hakim, the ruler of Kabul, was the son of Humayun by his wife Mah Chuchak Begam, and was therefore half-brother to Akbar, whose mother was Hamida Bano Begam. Mah Chuchak was murdered in Kabul in 1564 by Humayun's favourite general, Abul Maali.

[7] Arachosia, in olden times a province of the Persian empire, corresponded roughly with the south-eastern portion of Afghanistan. It was conquered by Alexander the Great, who founded its capital city, Alexandreia, now usually identified with Kandahar.

[8] Peruschi (*Informatione*, p. 14): ". . . facendogli ritirare sino all'Isole del mare de Vengala." This curious expression probably denotes the delta of the Ganges, which is so intersected by rivers and creeks that it may almost be described as a collection of islands. Ralph Fitch, in his description of this part of Bengal, wrote, "They be all hereabouts rebels against their king Zelabdim Echebar; for here are so many rivers and ilands, that they flee from one to another, whereby his horsemen cannot prevaile against them" (Foster's *Early Travels in India*, p. 28).

[9] This was Shah Tahmasp I. He reigned from 1523 to 1577, and was an ardent apostle of the Shiah faith.

[10] i.e. Ali, the adopted son of Muhammad, whose claim to succeed to the Khalifate on the death of the Prophet gave rise to the Shiah schism.

[11] i.e. the province of Gujarat (see note 4, ch. VI).

[12] The Portuguese usually referred to the kingdom of Vijayanagar as 'Narsinga,' from the name of the king, Narasingh, who reigned when they first came to India.

[13] With Monserrate to guide him, du Jarric had no excuse for making the Tapti and the Narbada flow into the Ganges. The description in the *Relaçam*, which is literally translated by Peruschi, though he mis-spells the names of the rivers, is as follows: "Industan is watered by ten rivers called as follows: the Taphi, which passes

through Currate; the Narvada, passing through Baroche; the Sambel, which flows into the Jamona; the Jamona, which passes into the Ganga; the Ganga with its mouth in Bemgala; the Çatanulge, Beha, Raoy, Chenao, Behet, and the Indo which the last five join." 'Rebeth' is evidently a perversion of Behet, or Behat, the old and correct name of the Jhilam. 'Behet' is from the Sanskrit *Vitasta*, or *Bedasta*, which the Greeks corrupted into Bidaspes, or Hydaspes (*vide* Yule's *Glossary*, p. 81). Amongst ancient names of the Sutlej, Yule gives *Satadru*, *Satudri*, and *Sitadru;* an old English name appears to have been 'Satanledge' (*vide Memoirs A.S.B.*, 1914, p. 592). By the process of elimination, we arrive at the conclusion that the Cebcha is the Beas, or Beha, the only river left. I suggest that Peruschi misread the two names 'Çatanulge Beha' as 'Catanul Gebeha,' and that from these distortions arose the monstrosities we find in the text.

[14] Akbar's fighting strength was represented by a small standing army, paid and equipped out of imperial funds, *plus* a large irregular force consisting of troops furnished by his captains, or *Mansabdars* (lit. 'office-holders'). The official 'grading' of the *Mansabdars* was one of the administrative reforms instituted in the years 1574–5. They were then divided into thirty classes, ranging from commanders of 10 to commanders of 5000. There were higher commands, of 7000, 8000, and 10,000; but these were, with rare exceptions, only conferred on Princes of the blood. In each case the numbers represented the rank of the commander, rather than the strength of the contingent he was expected to furnish, which was considerably less, sometimes not more than a tenth, of his nominal command. Indeed, the rank of Mansabdar was frequently conferred without any military obligation at all, on persons whom the king wished to honour. The *mansabdari* system, therefore, not only served a military purpose, but constituted a kind of order of knighthood. The salaries attached to the various grades ranged from 75 rupees a month for commanders of 10, to 30,000 rupees for commanders of 5000, or, as it were, 'grand commanders' of the order.

Neither Abul Fazl, the author of the *Ain-i-Akbari*, nor Badaoni, the two principal authorities on Akbar's military administration, makes any mention of commanders of 12,000 or 14,000. But du Jarric's figures are those given by Monserrate, and cannot, therefore, be lightly set aside. Monserrate accompanied Akbar on his military expedition to Kabul in 1581, and his figures are doubtless based on the composition of the force employed on that occasion. It must be remembered that, at this juncture, Akbar's throne was in very imminent danger; for while his dominions were being invaded from the west, a formidable rebellion was raging in Bengal, the two together constituting a deep-laid conspiracy to place his brother Muhammad Hakim, the ruler of Kabul, on the imperial throne. In such an emergency Akbar must have needed the help of every man he could lay his hands on; and it is, therefore, quite conceivable that his captains were called upon to take the field with contingents larger than those they were normally expected to maintain. The number of troops employed during these troubles is given in the *Relaçam* as follows: "In his campaign against his brother, the Prince of Qhabal, he left 10,000 men in garrison in Cambaia, and 12,000 in Fatipur with his mother. To the frontiers of Bemgala he sent against the rebels a foster brother of his own, one of his relations, with 20,000 horse, and some four or five captains, each with six, five or four thousand horse, besides some infantry and camp-followers for the baggage. In all the towns he left the necessary garrisons, and took with him about 50,000 picked men, besides an infinite number of infantry and camp-followers."

[15] Du Jarric's authority for this statement was a letter written by the Father Provincial of Goa in November, 1591, which was published at Rome in 1592 by an Italian Father named Spitilli, together with another letter by the same writer. Extracts from both these letters are given by Maclagan in his account of the Jesuit Missions (*J.A.S.B.*, Vol. 65). The passage referring to the elephants is as follows: "Father Anthony Monserrate states that when the Emperor took him on an expedition which he at one time made, he had with him five thousand fighting elephants exclusive of those used for baggage, and that in the whole empire there are fifty thousand elephants stationed for war-like purposes at various centres." The statements here attributed to Monserrate do not appear in his works. In the *Relaçam*, however, he says, in reference to the Kabul campaign, that, after the Indus had been crossed, the king's second son "was sent ahead with 15,000 horse and 1500 elephants"; so that the number of the latter animals taken on the expedition must have been very large. The statement that Akbar maintained 50,000 war-elephants is also made by Peruschi.

[16] These are described in the *Relaçam* as follows: "He [Akbar] had also with him fifty elephants, each with four musketeers, placed on certain appliances, like children's cradles, with a balcony which they can turn in any direction they like. These musketeers discharge bullets of the size of an egg." The method here described of arming elephants was not peculiar to the armies of the Mogul kings. In the *Chronicle* of Fernão Nuniz we read that the war-elephants of Vijayanagar "go with their howdahs (castellos) from which four men fight on each side of them, and the elephants are completely clothed, and on their tusks they have knives fastened, much ground and sharpened, with which they do great harm." Varthema, who gives a detailed description of

the Vijayanagar war-elephants, says: "They fasten to the trunk a sword two *braccia* long, as thick and as wide as the hand of a man. And in this way they fight. And he who sits upon his neck orders him: 'Go forward,' or 'Turn back,' 'Strike this one,' 'Strike that one,' 'Do not strike any more,' and he understands as though he were a human being." If the custom of attaching a sword to the trunk, and daggers to the tusks, of an elephant actually prevailed, as Monserrate states in the *Relaçam*, in the Mogul army, it is curious that no mention is made of it in the *Ain-i-Akbari*. I have not found the practice referred to by any Muhammadan writer, nor have I seen it depicted in any Mogul battle-picture. Irvine says nothing about it in his *Army of the Indian Moguls*.

[17] This apparently refers to Akbar's twin sons, Hasan and Husain, who died in infancy in 1564 (see Smith's *Akbar*, p. 75). The building of Fathpur-Sikri was commenced in 1569. Monserrate says in his *Commentarius* that when Akbar took up his residence at Agra, he found the city full of evil spirits, who molested all classes of the people, and even his own children were amongst their victims: "Nam absoluto jam opere, ubi Rex nouam arcem, et aulam incolere cœpit, lemures diuino id permittente numine, domos percurrere, rursum prorsum cursitare, omnia conuellere, mulierculas, et pueros territare, lapidis jacere, omnibus denique nocere instituunt. Ac fuissent fortasse, haec in commoda, si latius se non fuissent, ferenda. Verum in Regis liberos, Daemonis sese effudit audacia: quos biduo, aut tribuo postquam nati essent, enecabat. Et binos, aut tirnos eripuit." (*Memoirs of the A.S.B.*, 1914, p. 562).

[18] This date is incorrect. The first Jesuit Mission arrived at Fathpur in February, 1580. Two years before this, Akbar had been visited by a Christian priest named Julianus Pereira, the Vicar-General in Bengal, whose "zeal in explaining the law of the Gospel, together with the excellence of his conduct, disposed Akbar to regard our faith with increasing favour" (*Relaçam*). According to Father Hosten, however. this priest was not a Jesuit.

[19] The description in the *Relaçam* is as follows: "Akbar is a fine-looking, broad-shouldered man, but bow-legged, and of a swarthy complexion. His eyes are large, but with narrow openings, like those of a Tartar or Chinaman. He has a broad, open forehead; and his nose, except for a slight lump in the centre, is straight. The nostrils are large, and on the left one there is a small wart. He is in the habit of carrying his head slightly inclined to the right side. Like the Turks, he shaves his beard; but he wears a small neatly-trimmed moustache." This portrait is practically identical with that which Jahangir gives us in his *Memoirs*, except for the inadequate allusion to Akbar's wart.

Jahangir, evidently a connoisseur in such matters, does the royal excrescence more justice. " My father," he writes, " had on the left side of his nose a fleshy mole, very agreeable in appearance, of the size of half a pea. Those skilled in the science of physiognomy considered this mole a sign of great prosperity and exceeding good fortune " (*Tuzuk-i-Jahangiri*, i. p. 33).

[20] Monserrate says that when the Fathers went to the palace on the evening of their arrival at Fathpur, they found the King and his sons in Portuguese dress, which they had assumed as a compliment to their guests : " More Lusitanicis pallium purpureum, aureis fibulis induit, filiosque eodem vestibus, et pileis (caps) Lusitanicis prodire jussit, ut ea re hospitibus gratificaretur " (*Memoirs of the A.S.B.*, 1914, p. 559).

[21] *Il estoit melancholique de sa nature, et subiect au mal caduc ;* or, in the Latin version of Matthia Martinez, *Natura erat melancholicus, et epileptico subjectus morbo.* I have been unable to trace du Jarric's authority for this statement. It is not made by Monserrate, nor is it to be found either in Guzman's *Historia* or in the *Informatione* of Peruschi. Possibly du Jarric took it from the notes on the *Historia* made by Father Laertius (see p. xxviii). There is nothing improbable in the statement itself. That Akbar suffered at times from some form of mental depression, there appears to be no doubt ; and if Abul Fazl's statement (*Akbarnama*, tr. Beveridge, p. 1125) that Murad developed epilepsy, is to be trusted, it may be concluded that the disease, which is well known to be hereditary, was in the family. It may even be that Humayun's fatal fall was due to a seizure of this nature. The statement that Prince Murad developed epilepsy is also made in the *Maasir-ul-Umara* (see Mr. Beveridge's translation, p. 120).

[22] In the *Commentarius*, Monserrate states that he and Father Aquaviva were invited to witness one of these gladiatorial combats, and that they not only refused to do so, but severely reprimanded Akbar for countenancing so inhuman a practice. According to V. A. Smith, the ' gladiatorii ludi ' were continued by Jahangir and Shah Jahan.

[23] It is not the panther (*felis pardus*), but the hunting leopard (*felis jubata*) which was, and is still trained in India for hunting purposes. The latter animal is now generally called a ' cheeta ' ; though this name, which means ' spotted,' is frequently given to the panther, and to its close relative the leopard (*felis leopardus*).

[24] Apparently the office of the *Mir-i-Arz*, or *Barbegi*, is here referred to. According to Blochmann (*Ain*, I, p. vi) the *Mir-i-Arz* was " an officer who presents people at court, their petitions, &c." Abul Fazl says (*ibid.*, p. 251) that this officer was fully acquainted with all the ceremonies of the court, and that it was through him, and the officer in command of the guard for the day, that all the orders of the King

were made known. These two officers, he adds, "are day and night in attendance about the palace, ready for any orders His Majesty may issue."

[25] The duties of a *waqái-navis* (lit. 'news-writer'), or royal scribe, are given in the *Ain-i-Akbari*. There appear to have been fourteen such officers, who came on duty in rotation, two at a time. It was their business to write up the *yad-dasht*, or daily record of all that the king said or did in the course of the twenty-four hours. If they did their work conscientiously, they must have had a very busy time; for the *yad-dasht* was a record not only of the king's public acts and utterances, but of countless matters of a personal or private nature, such as "what His Majesty eats and drinks; when he sleeps and when he rises; the etiquette in the state hall; the time His Majesty spends in the harem; when he goes to the general and private assemblies; when he marches and when he halts; vows made by him; his remarks; what books he has read to him; what alms he bestows; what presents he makes . . ." (*Ain*, I, p. 258).

[26] Du Jarric presumably means 'impaled.' In the *Commentarius* of Monserrate the punishments are referred to as follows: "Qui capitale commiserunt, aut pedibus elephantum proterendi proijiuntur, aut palis infiguntur, aut suspendio enecantur. Raptores et adulteri, aut jugulantur, aut in furcam aguntur."

[27] This was Khwaja Shah Mansur, who was finance minister when the first Jesuit mission arrived at Akbar's court. Shah Mansur took a leading part in the conspiracy mentioned on page 32. Three times he was found to be in treasonable correspondence with Mirza Muhammad Hakim, the ruler of Kabul. The letters discovered on the last occasion may have been, and in all probability were, forged by his enemies, with a view to compassing his downfall; but of his guilt on the two first occasions there appears to be little doubt. The question is fully discussed by V. A. Smith on pages 195–7 of his *Akbar;* but reference should also be made to the account of the Kabul campaign in *J. & Proc. A.S.B.*, Vol. XI (1915), in which the case *for* Shah Mansur is very strongly put.

NOTES TO CHAPTER II

The First Mission to Mogor

[1] The first paragraph of this chapter is based on the *Informatione*, and the remainder on Guzman's *Historia* (Bk. III, chs. xxviii–xxx).

[2] Cabral was already known to Akbar, to whose court he had been sent as ambassador in 1573. Akbar was at that time engaged in the siege of Surat, then held by his rebellious kinsmen, the Mirzas; and having heard that the Portuguese were taking steps to assist the defenders, he made friendly overtures to Don Antonio de Noronha, the Viceroy at Goa, who thereupon despatched an embassy under Antonio Cabral (or Cambral) to meet the Emperor at Surat. Owing to the skill with which Cabral conducted the negotiations, a peaceful settlement was arrived at, and was shortly followed by the capitulation of the town. Monserrate says in his *Relaçam do Equebar* that Akbar "was first drawn to our religion by the courteous behaviour and fearlessness of the Portuguese who accompanied Cabral on his mission to Surat." The circumstances which led to Cabral's second embassage in 1578 are somewhat obscure. According to V. A. Smith (*Akbar*, p. 137), Akbar's relations with the Portuguese had again become strained, and an embassy was sent to Goa to arrange matters. "In 1578 the Viceroy (Dom Diogo de Menezes) responded by accrediting to Akbar's court as his ambassador the same Antonio Cabral who had conducted the satisfactory negotiations in 1573. He spent some time at Fathpur-Sikri, and was able to give the Emperor a considerable amount of information concerning Christian manners and customs; but, being a layman, he was not in a position to expound with authority the deeper matters of the faith." Du Jarric does not appear to have known that Cabral conducted two embassies to the Mogul court.

Abul Fazl's account of the siege of Surat in 1573 contains the following interesting passage: "One of the occurrences of the siege was that a large number of Christians came from the port of Goa and its neighbourhood to the foot of the sublime throne, and were rewarded by the bliss of an interview (*mulazamat*). Apparently they had come at the request of the besieged in order that the latter might make the fort over to them, and so convey themselves to the shore of safety. But when that crew saw the majesty of the imperial power, and had become cognisant of the largeness of the army, and of the extent of the siege-train, they represented themselves as ambassadors and performed the *kornish*. They produced many of the rarities of their country, and the appreciative Khedive received each one of them with special favour and made inquiries about the wonders of Portugal and the manners and customs of Europe. It seemed as if he did this from a desire of knowledge, for his sacred heart is a depôt of spiritual and physical sciences" (*Akbarnama*, tr. H. Beveridge, Vol. III, p. 37).

[3] The Fathers in question were Anthony Vaz and Peter Dias. In his *Missione al Gran Mogor*, Father Daniel Bartoli states that these two priests "having come to preach in his (Akbar's) dominions in Bengala, and finding that the Christians there defrauded his royal exchequer of the taxes they rightly owed for anchorage, and of the annual imposts agreed upon between them, obliged them to make restitution. A large sum was recovered, and the King, wise as he was, on hearing of it from his ministers, marvelled at the measure, and highly commended the probity of the Fathers, as also the holiness of the Christian law, since it would not allow its followers any disloyalty or injustice even towards foreigners and enemies" (see *A.S.B. Memoirs*, Vol. III, p.540).

In the *Relaçam* of Monserrate he is called Pero Tavares, and is described as "the Captain of Port Pequino." Porto Pequino and Porto Grande, the 'Little Haven' and the 'Great Haven,' were the names by which the Bengal ports of Satigam and Chatiyam (Chittagong) were commonly known to the Portuguese (see *Hobson-Jobson*, p. 727). There can be little doubt that, as Mr. Beveridge has suggested, Tavares is to be identified with the person called Partab Bar in the *Akbarnama* of Abul Fazl. The reference is to the account of the 23rd year of the reign (1578), in which it is stated that, along with the tribute from Bengal, there came to Akbar's court "a European named Partab Bar, one of the chief merchants of the ports of Bengal, who was accompanied by Basurba, his wife: he was graciously received at court, and his sound sense and upright conduct won the favour and esteem of the Emperor" (*E. & D.*, VI, p. 59). Partab Bar is a very close approximation to Pero Tavares. For suggested explanations of the name Basurba, see Mr. Beveridge's note on page 383 of his translation of the *Akbarnama*.

[5] Up to this point du Jarric has followed (practically translated) Peruschi; but either the extract he was using here came to an abrupt end, or his copy of the *Informatione* was mutilated; for, in the very next line, Peruschi refers to the priest as Padre Giuliano Pereira. The remaining portion of this chapter is a translation of pages 243–248 of the *Historia*, in which the priest's name is not mentioned.

It appears from the *Relaçam* of Monserrate, from which Peruschi took the name, that Pereira afterwards had charge of the bishopric of Cochin. In the *Oriente Conquistado* of de Sousa he is referred to as a man who " possessed more virtue than letters, hence, after answering what he knew, he said that he was a dunce compared with the men of letters to be found at Goa, and that His Majesty might call for some to be fully informed of the mysteries of the Gospels." In the *Commentarius*, Monserrate styles this priest Aegidius, which is the Latin form of Giuliano, or Julianus.

[6] The word *cazique* (variously spelt *casis*, *caxis*, *caciz*, etc.) was used by Spanish and Portuguese writers to signify a Muhammadan priest or *mulla*. According to Yule (*H.J.*, p. 169), " it may be suspected to have arisen from a confusion of two Arabic terms—*kādi* [i.e. *kazi*, a Muhammadan civil or criminal judge] and *kashish* or *kasis*, a Christian Presbyter." On page 146 the word is spelt *coxi*, and is wrongly used to designate a Hindu divine ; at any rate, I can suggest no other explanation of the term *coxi*.

[7] Du Jarric evidently means the King's *Amiru-l-hajj* or *Mir-i-kafila*, the officer in charge of pilgrims to Mecca. This office was generally held by a man of high rank and dignity. The person here referred to is Sultan Khwaja, who had been appointed Amiru-l-hajj in 1577, and had conducted a numerous party of courtiers to the holy shrine (*Ain-i-Akbari*, I, 423). According to Abul Fazl and Badaoni, Sultan Khwaja afterwards became a follower of Akbar's new religion, the *Din Ilahi*. His daughter was married to Prince Danyal.

[8] Tavernier says that the Jesuit Fathers at Goa were known as Paulists, " on account of their grand church dedicated to St. Paul " (*Travels*, ed. Ball, I, p. 197). It was, however, not the church, but the College of St. Paul, which gave rise to the name Paulists. This college was originally an ordinary lay seminary, but was taken over and converted into a Jesuit institution by St. Francis Xavier. Many Jesuit priests were trained in the college, which was looked upon by the Fathers of the Society as their Indian *Alma Mater*. Du Jarric describes it as the fountain-head of the missionary movement, " du quel toutes les autres maisons, lieu de residance, ou Colleges que nous avons en l'Inde Orientale, sont sortis, comme des Colonies ; par consequent nous pouuons dire en quelque façon, que tout le bien, qui esté faict en Orient par le moyen de ceux de nostre compagnie, prend sa source de là, comme d'une fontaine . . . et partant ce n'est pas sans raison, qu'on les appelle presque par tout l'Orient les Peres de S. Paul, comme si tous estoient habitans de ce College " (*Histoire*, I, p. 307).

[9] His real name was Peres or Pires. According to Bartoli he was an Armenian Christian. In 1582 he married an Indian wife. We learn from a letter written by Aquaviva, that Akbar himself was present

at the marriage, and interpreted to the bride the sermon which he (Aquaviva) delivered on the occasion (see *J.A.S.B.*, LVI, p. 57).

[10] The King's ambassador reached Goa in September, 1579, and was received with great honour. "The same celebrations were accorded him," says Bartoli in his *Missione al Gran Mogor*, "which were customary on the arrival of Viceroys newly come from Europe to take up the government of India. . . . The ambassador was conducted from the *S. Iago* which lay two or three nautical miles off Goa, made his solemn entrance, the whole of the Portuguese nobility welcoming him. A part of them met him as he alighted on the shore; the rest expected him at the palace. A great train of cavaliers then accompanied him to our College of St. Paul, where he presented to the Provincial the letters of his King with the amplest patents, so that, from their first entrance into the states of his Crown up to their arrival at his court of Fatepur, the Fathers who were to be sent might be received, provided for and, if need be, protected as persons belonging to His Majesty's own household, by the Viceroys and the Governors of the Provinces through which they would pass." De Sousa (*Oriente Conquistado*, II, 150) says that the Portuguese Viceroy was at first unwilling to comply with Akbar's request, fearing that he meant to hold the Fathers as hostages, "and thus oblige the Captains of Damaò, Dio, and of the armadas of the North to overlook his encroachments," and that it was only after the Provincial had assured him that his apprehensions were baseless, "while there appeared solid hope of greater conquests to the Faith and of advantages to the State," and after the matter had been referred to and approved by a council of Bishops, that he finally decided to despatch the Mission.

The above quotations from Bartoli and de Sousa are from the passages translated by the Rev. H. Hosten in his introduction to the text of the *Commentarius* of Monserrate (*Memoirs A.S.B.*, III, 1914).

[11] Father Rudolf Aquaviva had just reached Goa when Akbar's embassy arrived. He was then only 30 years of age. After joining the Jesuit Society he had insisted, despite his delicate health, on being sent to aid in spreading the Gospel in the East. He at once asked to be sent to the Great Mogul's court, and was appointed leader of the Mission. On his return to Goa in 1583, he was sent to Salsette, where he was killed a few months later by a Hindu mob. An interesting biographical sketch of Aquaviva is contained in Father F. Goldie's *First Christian Mission to the Great Mogul.*

[12] Father Anthony Monserrate was not only a zealous and courageous missionary, but a scholar and a man of letters. He first came into prominence during the great plague which devastated the city of Lisbon in 1569, when he displayed fearless devotion in ministering to

the sick. He accompanied the first Mission to Akbar's court for the double purpose of sharing its labours and writing its history. His *Mongolicæ Legationis Commentarius*, or narrative of the first Jesuit Mission, constitutes one of the most important of our primary sources for the history of Akbar's reign. In Part II of his *Histoire* (pp. 224–238) du Jarric gives a detailed and interesting account of Monserrate's capture by Arabs off the coast of Arabia in 1588, and of his subsequent adventures, until finally ransomed six and a half years later. The complete Latin text of the *Commentarius*, edited by Father Hosten, is contained in Vol. III of the *Memoirs of the Asiatic Society of Bengal.*

[13] Father François Henriqués was a Persian convert, selected probably on account of his knowledge of the Persian language. He does not appear to have been a success. He returned, or was recalled, to Goa before the termination of the Mission.

[14] The route followed, which was through Khandesh, Ujjain, Sarangpur, Sironj, and Gwalior, is given, with other details of the journey, in de Sousa's *Oriente Conquistado*, and the *Commentarius* of Monserrate. A good account of the journey may also be read in Murray's *Discoveries*, II, p. 83 *et seq.*

[15] According to Goldie (*First Christian Mission*, p. 63), this was the new Royal Polyglot Bible of Plantyn, printed for Philip II, 1569–1572. Father Goldie evidently refers to the *Biblia Montani*, edited by Father B. Arias Montanus, and printed at Antwerp, 1569–1573, by Christopher Platinus. This Bible was published in eight (not seven, as stated by Goldie) folio volumes. The four languages are Hebrew, Chaldee, Latin, and Greek. The Old Testament is contained in the first four volumes, and the New in the fifth. The last three volumes are filled by the " apparatus sacer." There is a fine and complete copy of the *Biblia Montani* in the library of the British Museum, which is said to be the copy presented by the printer to Matthias, Archduke of Austria, afterwards Emperor. For an account of the editor and his work, see Hurter's *Nomenclator*, Vol. I, pp. 145–7. Monserrate clearly states in the *Commentarius* that the Bible presented to Akbar was in seven volumes ; so, if the above identification is correct, Akbar's copy must have been incomplete.

[16] This picture adorns the altar in the Borghese Chapel in the Church of S. Maria Maggiore at Rome. It is one of the pictures attributed to St. Luke, and is supposed to possess miraculous powers. It is said that in the year 590, when Rome was devastated by cholera, Pope Gregory the Great caused this picture to be carried in procession through the streets, and that the disease straightway disappeared from the city. A similar procession took place in 1860 after the victories of Garibaldi, which were attributed to the miraculous influence of the picture.

[17] This was doubtless the dispute referred to by Abul Fazl in the *Akbarnama;* "One night," he says, "the *Ibadat-Khana* was brightened by the presence of Padre Radalf, who for intelligence and wisdom was unrivalled among Christian doctors. Several carping and bigoted men attacked him, and this afforded an opportunity for a display of the calm judgment and justice of the assembly! These men brought forward the old received assertions, and did not attempt to arrive at the truth by reasoning. Their statements were torn to pieces, and they were nearly put to shame; and then they began to attack the contradictions in the Gospel, but they could not prove their assertions. With perfect calmness and earnest conviction of the truth, the Padre replied to their arguments . . ." (*E. & D.*, VI, p. 60).

NOTES TO CHAPTER III

'What is Truth?'

[1] The first 11 paragraphs of this chapter are based on the *Informatione* (pp. 34–40), and the remainder on chapter xxxi of the *Historia*.

[2] This is incorrect. Salim was born in 1569; in 1582, therefore, he was 13, or by Hijri reckoning, 14 years of age. He was named after the saint Shaikh Salim Chisti, in whose house he was born. "After my birth," he wrote in his Memoirs, "they gave me the name of Sultan Salim, but I never heard my father, whether in his cups or in his sober moments, call me Muhammad Salim, or Sultan Salim, but always Shaikhu Baba" (*Tuzuk-i-Jahangiri*, I, p. 2). Murad, nicknamed Pahari, was born in 1570, and was, therefore, 12 years old at this time. Dan, or Danyal, was born in 1572.

[3] Murad's education was first entrusted to Monserrate and afterwards to Aquaviva. In a letter to the General of the Order, dated April, 1582, Aquaviva wrote: "We hope to see some fruit from the Emperor's second son, Pahari, a boy of 13 years of age, who is learning the Portuguese language, and therewith the things relating to our faith, and who shows himself well disposed thereto, and who is of great natural genius and has good inclination. Father Monserrat was his teacher, and now I am" (*J.A.S.B.*, VI, p. 55). How bitter the fruit proved, Aquaviva was never to know.

[4] The complete formula with which the Muhammadan school-boy should commence his exercises is *Bismillahi 'r-rahmani 'r-rahim:* "In the name of God, the Compassionate, the Merciful." This formula, or more frequently the word *bismillah* alone, is repeated at the commencement of any new work. It serves as a grace before meals, and is used at the beginning of all books. The incident in the text seems to be referred to by Badaoni. "Learned monks," he says, "came from Europe, who go by the name of *Pádre*. They have an infallible head called *Pápá*. He can change any religious ordinances as he may think advisable, and kings have to submit to his authority. These monks brought the Gospel, and mentioned to the Emperor their proofs of the Trinity. His Majesty firmly believed in the truth of the Christian religion, and wishing to spread the doctrines of Jesus, ordered Prince

Murád to take a few lessons in Christianity by way of auspiciousness, and charged Abulfazl to translate the Gospel. Instead of the usual *Bismilláh-irrahmán-irrahím*, the following words were used—

Ai nám i tu Jesus o Kiristo,

which means 'O thou whose name is gracious and blessed'; and Shaikh Faizi added another half, in order to complete the verse—

Subhánaka lá siwáka Yá hú.

(We praise Thee, there is no one besides Thee, O God!)

These accursed monks applied the description of cursed Satan, and of his qualities to Muhammad, the best of all prophets—God's blessings rest on him and his whole house!—a thing which even devils would not do" (*Ain*, I, p. 182).

[5] The corresponding passage in the *Informatione* is as follows: "Finalmente disse a i Padre, che la lor legge gli piaceua molto: ma che non poteua credere quelli due articoli della Trinitatà, & della Incarnatione: & che, se gli facessero penetrare, & intendere questi, voleua essere Christiano; & che, se percio fusse necessareo di lasciare il Regno, lo farebbe."

[6] The Koran is full of allusions to the Old and the New Testaments; but I know of no passage in which either the possession or the reading of these books is forbidden. The statement in the text appears to be one of the many examples which the Jesuit writings afford of the ignorance of the Fathers on matters pertaining to the faith of Islam.

[7] On the extent to which slavery prevailed in India at this period, see Moreland's *India at the Death of Akbar*, especially chapters III and IV. The position and treatment of slaves is referred to by Abul Fazl in the 6th *Ain* (Blochmann, I, p. 253). Akbar, we are told, objected, from religious motives, to the use of the word *bandah* (slave), and spoke of the class always as *chelahs*, or 'faithful disciples.' He also permitted many *chelahs* to "chose the road to happiness" by joining the *Din Ilahi*. There were both Indian and foreign slaves. The chief market for the latter was at Goa, in which city, according to Linschoten, slave labour was extensively employed. Abul Fazl gives the pay of the lowest class of slave as 1 *dam* per day, or less than a rupee a month. It was only in 1843 that slavery was finally abolished in India by legislation.

[8] Amongst Muhammadans it is considered a highly meritorious act to assist in carrying the dead to the place of interment.

[9] This is the Jesuit version of the story, for a fuller account of which see the *Commentarius* of Monserrate, pp. 564–6. According to Abul Fazl (*E. & D.*, VI, p. 60), the challenge emanated from the Fathers, and was declined by the "black-hearted and mean-spirited" Mullas, who "answered only with angry words." Badaoni reverses the story.

NOTES TO CHAPTER III

"The fire," he says, "was made. The Shaikh pulled one of the Christian priests by the coat, and said to him, 'Come on, in the name of God!' But none of the priests had the courage to go" (Blochmann, *Ain*, I, p. 191). See also Smith's *Akbar*, p. 176.

[10] This was probably Hakim Ali who attended Akbar during his last illness. "In the 40th year, Ali was a commander of 700, and had the title of *Jálinús uzzamání*, 'the Galenus of the age.' His astringent mixtures enjoyed a great reputation at court. He treated Akbar immediately before his death. It is said that the Emperor died of dysentery or acute diarrhœa, which no remedies could stop. 'Alí had at last recourse to a most powerful astringent, and when the dysentery was stopped, costive fever and strangury ensued. He therefore administered purgatives, which brought back the diarrhœa, of which Akbar died. . . . Jahangir says of him that 'his subtlety was greater than his knowledge, his looks better than his walk of life, his behaviour better than his heart; for in reality he was a bad and unprincipled man.' Once Jahangír hinted that 'Alí had killed Akbar. On the other side, it is said that he spent annually 6000 rupees on medicines for the poor" (*Ain*, I, p. 467).

[11] The rebellion had already commenced when the Jesuit Mission reached Fathpur at the end of February, 1580. The Governor of Bengal, Muzaffar Khan, was murdered in April; but it was not till the beginning of the following year that Muhammad Hakim marched from Kabul into the Panjab. Akbar set out on his campaign against his brother in February, 1581. He entered Kabul in August, and was back again at Fathpur before the close of the year.

[12] Akbar's treatment of the Fathers at this time was probably dictated by policy, rather than by any violent change in his personal feelings towards them, or in his attitude either to Christianity or to Islam. He was, in fact, in an extremely critical situation, and one which demanded that, for the time at any rate, his unpopular religious views should be kept in the background. That the Fathers were not entirely banished from his favour is proved by the fact (unknown apparently to du Jarric) that he took Monserrate with him on the Kabul expedition. We are told that Father Rudolf also wished to accompany the Emperor. "But Akbar thought it well not to irritate the Muhammadans in a moment of danger, and would only allow Father Montserrat to accompany him, as the tutor of his son, Murad." (Goldie, *First Christian Mission*, p. 83).

[13] *Vide* note 14, ch. I. Detailed accounts of the Kabul campaign are to be found in Monserrate's *Commentarius*, and in the *Akbarnama* of Abul Fazl.

NOTES TO CHAPTER IV

Father Rudolf Aquaviva

[1] This chapter, with the exception of the last four paragraphs, is almost a literal translation of chapters xxxii and xxxiii of the *Historia*.

[2] Father Monserrate set out for Goa in April, 1582, and his departure may be said to mark the close of the first Jesuit Mission. Father Rudolf Aquaviva remained at Fathpur till the following February, when he too left for Goa, where he arrived in the month of May. Akbar sent, at the same time, a letter to the Provincial, in which he thus referred to Rudolf's departure: "As the said Father is very learned and versed in the wisdom of the ancients, and as I love him much and see that he is wise and learned in the faith, I wish to devote every hour to conversation with him. For these reasons I have sometimes refused the leave which he asked for and which your Reverence also in your letter desired. But now I give him leave to go: and as my intention is that our friendship should increase from day to day it is meet that your Reverence should do your part towards preserving it by sending Father Rodolfi back to me, with several other Fathers, as soon as possible, for I wish the Fathers of your Society to be with me, and I take great delight in them. I have told the Father many things by word of mouth that he might repeat them to your Reverence, the which you will consider well" (*J.A.S.B.*, LXV, p. 59).

[3] In a letter written to the General of the Company in 1598, Xavier tells how, on one occasion, the Prince, after talking at great length of the bodily afflictions which the Christians were wont to undergo, confirmed his account by referring to Father Aquaviva "whose intimate friend he had been, saying how one night when sleeping near him he heard a sound as though he were moving in the far end of his room. When the sound ceased he entered the Father's room and found there a whip so covered with blood that drops were falling on the floor. He asked him what the sound meant. The holy Father, however, tried to cover with a laugh what the flush on his face and the modesty of his eyes plainly betrayed" (*J.A.S.B.*, VI, p. 75).

[4] It was about this time (i.e. in 1582) that Akbar first publicly promulgated his new religion, the *Din Ilahi*, or 'Divine Faith.'

NOTES TO CHAPTER V

The Second Mission

[1] This chapter, like the corresponding chapter (xxxiv) of Guzman's *Historia*, reproduces almost word for word the reports sent to Rome in 1590 and 1591 by the Provincial at Goa. Italian translations of both these reports were published at Rome in 1592 by Spitilli. A Latin version of the same appeared at Antwerp the following year.

[2] In the Provincial's letter on which this chapter is based the corresponding passage is: "Fana urbis, in qua residet, universa (Moscheas vocant) in stabula equorum, & elephantorum receptacula convertit, majoris apparatus bellici prætextu. Postmodum vero Alcoranos (turres sunt fanis injectæ, ex quibus sacrificuli voce præalta Mahometum inclamant) evertit, affirmans quod cum inutilia essent fana, & orationi inidoneæ, frustra prædictæ turres subsisterent."

The term generally used by Portuguese writers of the period for a *manar*, or minaret, was not 'alcoran,' but 'alcorana'; and it is the latter word which has obtained a permanent place in the Portuguese vocabulary. Lacerda's dictionary defines it as "a slender and high turret in which the ministers of Alcoran said or read aloud their prayers." The same meaning (and the same misconception of the *muazzin's* call) is to be found in modern Portuguese dictionaries. Examples of the use of the term are common in the works of Castañeda, Barros, Teixeira, and other early Portuguese authors. It was borrowed by the English traveller Herbert, who, in his *Travels* (p. 164, 3rd ed.), describes "the alcoranas of Mosques" as "high, slender, round steeples or towers, most of which are terraced near the top like the Standard in Cheapside, but twice as high." In an earlier chapter of the *Histoire*, the same term is used, not of the *manar* of a mosque, but of the mosque itself.

This name for a minaret appears to have originated with the Portuguese. I have discovered no instance of its use prior to the 16th century. Mr. Fennell (*vide* his *Dictionary of Anglicised Words and Phrases*) regards it as quite distinct from *alquran*, the Koran, and derives it from *al-qorun*, 'the horns,' or *al-qiran*, 'the vertices.' Yule, who offers no explanation, quotes, but does not endorse this derivation (*Hobson-Jobson*, p. 11). The above-mentioned passage in the *Histoire* indicates, I think, that Mr. Fennell is wrong, and that in the word 'alcorana' we have nothing more than a misapplication of the name of the Sacred Book of Islam. In the chapter referred to, du Jarric tells how, during the Mission to Ormuz (*circa* 1549), Father Gaspar Barzé was permitted, as a great favour, to enter the principal mosque of the city. The people, he says, took the Father "au plus grand & plus magnifique temple de Mahomet, appelle Coran, ou Alcoran : ce que signifie en langage Arabique une chose sacrée, & pource appellent-'ils leur Loy Alcoran, & donnoyent a ce temple le mesme nom ; parce que c'estoit le plus sainct & sacré a leur jugement, qu'ils eussent en toutes quartiers." This strongly suggests that 'alcorana' was the outcome of a confused association of ideas, combined with ignorance of the Arabic tongue. Teixeira's explanation seems to favour the same view. After describing a minaret and the purpose for which it is used, he adds : "y porque al libro de la setta de Mahamed llaman Koran o Alkoran, se dió el mismo nombre al lugar hesho parapredicarlo" (*Relacion*, p. 113).

It is quite conceivable that the first Portuguese settlers were wrongly informed, or even hoaxed. They took little trouble to obtain accurate information about the people of India, while their credulity was astounding. When Da Gama and his followers landed on the West Coast in 1499, they were told that the Hindu temples at Calicut were Christian churches, that the officiating priests were styled 'kaffirs,' and that a Nayar wore a top-knot to show that he belonged to the Christian religion ; and after knocking about for three months in Malabar, they carried this priceless information back with them to Portugal (see my *Scenes and Characters from Indian History*, pp. 90–92). It would have been an easy task to persuade these early adventurers that 'alcorana' was the correct name for a minaret ; but that the Jesuit Fathers, who professed to be, and in many cases undoubtedly were scholars, should have allowed themselves to be imposed upon to the extent revealed in the above quotations, seems almost incredible. Their ignorance in this instance was, however, characteristic of their general attitude towards the religions of the East. To them these alien creeds were things to be uprooted rather than studied. Islam was an evil growth ; and they took as little trouble to master its terminology as they took to comprehend the nature of its doctrines, and the significance of its rites.

Dalgado in his *Glossario-Luso-Asiatico* gives a number of examples of the use of 'alcorana,' but throws no further light on its origin. His first example is taken from the *Itinerario* of Antonio Tenreiro, to which he assigns the date 1529. This date is incorrect. The original edition of the *Itinerario* was published at Coimbra in 1560.

NOTES TO CHAPTER V

[3] The desecration of the mosques is referred to by Badaoni, who says that they were "changed into store-rooms, or given to Hindu chaukidars" (*Ain*, I, p. 200); but the destruction of the minarets and the dispersal of the royal *harim* are not confirmed by other writers. The Provincial gained his information from Leon Grimon, who, in 1590, carried to Goa Akbar's request for the despatch of a second Mission. Grimon's tale of Akbar's zeal for the faith evidently lost nothing in the telling.

[4] There can, I think, be little doubt that Leon Grimon is to be identified (as Maclagan suggests) with the Padre Farmalíún mentioned by Abul Fazl. In his account of the 35th year of the reign, the identical year (i.e. 1590) in which Grimon carried Akbar's letters to Goa, the author of the *Akbarnama* says: "At this time, Padre Farmalíún arrived at the Imperial Court from Goa. He was a man of much learning and eloquence. A few intelligent young men were placed under him for instruction, so that provision might be made for securing translations of Greek books and of extending knowledge" (*E. & D.*, VI, p. 85). Leon Grimon was a Greek, and hence the use Akbar made of him. His name, in the Persian text used by Professor Dowson, is spelt فرمليون (farmaleon). A very slight alteration turns this into غرمليون (ghrimaleon or ghramaleon), which may very possibly have been the word that Abul Fazl wrote. The 'g' of Grimon was probably sounded very like the Persian غ (*ghain*).

Grimon subsequently set out with Goes on his mission to Cathay, but was unable to endure the hardships of the expedition, which he abandoned at Kabul.

[5] *Seigneur de la Fosliere*. Du Jarric follows Guzman's spelling; but in the Italian version of Spitilli, which takes us a step nearer to the original, we find *Signore della Fostiera*. Maclagan (*J.A.S.B.*, LXV, p. 60) suggests that *Fosliere* is for 'Fasli era'; but this does not suit Spitilli's spelling; nor have we any reason to suppose that Akbar ever used such a title. Mr. C. A. Storey has suggested to me that *Signore della Fostiera* may be a translation, or an attempt at a translation, of one of the imperial titles. In the superscription of farmans, Akbar was usually styled 'Jalal-ud-din Muhammad Akbar Padshah Ghazi,' and the Jesuit version may be an attempt to translate the whole superscription, 'Jalal-ud-din' being rendered by 'exalted,' 'Akbar Padshah' by 'great King,' and 'Ghazi' by 'Signore della Fostiera'; but I can offer no explanation of the last word; the spelling is evidently corrupt.

[6] The reader may like to have Spitilli's version of this remarkable sentence. It runs as follows: "Et como adesso aspetto per mezzo suo altri Padri molto dotti, c'ho mandato à chiamare da Goa, doue lo

inuiai molti giorni sono, acciò me li conduca : ne quali confido, che da morte mi tormeranno à vita con la buona dottrina loro, si come il loro Maestro Giesù Christo venendo da cielo, in terra, diede la vita à molti resuscitãdoli da morte à vita."

[7] 'Canchena' is for *Khan-khanan*, the title held by Mirza Abdur Rahim Khan, the son of Bairam Khan, at this time commanding in Gujarat. Maclagan suggests that 'Raizza' may stand for Rai Singh of Bikanir (*Ain*, I, p. 357), and 'Giabiblica' for Raja Ali Khan of Khandesh. 'Giabiblica' might equally well stand for Shihabuddin Khan, who in 1590 was governor of Malwa (*Ain*, I, p. 332); but it is difficult to understand why either he, or Raja Ali Khan, should be styled Captain of Cambayetta. The identification of halting places are those given, or suggested, by Maclagan. For 'Guipar' Smith suggests Kharopar, and for 'Bitasser,' Kalaser, north of Bikanir. As the general direction of the route is sufficiently clear, it seems unnecessary to make any further 'shots.'

[8] In Spitilli's Italian version this passage is as follows: "Padri ch'andate per buoni camini, Fò sapere alle RR. VV. che io ho intenso tutte le leggi del mõdo si de Gentili de varie sette, come de Mori; eccetto quella di Christo, che è quella di Dio, & per tale conosciuta & pratticata. Et como io sento inclinatione all'amicitia & cõursatiõe de Padri, desidero, che da essi mi sia insegnata questa legge Christiana."

[9] In the translation of this letter given by Maclagan (*J.A.S.B.*, LXV, p. 61) this word is wrongly rendered 'Qazis' (see note 6, ch. II).

[10] *fust en deliberation de l'y renvoyer.* According to the report of the Provincial, dated Nov., 1591 (see note on p. 227), Father Christopher Vega actually was sent back. "When the Fathers saw that the Emperor had not decided as they expected, to embrace the Christian faith, they proposed to return to Goa, but were bidden by me not to do so. Father Edward Leïoton (who is one of the Fathers that remained there) being expressly ordered not to return, but to remain where he was. Father Christopher di Vega, who returned with Father Leïoton's consent, was sent back by me as he was a great favorite with the Emperor, and was told not to come away except it were under an oath that he would return" (*J.A.S.B.*, LXV, p. 63).

[11] Little is known about this second Mission beyond the details given in this chapter. At Goa it was regarded as a failure; but the actual cause of its sudden collapse is unknown. The Fathers were recalled early in 1592, while it was only in the previous November that the Provincial had reported that it had been decided to continue the Mission. Maclagan suggests (*J.A.S.B.*, LVI, p. 64) that there may have been a difficulty about the Father's accompanying Akbar to

Kashmir, whither he proceeded in the spring of 1592. Other difficulties are, however, hinted at in the Provincial's letter, which terminated as follows: "Ac jam nostri exercent pueros (uti antea diximus) in lectione & scriptione Lusitanica, similibusque officiis, commodam expectantes occasionem, qua cum Rege de rebus fidei familiarius & liberius agant, quod ne huc usque facerent, impedimento fuerunt belli ductores, qui perpetuo Regi adhaerent, & quibus absentibus ordinarie nulla audientia datur. Cumque hujus Regis ad fidem Catholicam traductio, maximi fit momenti necessum est, ut dextrè & suauiter procedatur." From this it is clear that, whatever Akbar's attitude towards the Fathers may have been, that of his nobles was distinctly hostile. It is quite possible, therefore, that the Fathers failed to display the tact and suavity which the situation called for, and that the opposition of the nobles became so powerful as to render the continuation of the Mission futile.

NOTES TO CHAPTER VI

Despatch of the Third Mission

[1] Du Jarric derived his materials for this and the following chapter from the report sent by the Provincial at Goa to the General of the Society at Rome in November, 1595. This report included a letter from Pinheiro written from Cambaya, another from Xavier written in August after the arrival of the Mission at Lahore, and a third, also from Lahore, dated 3rd September, from Pinheiro. All the above are reproduced in Peruschi's work. Du Jarric also made use of chapters xxxv and xxxvi of the *Historia*, which are based on the same letters.

[2] A *Profe* is a professed monk, one definitely enrolled as a member of a monastic order. In his description of Goa (*Histoire*, Part I), du Jarric wrote : " Nous avons en la mesme cité de Goa, une maison de Profes, là ou demeurent ceux, qui vivent d'aumosnes, selon nostre institut." The house, he adds, was well built, and in the centre of the town. It was ordinarily occupied by about 40 persons, who were supported by the liberality of the inhabitants.

[3] " There can be little doubt," says Maclagan, " that the members of the party were picked men. Jerome Xavier had entered the Society at Alcala twenty-six years previously, and had spent most of his service in India, firstly as Rector at Bassein, then at Cochin and finally at Goa. Without possessing the enthusiastic asceticism of Aquaviva, he was an earnest man of mature age, who had spent most of his life in teaching and who had enjoyed positions of trust. For twenty-three years he was to remain at the Mogul court ; sometimes in favour, sometimes in prison ; working sometimes for the spiritual conversion of Emperors, at other times for the material advancement of his compatriots : maintaining on the whole a prominent and honoured position, but like most of those who have striven with native courts, finding himself little more advanced at the end than at the beginning. At last in 1617, he returned to Goa, and died there on the 17th June of that year, being at the time Archbishop elect of Cranganore " (*J.A.S.B.*, LXV, p. 64).

Benoist de Goes, one of the most remarkable of the early Jesuit missionaries, was born in the Azores in 1562. He came to India as a soldier, and appears at first to have lived a somewhat dissipated life. Yule suggests that he was a youth of good family " who enlisted for the Indies in consequence of some youthful escapade." At the age of twenty-six, however, he became a reformed character, and joined the Jesuit Society. After eight years' work with the Mission at Lahore, he was selected by the Provincial of Goa to explore the countries of Tibet and Cathay and discover the Christian communities reported to be dwelling in those regions. He departed on this mission early in 1603. Accompanied only by a single companion, he travelled for four years through the heart of inner Asia, and in 1607, after incredible hardships, reached the town of Sao-chu on the frontiers of China. Here for seventeen months he was detained as a prisoner. He contrived to communicate with the Jesuit Mission at Pekin, and friends were sent to his assistance; but he died before they could reach him. All his papers, including his diaries, were lost. A brief account of his adventures, based on such information as his companion could supply, was written by Father Matthew Ricci of the Pekin Mission. "Had Benedict's diary," says Yule, "which he is said to have kept in great detail, been spared, it would probably have been, to this day, far the most valuable geographical record in any European language on the subject of the countries through which he travelled, still so imperfectly known" (*Cathay and the Way Thither*, II, p. 536). Father Ricci's account is contained in Yule's book, and some additional details, relating mainly to the traveller's imprisonment at Sao-chu, are given by du Jarric (*Histoire*, III, pp. 145–162).

Emmanuel Pinheiro was born in the isle of S. Michel in 1556, and joined the Society in 1573. He spent in all twenty-three years in India, and died at Goa in 1618. "He seems," says Maclagan, "to have been the first of the Jesuits on these missions to turn his attention seriously to the people rather than the court, and he was for many years pastor of a considerable congregation in Lahor; but he also exercised a certain amount of influence with the Emperor." Pinheiro's activities were, however, by no means confined to the mission field. He was specially employed by the Portuguese authorities at Goa to counteract the influence of the English travellers who visited the Mogul court both before and after the death of Akbar. From the accounts left to us by Fitch, Mildenhall, Hawkins, and Finch, he appears to have been a past master in the arts of intrigue, and thoroughly unscrupulous in the means he adopted to discredit the English in the eyes of the Emperor, and to defeat their efforts to obtain a commercial footing in India.

[4] Cambay, or Kambayat, as it was called by Muhammadan writers, was at this time the chief sea-port of Gujarat, and one of the busiest trading centres in the East. The city, or what is left of it, is situated at the north-eastern extremity of the gulf of the same name. William Finch, who visited Cambay between 1608 and 1611, describes it as

the mart of Gujarat, " and so haunted by the Portugals that you shall often find two hundred frigates at once riding there. It aboundeth with all sorts of cloth and rich drugges. The bay is 8 cos over, dangerous to pass by reason of the great bore which drowns many, and therefore requires guides skilfull of the tides." The town lost its importance as a port owing to the shallowness of the water at the head of the gulf, which prevented the approach of large vessels. The kingdom of Gujarat was annexed by Akbar in 1572. In 1583 the ex-King, Muzaffar Shah, made a determined effort to recover his throne. He was severely defeated the following year by Abdur Rahim Khan-khanan, but managed to evade capture for nearly eight years. He died (probably by his own hand) whilst being conducted to Lahore at the end of 1592. The Jesuit writers frequently give the name Cambaya to the kingdom, or province of Gujarat. According to Col. Tod, the original Hindu name of the city was *Khambavati*, ' City of the Pillar ' (see *Hobson-Jobson*, p. 150), which accounts for such spellings as ' Cambaet,' ' Cambayetta,' etc.

[5] Prince Murad was at this time Governor of Gujarat. War against the Deccan Sultanates had been determined on in the previous year, and the Khan-khanan, with whom Murad was to co-operate, was already advancing from Malwa. Eventually the two forces met and proceeded, towards the end of the year (1595), to invest Ahmadnagar. Owing to the discord which arose between the two commanders, and also to the gallant defence of the city by Chand Bibi, the operations were unsuccessful, and, early in the following year, terms, which Abul Fazl describes as ' unworthy,' were agreed upon. Chand Bibi ceded to the Mogul the province of Berar, and was left in victorious possession of Ahmadnagar.

[6] Malik (Melique) was a title given to the rulers of Nizam-ul-Mulkiya (Ahmadnagar), at this time one of the most important of the Sultanates of the Deccan. " Texeira says that the King of Decan was formerly by the inhabitants called Nezal ul Malucho, that is, the *Lance of the Kingdom*, and also Malik, or Melik, which signifies King " (Ogilby, *Asia*, I, p. 245). Maclagan supposes the word Melique to refer to Malik Ambar (*J.A.S.B.*, LXV, p. 80); but it was not until after the fall of Ahmadnagar in 1600 that Malik Ambar raised himself to the position of ruler of the unconquered portions of the Ahmadnagar kingdom. It seems, therefore, more likely that Melique or Malik is here used to designate the ruling King, who at the end of 1594 was Ibrahim, the son of Burhan-ul-Mulk II. After the death of Ibrahim in 1595, the management of affairs was mainly in the hands of Chand Bibi, the sister of Burhan-ul-Mulk, who at the time of the siege of Ahmadnagar by Prince Murad was acting as regent for her grand-

nephew Bahadur. It was the latter who was captured when the fortress fell in 1600 (see note 5, ch. IX).

[7] Evidently the Persian *mahmudi*, a silver coin current in Surat and in the province of Gujarat. Moreland says that a *mahmudi* was worth about 11d. in Akbar's day, but was subject to considerable fluctuations. Terry put the value at 8d., and Tavernier at 20 *paisa*. Assuming the French *livre* to have been worth 2s. (it was ⅓ of an *écu*, which was generally reckoned as equal to 6s.), the *mahmudi* was worth, according to du Jarric's figures, about 10d.

[8] The serious disagreement between Prince Murad and the Khan-khanan, who was associated with him in command of the forces sent to operate against Ahmadnagar, is referred to at length by Abul Fazl (*vide E. & D.*, VI, p. 92).

[9] Complete abstension from worldly affairs (*i'tikaf*) is usually limited to the last ten days of the fast, and is practised only by the strictest and most devout Moslims. The fast takes place during Ramazan, the ninth month of the Muhammadan year. All orthodox Muhammadans fast from dawn to sunset throughout the entire month. Only the sick, pregnant women, and young children are exempt from this observance.

[10] Ahmadabad was the capital of Gujarat; the English traveller Withington (1612–1616) describes it as being "verye neare as bigge as London, walled rounde with a verye stronge wall, scituate in the playne by the river-syde. Here are marchaunts of all places resydinge, as well Chrystians as Moores and Gentills. The commodities of this place are cloth of gould, silver tissue, vellvets (but not comparable to ours), taffetase and other stuffes, and divers druggs, with other commodities" (see Foster's *Early Travels in India*, p. 206).

[11] Ogilby (*Asia*, I, 210) says this tomb was at a village called Zirkes, or Sirkesia, and describes it as follows: "This structure is said to be the tomb of one Cacis, tutor to one of the Kings of Zurrate, to whom they ascribe great sanctity and wonders; and that the said King, who with three other Kings, lies buried in another chapel, built the same in commemoration of his tutor. At a certain time of the year most of the Mahumetans come hither in pilgrimage, firmly believing thereby to obtain pardon for their sins. On one side of it is a large pond." In the days of Akbar, Sarkhej was a place of some importance, and was specially noted for the production of indigo. It was visited by Tavernier, who also mentions a wonderful Pagoda he saw there (*Travels*, Bk. I, ch. v). The name has been spelt in many ways: Sarquesse, Surkeja, Sarkés, etc.

[12] A woman who performs the *hajj* must do so in company with her husband, or, if he cannot, or will not accompany her, she may go with a *mahram*, that is, a near relative with whom it is unlawful to marry.

If she has sufficient means for the journey, and can find a *mahram* to escort her, her husband cannot prevent her from making the pilgrimage (see Hughes' *Dictionary of Islam*, p. 156). The idea of a temporary husband probably arose from a misconception of the latter dispensation. The Fathers, as I have elsewhere remarked, made no effort to acquaint themselves with the customs of Islam, which they frequently misrepresent.

[13] Patana (Pattan) is distant about sixty miles from Ahmadabad; so that the caravan must have covered, on an average, something like twelve miles a day.

NOTES TO CHAPTER VII

THE FATHERS AT COURT

[1] See note 1, ch. vi.

[2] Prince Salim was twenty-six years old at this time (see note 2, ch. III).

[3] This was Prince Khusru, who was born in 1587, and was, therefore, eight years of age.

[4] Maclagan (*J.A.S.B.*, LXV, p. 69) has the following note on these books: " S. Thomas is Aquinas. Soto is probably Domingo de Soto, a scholastic writer of the sixteenth century. S. Antoninus of Forciglione lived 1389–1459. Sylvester may be the second Pope of that name, a considerable writer on theology (d. 1003). Navarrus is perhaps Father Juan Aspidueta, surnamed Navarro, Jesuit Missionary in Brazil and a connection of the Xaviers (d. 1555). Cardinal Cajetan (1470–1534), who cited Luther at Augsburg, was a writer on Aquinas and other subjects. The Commentaries are those of the great Albuquerque published by his son in 1557. The Exercitia Spiritualia are the Devotions issued by Ignatius Loyola and the 'Ars' appears from du Jarric's translation to have been a Latin Grammar."

[5] We are told in Pinheiro's letter of September 3rd, 1595 (see p. 232), that this was the *Vicerex Canaha frater consobrinus Satamas*, that is Muzaffar Husain Mirza, cousin of Shah Abas (Satamas), who surrendered Kandahar (Canaha) to Akbar early in 1595.

[6] This is a mistake. The letter from which du Jarric now begins to quote is that of Pinheiro, dated Sept. 3, 1595.

[7] C.f. Badaoni (*Muntakhab-ut-tawarikh*, Vol. II, p. 314): " And in contempt of Islam ceasing to consider swine and dogs as unclean, he kept them in the *haram* and under the fort, and regarded the going to look at them every morning as a religious duty."

[8] C.f. Badaoni, who says, " a lot of low and mean fellows put piously on their necks the collar of the Divine Faith, and called themselves disciples, either from fear, or hope of promotion " (*Ain*, I, p. 185). Abul Fazl, on the other hand, states that Akbar admitted new disciples with caution, and even reluctance. " He even keeps back," he says, " many who declare themselves willing to become his disciples. He often says, ' Why should I claim to guide men, before

I myself am guided?' But when a novice bears on his forehead the sign of earnestness of purpose, and he be daily enquiring more and more, His Majesty accepts him, and admits him on a Sunday, when the world-illuminating sun is in its highest splendour. Notwithstanding every strictness and reluctance shewn by His Majesty in admitting novices, there are many thousands, men of all classes, who have cast over their shoulders the mantle of belief, and look upon their conversion to the new faith as the means of obtaining every blessing." The ceremony of initiation is then described: "At the above-mentioned time of everlasting auspiciousness, the novice with his turban in his hands, puts his head on the feet of His Majesty. . . . His Majesty, the chosen one of God, then stretches out the hand of favour, raises up the suppliant, and replaces the turban on his head, meaning by these symbolical actions that he has raised up a man of pure intentions, who from seeming existence, has now entered into real life. His Majesty then gives the novice the *Shact*, upon which is engraved the 'Great Name,' and His Majesty's symbolical motto, *Allahu Akbar*. This teaches the novice the truth that 'The pure Shact and the pure sight never err'" (*Ain*, I, p. 165). The Persian word *shast* signifies 'aim'; it also means anything round, such as a ring, and is applied to the Brahminical thread. In this case it evidently refers to the badge of initiation given to converts. Blochmann supposes it to refer to the likeness of Akbar which, according to Badaoni, disciples of the New Faith wore on their turbans (*Ain*, I, p. 166). Badaoni is never tired of displaying his contempt for those who took the 'shact.' He concludes a list of distinguished Mussalmans who became converts in the year 1004 A.H. with the words: "They all accepted the four degrees of faith, and received appointments of Commanders from One Hundred to Five Hundred, gave up their beards agreeably to the rules, and thus looked like the youths in Paradise. The words *mutarash i chand*, or 'several shavers,' express the *tarikh* of this event" (*ibid.*, p. 208). The initiation ceremony is also described by Jahangir in his Memoirs (*Tuzuk-i-Jahangiri*, I, p. 60).

[8] This appears to be the name by which the Jain ascetics of Gujarat were known. Thevenot, who describes the sect (*Voyages*, Bk. III, ch. XXXVI), calls them Vartias. The name is probably the Sanskrit *vrati*, 'an ascetic,' 'a devotee.' The Fathers came into contact with the sect on their way through Gujarat. Du Jarric appears here to be quoting from Pinheiro's letter, not Xavier's. In the former the Verteas are thus referred to: "He (Akbar) follows the sect of the Verteas who live together like monks in one body and undergo many penetential observances. They eat nothing that has had life. Before they sit down they clean the spot with cotton brushes, in case they should

sit on and kill some insect. These Verteas hold that the world has existed from all eternity; though some of them deny this and hold that many worlds have existed in the past. They have also other foolish and ridiculous tenets, with which I need not trouble Your Reverence" (*J.A.S.B.*, LXV, p. 70). In Part I of the *Histoire* (pp. 494–6), du Jarric describes at some length the doctrines and usages of the Verteas. His description is very similar to that given by Thevenot.

For an account of the Jain *gurus* who visited the court of Akbar, and the extent to which the latter was influenced by their doctrines, see Smith's *Akbar*, pp. 166–168.

[10] From Pimenta's report of Dec., 1599 (see p. 241), we learn that these were the children of Mirza Shahrukh, the exiled King of Badakshan, who had taken refuge at the court of Akbar (*Ain*, I, p. 312).

[11] It was not until seven years later, i.e. in 1602, that Akbar was induced to issue a farman under his own hand and seal, granting permission to any of his subjects who so desired to accept Christianity (see ch. xv below). I have found no copy of the Cambay farman issued at this time. The following, however, will serve as an example of Akbar's 'letters-patent.' It is a copy of a similar mandate issued three years later (1598), granting permission for the building of a church at Cambay:—

> " (Tughra) Farman of Jalal-ud-din Muhammad Akbar,
> Padshah, Ghazi.
>
> Whereas it has reached our eminent and holy notice that the Padris of the Holy Society of Jesus wish to build a house of prayer in the city of Cambay; therefore an exalted royal mandate proper to be submitted to, has received the dignity and the honour of being issued, to the effect that the dignitaries of the city of Cambay should in no case stand in their way, but should allow them to build a church so that they may engage themselves in their own worship. It is necessary that the order of the Emperor should be obeyed in every way. Written on the 25th of the month of Farwardin in the 42nd year of the Ilahi era. Enough."

The above is taken from Father Felix's paper on the Mughal Farmans, published in the *Journal* of the Panjab Historical Society for 1916. The word *tughra* is the name of a particular style of caligraphy. The royal titles were usually written in the *tughra* character, and hence the word was also used to denote the titles themselves. The body of the farman was usually written in the *nastalik*, or round-hand style. The royal seal was placed on the right-hand side of the *tughra* lines.

[12] We read in the 35th chapter of Guzman's *Historia* (Vol. I, p. 259) that when the Fathers passed through Cambay in 1594, on their journey to Lahore, certain of the Gentiles and leading men of the town told Xavier that "si el Emperador su señor diesse licencia para que se predicasse la ley de Dios, holgarian de ser Christianos y baptizarse, y assi yua el Padre determinado, de pedir esta licencia al Emperador."

[13] The passage referred to runs as follows: "Les Peres Antoine Machade & Pierre Paëz de nostre Compagnie avoyent esté enuoyez là, ainsi que les lettres qu'on escriuit du 2. de Decembre l'an 1599 asseurent; ou il est aussi porté, que leur arrivée avoit merueilleusement resiouy non seulment les Chrestiens, qui habitent là: may encore les Payens; si bien qu'vn bon marchand Portugais auoit promis de faire à ses depens tous les frais, qu'il faudrait pour eux; voire qui plus est les Baneanes, qui sont certains marchans Payens des mieux entendus au fait du commerce, vouloient prendre charge de les nourir, & demandoyent instamment leure demeure en Cambaya. L'Archeuesque de Goa fust si aise de cette nouvelle, qu'il communiqua à ceux qui furent deputez à ceste mission ou voyage, tous ses pouvoirs, & facultez: afin de faciliter d'auantage la conuersion de ce peuple" (*Histoire*, I, p. 496). The Mission, however, met with much opposition, and appears to have come to a speedy termination. We hear of no further attempt to convert the people of Cambaya until Father Gaspar Soarez visited the town in 1605 (see *Histoire*, III, pp. 221 *et seq.*). Father Felix states (*Journal of the Panj. Hist. Soc.*, 1916, p. 9), I know not on what authority, that the Mission organised in 1595 did not even start.

[14] There is evidently some confusion here. At this time the Fathers received only verbal permission to make converts in Lahore.

NOTES TO CHAPTER VIII

On Tour with the King

[1] The primary authorities for the visit to Kashmir (May to November, 1597), and other events dealt with in this chapter, are :—

(1) A long letter from Father Xavier to the General of the Society, written from Lahore early in 1598.
(2) A letter from Father Pinheiro written "some time after Whitsuntide" (Maclagan, p. 79), 1599.
(3) The report of the Provincial (Father Pimenta) sent to the General of the Society in December, 1599. This report contains extracts from Xavier's letter, and from other letters received from the same Father, and from Pinheiro.

Chapters xxxviii and xxxix of Guzman's *Historia* are based on the same letters. Du Jarric took his account partly from Guzman, and partly from the letters themselves, considerable portions of which he translates. All the above-mentioned letters are contained in Hay's *De Rebus Japonicis, etc.*

Father Nicolas Pimenta, another of whose letters will be referred to in the next chapter, entered the Company in 1562, at the age of sixteen. He was for some years teacher of theology at Evora and Coimbra, and was afterwards (in 1596) sent to India as Visitor. He was placed in charge of the Provinces of Goa and Malabar, and remained in India till his death, which took place at Goa in 1614.

[2] Compare Guerreiro, Part I, p. 15, where he states that Akbar's devotion to the sun was so great that "antre dia, & noyte lhe reza dez mil orações por hum Rosario que tem de pedras preceosas, das mais linhas, & finas do mundo, como Rubis, Diamates, Perlas, Topazeos, & outras q̃ por todas faze mil & quinhetas; as cotas dos estremos se diz valerao hu conto de ouro pella fineza das pedras, & affirma o irmão Bento de Goes que muytas vezas vio, & tene na mao este Rosario que se mao pode encarecer a gram valia delle."

[3] This is amply corroborated by Badaoni, who tells us that the people used to come every morning "opposite to the window near which his Majesty used to pray to the sun, and declared that they had made vows not to rinse the mouth, nor to eat and drink, before they

had seen the blessed countenance of the Emperor. And every evening there was a regular court assembly of needy Hindus and Musalmans, all sorts of people, men and women, healthy and sick, a queer gathering and a most terrible crowd. No sooner had his Majesty finished saying the thousand and one names of the 'Greater Luminary,' and stepped into the balcony, than the whole crowd prostrated themselves. Cheating, thieving Brahmans collected another set of one thousand and one names of 'His Majesty the Sun,' and told the Emperor that he was an incarnation, like Ram, Krishna and other infidel Kings; and though Lord of the world, he had assumed his shape, in order to play with the people of our planet" (*Muntakhab-ut-tawarikh*, Vol. II, p. 336).

[4] Badaoni, though he thoroughly disapproved of these religious speculations, gives a remarkably accurate description of Akbar's state of mind at this time. "His Majesty," he says, "collected the opinions of every one, especially of such as were not Muhammadans, retaining whatever he approved of, and rejecting everything which was against his disposition, and ran counter to his wishes. From his earliest childhood to his manhood, and from his manhood to old age, his Majesty has passed through the most various phases, and through all sorts of religious practices and sectarian beliefs, and has collected everything which people can find in books, with a talent of selection peculiar to him, and a spirit of enquiry opposed to every [Islamitic] principle. Thus a faith based on some elementary principles traced itself on the mirror of his heart, and as the result of all the influences brought to bear on his Majesty, there grew, gradually as the outline on a stone, the conviction in his heart that there were sensible men in all religions, and abstemious thinkers, and men endowed with miraculous powers, among all nations. If some true knowledge was thus everywhere to be found, why should truth be confined to one religion, or to a creed like the Islam, which was comparatively new, and scarcely a thousand years old; why should one claim a preference without having superiority conferred on itself?" (*Ain*, I, p. 179).

[5] This apparently refers to the failure of Murad's attempt to reduce the fortress of Ahmadnagar, early in the year 1596. The feast of the *Nauroz* commenced on the 1st of the solar month *Faridun*, coinciding with the spring equinox, and lasted for eighteen days. The news must, therefore, have reached Akbar late in March or early in April. According to Abul Fazl, the "unworthy treaty" which Murad concluded with the defenders was signed on the 11th of the preceding month, *Isfandarmuz* (*E. & D.*, VI, p. 94).

[6] Du Jarric does Prince Murad too much honour. He was not slain in battle, but died of *delirium tremens* in 1599. The same mistake is made by Ogilby (*Asia*, I, p. 245) and also by Catrou (ed. 1709,

p. 167). Ogilby is, however, obviously quoting 'Jarrick,' and Catrou very likely followed Ogilby. At first sight the statement looks like a deliberate attempt on the part of some Jesuit writer to conceal the fact that Murad, the promising and docile pupil of Monserrate and Aquaviva, took to evil courses, and drank himself to death before he reached the age of thirty. But a comparison of the text account with that of the *Historia* indicates, I think, that du Jarric mis-read or mis-interpreted his authority. The passage in the *Historia* (ch. XXXVIII, p. 266) runs: "le (i.e. to Akbar) vimiera muy malas nueuas de la guerra que estaua haziendo el Principe su hijo segundo, en los fines de Cambaya, contra un hijo del Meliche, señor de Chaul y de otras islas: porque le mataron alli casi veynta mil hombres, y los mejores capitanes que tenia": which clearly means that the bad news which reached Akbar from the seat of war was the loss there of twenty thousand men, and the best captains that he had. Subsequently (p. 269) Guzman says: "Este Principe murio en aquella guerra"; he would not have written *murio* had he meant to imply that Murad was killed.

[7] See *Histoire*, II, pp. 692–3, where we are told not only that fire consumed the palace of the King of China, as a punishment for his indifference to the welfare of his soul; but that in the previous year (1596) the superb edifices built by Taïcosama, the then ruler of Japan, "pour monstrer sa grandeur & magnificence," were utterly destroyed by an earthquake, in consequence of his refusal to permit the preaching of the gospel in his capital. "Dieu voulant," as du Jarric piously observes, "aduiser ces trois grands Monarques quasi en mesme temps, qu'ils n'auoyent pas icy de cité permanente, ny demeure stable & asseurée: à celle fin qu'ils ny attachassent pas leur cœur: & par mesme moyen leur faire cognostre qu'il y a un plus grand Seigneur qu'eux, qui commande au ciel & en terre, pouvant chastier & humilier les plus grands Princes du monde, quand bon luy semble."

The fire at Lahore is thus referred to by Abul Fazl, in his account of the 42nd (Ilahi) year of the reign: "Suddenly some rue was burnt in the face of fortune. Fire seized the preparations for the New Year's feast, and the flames went from the court-yard to the holy mansion. Apparently, a spark from the royal bedchambers set fire to an awning, and then there arose a conflagration. Efforts were made for several days to extinguish the fire. . . . A remarkable thing was that there was a similar fire in the quarters of the Prince Murad in the Deccan" (*Akbarnama*, tr. Beveridge). A detailed account of the fire, from which the text version appears to be taken, is given in the *Annuæ Literæ Societatis Jesu, anni* 1592. These letters (translated into Latin by Father Sebastian Beretari) were published at Florence in 1600. The account is to be found on page 570.

[8] Kashmir was annexed by Akbar in 1586.

[9] Yule (*Cathay, and the Way Thither*, II, p. 535) says: "I do not know what the name Rebat is intended for (proper names in du Jarric being often sadly mangled), perhaps for Tibet." Yule was right in his conjecture, but wrong in attributing the mangling to du Jarric; this had already been done by Pimenta, who, in his report of December, 1599, wrote: "Mihi quoque dum in Caximiri agebam, nunciatum est, esse in regno Rebat multos Christianos & ecclesias, etc...." That Tibet is the country referred to is proved by Xavier's letter of 1598 on which the text account is based. The passage runs: "Regio hæc perfrigida est, eamque algidam magis reddunt altissimi quibus cingitur, montes: sed cum regno Tebat (quod illi ab Oriente adjacet . . .) collata, temperatior, ita ut a gelidis montibus regni Tebat mense Maio gregatim & per acies infinita prope anserum sylvestrium agmina advolent, & in flumina, que juxta urbem Cascimirium tanquam calidam magis manant & fluunt, se immittant." Xavier's letter is quoted in full in Hay's *De rebus Japonicis, etc.* Du Jarric, who is very careful to reproduce the spelling of his authorities, evidently did not use the original letter.

The statement that the King of 'Rebat' was on friendly terms with Akbar is confirmed by Abul Fazl. "From the time," says that writer, "that Kashmir had been included in the Empire, the ruler of that country (Tibet) had continually made supplications." We learn, from the same source, that the King of Tibet sent his daughter to Akbar's court.

[10] Cf. Ogilby (*Asia*, I, p. 201): "The chief town of this country (Kashmir) bears the same denomination with the kingdom." In a previous passage (p. 199) he has stated that "Jarrick gives the name of Syranacar both to the chief city of this kingdom, and to the country itself"; but I have been unable to trace the reference to du Jarric. Amongst the people of the valley, the name Kashmir is, to this day, given to the city of Srinagar.

[11] Probably the plane-tree (*Platanus orientalis*), known as the *boin* in Kashmir, where it flourishes and attains a great size. "It is especially valued," says Mr. W. R. Lawrence, "for making presses, and its fine grained wood is used for making boxes" (*The Valley of Kashmir*, p. 82).

[12] This famine commenced in the year 1595 and, according to Nur-ul Haqq, raged throughout Hindustan for more than three years. It was accompanied by a pestilence which "depopulated whole houses and cities, to say nothing of hamlets and villages." Grain, says the same writer, was so scarce that men ate their own kind, and the streets and roads were blocked with dead bodies (*E. & D.*, VI, p. 193).

Abul Fazl gives a brief account of the famine in the *Akbarnama* (*ibid.*, p. 94). The practice of selling children during periods of famine was common in India, and of long standing. It is noticed by Barbosa, Correa, Linschoten, and other writers both European and Indian. Barbosa narrates that during a famine on the Coromandel coast, children were sold for less than a rupee (see Moreland, *India at the Death of Akbar*, p. 266). The practice appears even to have been legalised; for Badaoni states that "at the times of famines and distress, parents were allowed to sell their children, but they might buy them again, if they acquired means to repay their price" (*Ain*, I, p. 207).

[13] i.e. the language commonly spoken by the people of 'Indostan,' as opposed to Persian, the language of the court. The name is now restricted, at any rate by Europeans, to the Urdu language (*vide* Maclagan, p. 72).

[14] "This picture or a copy seems to have been preserved for some time in Akbar's tomb at Sikandra. See Manuchi-Catrou, p. 135" (Maclagan, p. 76).

[15] Monserrate left Akbar's court in March or April, 1582, and returned to Goa (see note 12, ch. 11).

[16] In Xavier's letter he is referred to as Father Abraham de Georgiis, the Maronite, who had been killed "on his way to Prester John on account of his profession of the Christian faith" (Maclagan, p. 76). Father Abraham left Goa to join the Mission in Ethiopia in January, 1595. To avoid capture by the Turks, who kept a jealous watch on the Ethiopian coast to prevent the landing of Christians, the Father and an Abyssinian boy, who was his sole attendant, disguised themselves as Armenians. All went well till they arrived at Mazua, an island in the Red Sea, almost in reach of their destination. It was the holy month of Ramazan, during which every true Moslim fasts from dawn till sunset. One day, in the absence of the Father, the Abyssinian boy ventured to assuage the pangs of hunger during forbidden hours. The impious act was seen by some Turks, who, by dint of many blows, extracted from him the confession that he and his master were Christians. The Father was straightway seized and taken before the Turkish captain, who offered him the choice of Islam or death. The Father was true to his faith, and laid down his life with cheerful heroism. The story is told in full by du Jarric in a previous chapter (Part II, pp. 239–242). The martyrdom of Father Abraham George is amongst those depicted on the title-page of the *Histoire*.

[17] These wretched infants were incarcerated for four years. The experiment is thus described by Abul Fazl: "In the 24th year (1578), one of the occurrences was the testing of the silent of speech. There was a great meeting, and every kind of enlightenment was discussed.

H. M. said that speech came to every tribe from hearing, and that each remembered from another from the beginning of existence. If they arranged that human speech did not reach them, they certainly would not have the power of speech. If the fountain of speech bubbled over in any one of them, he would regard this as Divine speech, and accept it as such. As some who heard this appeared to deny it, he, in order to convince them, had a *serai* built in a place which civilized sound did not reach. The newly born were put into that place of experience, and honest and active guards were put over them. For a time tongue-tied wetnurses were admitted there. As they had closed the door of speech, the place was commonly called the Gang Mahal (the dumb-house). On the 29th (Amardad—9th August, 1582) he went out to hunt. That night he stayed in Faizabad, and the next day he went with a few special attendants to the house of experiment. No cry came from that house of silence, nor was any speech heard there. In spite of their four years they had no part of the talisman of speech, and nothing came out except the noise of the dumb. What the wise Sovereign had understood several years before was on this day impressed on the hearts of the formalists and superficial. This became a source of instruction to crowds of men" (*Akbarnama*, tr. Beveridge, p. 581). The story is also told by Badaoni, who says that "about twenty sucklings were taken from their mothers, for a consideration in money" (*Muntakhab-ut-tawarikh*, Vol. II, p. 296).

[18] In a subsequent letter (1604), describing the religious life of the Christians at Agra, Xavier wrote: "Every Friday evening in Lent, we have a sermon to the Christians; at the end we show them the crucifix which is placed, covered, on the altar, after which the Litany is recited, and then as many men as the church can hold (for here in Agra it is very small) take the discipline, while the Father recites the '*Miserere*.' When these have finished others take their place, until all have taken their turn. They take the discipline across the back, according to our custom: so do nearly all the Christians, old and new" (Maclagan, p. 90).

[19] Why the Fathers considered themselves in such imminent peril on this occasion is not very apparent. Father Xavier, from whose letter the text account is taken, seems to have been more anxious to set forth his own and Father Pinheiro's devotion, than to do justice to Akbar. His account, moreover, does not tally with what we are told in a later chapter of the *Histoire*. In the early part of Jahangir's reign we are again introduced to the Armenian, who now appears in the light of a hero, bravely withstanding all the attempts of the King to make him abandon Christianity for Islam. The incestuous marriage is again referred to; but the Armenian comes out of the affair very

differently. So far from his having induced Akbar to take up his case, we are told that it was Akbar himself, and one of his wives, who forced the unholy union upon him. The lady he married is described this time as the sister, not the niece, of his deceased wife. No reference is made to his conversion to the 'Divine Faith' (see *Histoire*, III, ch. XVII).

[20] Agra came into the possession of Akbar almost immediately after the defeat of Hemu at Panipat, in 1556.

[21] Akbar left Lahore for Agra towards the end of 1598, and remained at the latter city till July of the following year.

[22] The remainder of this chapter, with the exception of the last paragraph, is based on Pinheiro's letter of 1599.

[23] The Jesuit letters contain several references to the rumour that Akbar was poisoned. They do not, however, shed any new light on the subject, beyond establishing the fact that the rumour was widely current before Akbar died, and that suspicion had already fallen on Salim (see p. 204). The various stories to which the rumour gave rise are referred to, and discussed, by Mr. Smith on pages 324–326 of his *Akbar*. Van den Broecke's story, which Mr. Smith quotes, that Akbar took by mistake a poisoned pill which he intended for Mirza Ghazi Beg, is also told by Ogilby (*Asia*, I, p. 170), and by Peter Mundy (*Travels*, II, p. 103). According to Badaoni, this was not the first time that Akbar suspected Salim of trying to poison him. He says that, in the year 1591, "the Emperor's constitution became a little deranged and he suffered from stomach-ache and cholic, which could by no means be removed. In this unconscious state he uttered some words which arose from suspicions of his eldest son, and accused him of giving him poison, and said :

> 'Baba Shaikhu Ji since all this
> Sultanate will devolve on thee, why
> Hast thou made this attack on me :—
> To take away my life there was no need of injustice,
> I would have given it to thee, if thou hadst asked me'"

(*Muntakhab-ut-tawarikh*, tr. Lowe, II, p. 390). The story, at any rate as told by Badaoni, is not very convincing.

NOTES TO CHAPTER IX

At the Seat of War

[1] With this chapter we enter on Part III of the *Histoire*. Du Jarric brought his second volume to a close when he reached the end of Guzman's *Historia*. His account of the period 1600–1608 is based almost entirely on the *Relaçam* of Guerreiro (see p. xxxii). What may be called Guerreiro's narrative commences with the eighth paragraph of the chapter. The authority for the seven preceding paragraphs is the report sent to the General of the Society in December, 1600, by Father Pimenta, at that time acting as Visitor. This report was published at Rome in 1602 under the title, *Copia d'una* [*litera*] *del P. Pimenta, visitator delle Provincia d'Italia d'India Orientale al molto reverendo P. Claudio Acquaviva preposito Generale della Compagnia di Giessu, del primo Decembre*, 1600. A Latin version, of which I have a copy, was produced the same year (1602) at Maintz.

The Jesuit Letters relating to the years 1601–1603 have not been preserved, or, at any rate, their whereabouts are not known. For the events of this period we have, therefore, to depend on du Jarric and Guerreiro, who, unfortunately, seldom name their authorities. Our next first-hand evidence is Father Xavier's letter of September 6th, 1604 (see note 1, ch. xix).

Guerreiro's account of the siege of Asirgarh, which du Jarric reproduces, will be found in Part I of the *Relaçam*, pp. 7–9.

[2] This book, according to Maclagan (*J.A.S.B.*, LXV, p. 82), "was doubtless that which was ultimately called '*Speculum Veritatis*,' or '*Aina-i-Haqq-numa*.'" It would seem, however, that only a portion of the *Aina-i-Haqq-numa* is referred to, as this work, which consists of five Books, was not completed till 1609. It is dedicated to Jahangir "as a slight return for past favours, and a humble offering on the occasion of his accession" (*ibid.*, p. 111). Presumably, therefore, the work was still incomplete when it was presented to Jahangir, who ascended the throne in 1605. A detailed account of this and other works by Father Jerome Xavier is given by Maclagan (*ibid.*, pp. 111–113). In his letter of December, 1600, Pimenta calls this book *Lignum Vitæ*, and refers to it thus: "Opus est judicio meo pereruditum & prolixum, jamque grauiter laborat, ut illud in linguam

Persicam, adhibitis quibusdam illius idiomatis peritissimis, traducat. Tantos enim in ea progressus fecit hactenus dictus Pater ut ipsi Persæ cum voluptate eum loquentem audiant, & tantum non puritatem verborum, exquisitamque phrasin suspiciant."

[3] The Sanskrit word *ghat* signifies a mountain pass, but is now applied to the mountains themselves. This misuse of the word seems to have originated with the Portuguese, who took *ghat* to be equivalent to *serra*, a mountain range.

[4] This officer was Abdur Rahim, Khan-khanan. In Pimenta's report he is styled 'Xanacana.'

[5] This was the fortress of Ahmadnagar, the capture of which had been entrusted to the Khan-khanan and Prince Danyal. Pimenta says: "Antecedit eum in bellum Xanacana eius vicarius cũ aliis quinquaginta militum millibus. Et jampridem fortissimum regni Melique propugnaculũ, Rege adolescente in vincula coniecto, expugnavit." The statement that the young King was made a captive is a sufficient proof that the reference is to the fortress of Ahmadnagar. The name of the child King was Bahadur. He was a grand-nephew of Chand Bibi, who had governed Ahmadnagar as regent. After the fall of the fortress, Bahadur was sent to Gwalior, where he was kept a prisoner for the remainder of his life.

The Jesuit references to the Deccan campaigns are vague and inaccurate. It was before the fall of Ahmadnagar, not after it, as du Jarric implies, that Akbar occupied Burhanpur. The news of its fall reached him whilst he was engaged in the siege of Asirgarh (Syr). This siege commenced in April, 1600, and ended on 17th January, 1601. Ahmadnagar fell on or about the 18th August, 1600.

[6] i.e. Adil Khan, the ruler of Bijapur. The Portuguese usually called him Idalcan, and his kingdom Balagate (*vide* Yule's *Glossary*, p. 431). "There are," Faizi Sirhindi says, "three distinct States in the Dakhin. The Nizam-l Mulkiya (Ahmadnagar), Adil Khaniya (Bijapur), and Kutbu-l Mulkiya (Golconda). The settled rule among them was, that if a foreign army entered their country, they united their forces and fought, notwithstanding the dissensions and quarrels they had among themselves. It was also the rule, that when their forces were united Nizamu-l Mulk commanded the centre, Adil Khan the right, and Kutbu-l Mulk the left" (*E. & D.*, VI, p. 131).

[7] i.e. Burhanpur, the capital of the kingdom of Khandesh.

[8] Father Francisco Corsi, who went to Goa in 1599, remained in India until his death thirty-six years later. He was on intimate terms with Sir T. Roe and his chaplain Terry, and used to beg that their disagreement on religious matters might be kept from the King. Terry describes him as "a Florentine by birth, aged about fifty years, who

(if he were indeed what he seemed to be) was a man of severe life, yet of a fair and affable disposition : he lived at that Court as an agent for the Portuguese, and had not only free access unto that King, but also encouragement and help by gifts, which he sometimes bestowed, on him. . . . After his first acquaintance he visited us often, usually once a week. And as those of that Society, in other parts of the world, were very great intelligencers, so was he there, knowing all news which was stirring, and might be had, which he communicated to us" (*Voyage to East Indies*, ed. 1777, pp. 422–23).

[9] In Gujarat a man of the trading class was called *vaniyo*, from the Sanskrit *vanij*, a merchant. Catrou (ed. 1709, p. 68) describes the Banians as " the rigidest observers of the laws, and the most scrupulous in the point of abstinence from fish and flesh. As they have their residence chiefly in trading towns, and carry on the whole business of commerce, they are the more concerned to give good example to strangers and to the citizens, over whom they preside in the nature of governors. Their charity also, both for man and beast, is in no instances exceeded by any. Besides their hospitals erected for the sick and for orphans, they have founded others for cows, for monkeys, and for birds. The Banians would be the best of men, did not the fear of being defiled by any commerce with strangers render 'em unconversable, and their cunning somewhat dangerous to trade." Tavernier says that in business the Banians were " a thousand times worse than Jews, and more cunning than they are in all kinds of dodges and in malice when they wish for revenge " (*Travels*, ed. Ball, I, p. 136).

[10] Pimenta in his report styles this person ' Sultan Hamet, capitano di Cogi,' which was doubtless his proper designation. ' Cogi ' I take to stand for Goga, or ' Ghogeh,' a town on the inner shore of the Kathiawar Peninsula, and, in Akbar's time, a port of considerable importance. For Sultan Hamet's embassage to Goa, see chapter x.

[11] The person here mentioned is Mirza Muzaffar Husain, the son, not, as stated in the text, of the late king of Gujarat, but of Ibrahim Husain Mirza, who was defeated and slain in the Panjab in 1573. Soon after his father's death Muzaffar was captured by Akbar, whose service he eventually entered. In the year 1600, he was sent to besiege fort Lalang ; " but he quarrelled with Khwajah Fathullah, and one day, he decamped for Guzrat. His companions deserted him ; and dressing himself in the garb of a faqir he wandered about between Surat and Baglanah, when he was caught by Khwajah Waisi and taken before Akbar " (Blochmann, *Ain*, I, 464). If du Jarric's statement is correct, it must have been the force sent to bring in Mirza Muzaffar which Corsi joined. Pimenta's report, however, implies that Akbar sent out a force in charge of Mirza Muzaffar. Corsi, he says, was escorted by a force

che il Mogor mandana in compagnia di Meira Mustafar, figliolo del Re di Guzarato. He makes no reference to Muzaffar's attempt to abscond.

[12] This name is not once used by either Abul Fazl or Faizi Sirhindi, who, in their accounts of the siege of Asirgarh, invariably refer to the King as Bahadur, or Bahadur Khan. The latter must, therefore, have been the name which was familiar in Akbar's camp; and it is strange that a writer on the spot should not have used it. The name Miran was borne by most of the kings of Kandesh; but neither Bahadur, nor his predecessor Ali Khan, seems to have been generally known by it. In Pimenta's letter, the name appears as Omiranus.

[13] This evidently refers to the engagement, known as the battle of Supa, which took place early in 1597 between the Ahmadnagar forces and the imperial troops under the Khan-khanan. The action was fought on the banks of the Godavery, which separated Chand Bibi's territory from Berar. The battle was very fiercely contested, and though the Khan-khanan was left in possession of the field, his losses were so heavy that he was unable to follow up his victory. On this occasion the ruler of Khandesh, Raja Ali Khan, fought on the side of the Moguls. He was killed in the battle; and it was his son Bahadur Khan who, three years later, was besieged by Akbar in the fortress of Asirgarh. We are told that when the Imperial troops discovered that Raja Ali Khan was killed they plundered his camp, an act which so enraged his son Bahadur that from that time he consistently opposed Akbar (see *Indian Antiquary*, 1918, p. 179).

[14] Pimenta quotes Goes as his authority for this statement. The estimate of the number of guns is considerably in excess of that given by Faizi Sirhindi, who says that the number taken was 1300.

[15] Cf. *Akbarnama* (tr. Beveridge), III, p. 1166: "It is a custom of long standing that one of the Faruqis sits on the throne, and the others—brothers and relatives—remain in confinement. They spend their days in obscurity with their families." The author states that there were, at this time, as many as twenty-five descendants of Mubarak Shah in the fortress. Mubarak Shah reigned until 1566.

[16] Du Jarric's account of the siege of Asirgarh is taken from Part I of the *Relaçam* of Guerreiro, being, for the most part, a translation from the text of that work. The Jesuit story is so at variance with that of the Muhammadan chroniclers, that one might almost imagine it referred to a different episode. Ogilby actually was deceived, and narrates the capture of two fortresses, one named 'Hosser' and the other 'Sye,' nothing in the accounts which he read having suggested to him that these were the names of the same place. The fall of Hosser he attributes to a pestilence; and in the case of Sye, which he deals

with at much greater length, he quotes almost verbatim du Jarric's account (*Asia*, I, p. 237).

It is unfortunate that we do not possess the original Jesuit letters relating to this particular period. We know, however, that Father Xavier was present with Akbar's army during the siege; and it is therefore possible that it is on his letters that the text account is based. Mr. Vincent Smith had no doubt whatever that this was the case, and on the strength of his conviction proclaimed du Jarric's story to be "literally true, and deserving of acceptance as being the most authentic history of the events which led to the capitulation of Asirgarh" (*Akbar*, p. 276), and at the same time denounced the stories of the Muhammadan chroniclers as deliberate and systematic forgeries. Whether or to what extent this verdict is justified, the reader must judge for himself.

I have been unable to find any direct evidence in support of Mr. Smith's positive statements regarding the source of the text account. His assertions appear to have been based on the probabilities of the case and a misconception of the nature of du Jarric's composition, with which, as with the *Relaçam* of Guerreiro, he was very imperfectly acquainted, though he claims to have submitted the former to a critical examination. The statement (*Akbar*, p. 285) that it was du Jarric who summarised the letters of Xavier is manifestly incorrect, since, as I have said above, the account in the *Histoire* is nearly a word for word translation of that given in the *Relaçam*. Mr. Smith was apparently unaware that the latter work contained a detailed account of the siege; for he says (*ibid*., p. 282): "Guerreiro, who gives no details, confirms Du Jarric's (scil. Xavier's) statement that the capitulation was obtained by bribery"; and again (p. 469) he states that, in the *Relaçam*, the fall of Asirgarh "is briefly ascribed to corruption and the lavish expenditure of money." And yet, inexplicable though it seems, he makes references to, and quotations from Part I of the *Relaçam*, the actual volume in which the detailed account of the siege occurs.

Whatever, then, the primary source of the Jesuit story, it is clearly Guerreiro, and not du Jarric, who is responsible for its reproduction. This, of course, does not lessen the possibility that it is based on Xavier's letters: if anything, it increases it, since Guerreiro is more likely to have had access to such letters than du Jarric. Nevertheless, we are still left without any definite proof; and even if such proof were forthcoming, we should still, as it seems to me, be without adequate grounds for accepting the text account as absolutely and literally true, and denouncing as worthless fabrications all statements that are not in accord with it, including those made by writers who had far better opportunities than Xavier could have had of obtaining accurate information. Mr. Smith cites the account of the siege given in the *Akbarnama* as an example of Abul Fazl's deliberate perversion of the truth (*ibid.*, p. 460). In the note which follows, I have given my reasons for regarding this accusation as unfounded and inexcusable.

Apart from the question of external evidence, there are features in the Jesuit story itself which make it difficult to believe that it is based on the letters of Xavier, or indeed of any writer who was present during the siege. It contains, for example, no mention of the pestilence which broke out amongst the defenders. Though the exact nature and cause of the outbreak are variously stated by different writers, its severity and the heavy losses it entailed on the garrison are too well attested to admit of doubt. Faizi Sirhindi, who refers to it as one of the causes of the surrender, says that the disease caused paralysis of the extremities from the waist downwards and also attacked the eyes. Abul Fazl says 25,000 people died from it. Firishta puts the death roll at 40,000. Would Xavier, who must have heard much about the scourge from the Portuguese captives, have written an account of the siege without making even a passing reference to it? Again, the statement that Muqarrib Khan was put to death by Akbar, and the account given of the suicide of the Abyssinian Governor, are completely at variance, and chronologically irreconcilable with the narratives of the Muhammadan writers (see following note). To Mr. Smith, this is proof positive that these narratives are fabrications. To me it rather suggests that the writer responsible for the Jesuit version was not present during the siege operations, and that he based his account on second-hand information the reliability of which he made no effort to test. A third, though perhaps a minor point, is the use of the name Miran by the Jesuit writer, instead of Bahadur Khan, the name by which the King of Kandesh appears to have been known to the besiegers (see note 12 above).

Faizi Sirhindi's statement that Muqarrib Khan's death was self-inflicted is corroborated in the *Zafar-al-Walih*, an Arabic history of Gujarat, the text of which was published for the first time in 1910, under the editorship of Sir E. Denison Ross. The *Zafar-al-Walih*, the work of an enlightened and accomplished author, was written at the beginning of the 17th century. The description of the siege of Asirgarh, with which it closes, has, therefore, all the importance and interest which attaches to a contemporary narrative.

[17] Mr. Smith says (*Akbar*, p. 277) that the date of Miran's appearance before Akbar is not clearly stated. This is incorrect, as is also, I think, his assignment of the occurrence to the month of August. The date is clearly stated by Abul Fazl to have been the 30th of the Ilahi month Azar, i.e. about the 10th of December. As the same writer

dates other events of the siege accurately, we are justified in assuming that he is correct in this case. It was only twelve days previously, namely on the 18th Azar (about November 28), that the Maligarh fort, which commanded the main defences, was captured by the besiegers; and it was doubtless the loss of this important position that convinced Miran that it was useless to prolong the agony. "On the same day that Maligarh was taken," says Abul Fazl, "he (Bahadur Khan) awoke from his somnolence, and sent an ambassador to the author. He spoke of capitulating and of paying his respects (to Akbar). I did not accept the statements and made no reply, but at his earnest entreaty I sent on the envoy to court. On 23rd Azar, H.M. sent Ram Das to him, and on the fourth day he brought Muqarrib Khan, who was a chosen servant of his (Bahadur's). The purport of his message was that if the fortress and country were restored to him, and if the prisoners were released, he would hasten to submit. H.M. accepted the proposal and granted life and honour. Next day the Abyssinian (Muqarrib Khan) returned and petitioned, 'Now his (Bahadur's) request is that the Khan Azim M. Koka would take his hand and bring him to court.' This was agreed to, and he (M. Koka) came to Mali, and Bahadur Khan descended from Asir. On the 30th he rubbed his forehead on the threshold of fortune, and obtained deliverance from his various sorrows" (*Akbarnama*, tr. Beveridge, p. 1116).

It will be noticed that no attempt is made in the *Akbarnama* to disguise the fact that the unfortunate monarch was lured from his den by promises which were never intended to be fulfilled. It is obvious, therefore, that the author was not laying himself out, as Mr. Smith would have us believe, to hide his master's treachery. If any one knew the actual circumstances of Bahadur's submission, it was Abul Fazl; and as he had no apparent motive for dishonesty, we are justified in accepting his story of the negotiations, if not as 'literally true,' at any rate as the most authoritative that we possess.

The same may be said of his equally candid account of the events which followed. From this, we gather that the interval between Miran's submission on the 10th December, and the final surrender of the fortress on 17th January (Abul Fazl says the 7th Bahman, the corresponding Ilahi date), was largely employed in efforts to 'buy' the defenders, and that, in the end, the latter agreed to deliver up the fortress, provided that, to cover their shame, a letter should be forthcoming from Bahadur authorising the surrender. Bahadur yielded to pressure, and his letter was sent to the defenders, who, without more ado, handed over the keys of the fortress. The passage in the *Akbarnama* runs as follows:

"Though exertions were made to push on the batteries from near

Korhiaih, and leave was obtained for the bringing of great guns, yet secretly all men engaged in enticing the garrison. By soothing words they drew their hearts towards them. The latter represented that some writing of Bahadur should be obtained, addressed to such and such an one, so that no stain of a bad name might fall upon them for delivering up the fort. They also asked for a firman from H.M., securing their lives, their property, and their honour. This was granted. Bahadur Khan for some time hesitated to write, and made untrue remarks. When pressure was put upon him, he was compelled to write, and to put his seal on the writing. H.M.'s order was sent into the fort along with this writing, and the terrified ones had repose" (*Akbarnama*, tr. Beveridge, Vol. III, p. 1168).

As so eminent an authority on Indian history as Mr. Vincent Smith has denounced Abul Fazl's account of the capitulation of Asirgarh as a deliberate falsification of the facts of history, and as I have referred to the same account as being, in many respects, more reliable than others, not excluding the Jesuit version, it is as well that the reader should have before him the text of Mr. Smith's indictment, so that he may judge how far I am justified in ignoring it. On page 284 of his *Akbar*, after a paragraph proclaiming the unimpeachable accuracy of du Jarric's story, he proceeds as follows :—

"The conclusions necessarily follow that Akbar was guilty of perfidious violation of his solemn oath, that Asirgarh fell because the officers of the garrison were bribed, not because 25,000 people died of pestilence, and that the contrary statements of the official chroniclers are deliberate falsehoods.

"Even in an Asiatic country in the year 1600 perfidy such as Akbar practiced was felt to be discreditable, a deed not to be described in plain language by courtly historians. So too the failure of that perfidy to accomplish its purpose and the consequent inglorious resort to bribery were not things to be proud of, or fit to be inserted in the record of an ever-victorious sovereign. Nothing could be done except to tamper with history, which accordingly was done. Abul Fazl and Faizi Sirhindi neither knew nor cared what story the Jesuit Father might send to Europe. Their business was to supply matter suitable for Indian readers. Although they were not careful enough to agree in all details, they agree in hiding their master's treachery, in ascribing the capitulation wholly or in part to pestilence, in ignoring the request for a Portuguese siege-train, and in concealing the final recourse to bribery."

It is, I think, clear, from the extracts already given from the

Akbarnama, that the only one of Mr. Smith's allegations that can, with justice, be applied to Abul Fazl, is that relating to the request for a Portuguese siege-train, assuming, that is, that such a request was ever made. The statement that he attributed the capitulation either wholly, or in part, to pestilence is as devoid of foundation as the statement that he concealed the final resort to bribery. Abul Fazl does say that the garrison was attacked by a pestilence which killed 25,000 people; but nowhere in his account does he refer to it as the cause, or even as one of the causes, of the capitulation. "The story of the deadly pestilence is," Mr. Smith says, "an invention intended to conceal the discreditable means adopted by Akbar to gain possession of the greatest fort in India." If Abul Fazl did invent the pestilence, it is obvious that he did not do so for the reason here assigned, since he tells us himself that the garrison was tampered with.

Mr. Smith devotes a lengthy appendix (*ibid.*, pp. 297–300) to the elaboration of his charges. Of this it is necessary to read only the first paragraph, as it appears therefrom that he framed his indictment against Abul Fazl without even taking the trouble to read that writer's account of the siege. On the strength of Professor Dowson's statement that the history of Faizi Sirhindi is nothing more than a compilation based in part on the *Akbarnama* of Abul Fazl, he took the ill-judged course of trusting solely to the work of the former writer, and basing thereon his charges against the latter.

That Faizi Sirhindi did not take his account of the fall of Asirgarh from Abul Fazl, there could be no more conclusive evidence than the extracts from his work which Mr. Smith reproduces, and which he prefaces with the amazing statement that they are, save where differences are noted, "equivalent to passages from Abul Fazl's book." The incidents described in these extracts are, in most cases, not even referred to in Abul Fazl's book. The chief interest of Faizi's story lies in the very fact that it deals with many features of the siege about which Abul Fazl, in his more condensed account, says nothing. At the same time, the two stories are not, in the main, irreconcilable. The most glaring discrepancy is in the dates assigned to the fall of the fortress. Faizi places this on the 18th of the month Safar, 1009 A.H. (August, 1600), while Abul Fazl gives the correct date, namely, the 17th January, 1601. There can, however, be no doubt that this was an oversight on Faizi's part, for he has previously stated that the news of the fall of Ahmadnagar (which he correctly dates 18th Safar, 1009) reached Akbar whilst the siege of Asirgarh was in progress.

[18] Miran was apparently forced to make the *sijdah*, or complete prostration, a form of obeisance reserved for the Divinity alone, in the performance of which the worshipper touches the ground first with

his nose, and then with his forehead. It was after the promulgation of the *Din Ilahi* that the *sijdah* was introduced into the court ceremonial. Though Akbar countenanced and appreciated this form of salutation, he did not invariably exact it; and on finding that it gave great offence to orthodox Mussalmans, he forbade its use in the general assemblies. At the more private audiences, however, he expected the *sijdah* to be performed, and the practice was continued throughout the remainder of his reign, and during that of his successor, but was formally abolished by Shah Jahan.

[19] Smith says (*Akbar*, p. 279) that Miran failed to comply with Akbar's request that he should write such a letter. This is incorrect. He did comply; though it was after pressure had been brought to bear on him.

[20] This story is more picturesque than convincing. The son of the Abyssinian governor, here said to have been murdered by Akbar, is clearly the Muqarrib Khan referred to by Abul Fazl and Faizi Sirhindi. According to the latter writer, Muqarrib Khan was alive at the end of the siege; and we are led to infer that it was he who carried Bahadur's letter to the defenders. The same account states that when he (Muqarrib) entered the fort, he was so bitterly reproached by his father (Sidi Yakub) "for having thrown his master into bonds and surrendered the fort," that he drew his dagger and stabbed himself. Muqarrib's father, the writer adds, poisoned himself shortly afterwards (*vide* Mr. Beveridge's note on p. 1171 (Vol. III) of the *Akbarnama*). Faizi's story falls so naturally into its place, and has so much more the appearance of reality than that of the Jesuit writer, that I have no hesitation in regarding it as the more authoritative. The motive assigned in the text account for the suicide of the Abyssinian governor borders on the fantastic; while the reference, in his supposed oration, to the approach of winter (i.e. to the 'rains,' which commence early in July) is wholly inconsistent with Abul Fazl's definite statement that Bahadur's submission occurred in December.

Faizi Sirhindi's description of the manner of Muqarrib Khan's death is confirmed by the independent account in the *Zafar-al-Walih*. According to that work, after Muqarrib had gone to Akbar's camp, his father, Malik Yakub, who is described as old and blind, "assembled in the royal palace in the fortress all the sons of Mubarak Shah and their sons, and said to them, 'The fortress is as it was and the garrison is as it was. Which of you will accept the throne and will protect the honour of your fathers?' And not one of them answered him anything, and he said to them, 'Would to God that ye were women!' And they excused themselves; and it happened that as he was defending the fortress there came up to it his son Muqarrab Khan with a message from the King, and Malik Yakub said to his son, 'May God not show me thy face. Go down to Bahadur and follow him.' And he obeyed his order, until at length in the assembly of Abul Fazl he stabbed himself in the belly with his dagger, in abasement that his father was not content with him, and he died. But Malik Yakub Sultani, when he despaired of all the offspring of Mubarak Shah, went out to his house, made his will, bathed himself, and had his shroud brought. Then he summoned his family and went out to the Mosque which he had built, and prayed, and distributed benefits and gave alms, and he caused to be dug a grave in a spot which he desired, and then he ate opium, for his jealous patriotism was strong upon him, and he died and was buried there." This admirably translated passage is quoted from Lt.-Col. Sir T. Wolsey Haig's account of the Faruqi Dynasty of Khandesh, published in the *Indian Antiquary* for 1918 (p. 182). The picture presented I believe to be substantially true. The author of the Jesuit story appears to have discovered it in fragments, and, in the process of reconstructing it, to have put all the pieces in their wrong places.

[21] The corresponding phrase in the *Thesaurus* is, *Cui Xaverius ait . . .*, which Mr. Smith, who translates the whole of this passage (*Akbar*, p. 280), renders, or misrenders, "Xavier, a shrewd politician, artfully replied. . . ." I point this out for du Jarric's sake, as I am sure he would wish to dissociate himself from Mr. Smith's compliment.

[22] This circumstance is not mentioned by the Muhammadan writers. Abul Fazl, whose account of the latter part of the siege is very brief, merely states: "As it was not imagined that the ruler of Khandesh would shut his gates in the face of the World's ruler, a siege-train had not been brought. Though, after arrival, by a thousand efforts some guns were brought from Parnala, Gawal and Ahmadabad, yet from inattention they were not of much use." It is very likely that Akbar did ask the Fathers to aid him in getting guns from Goa; and it does not seem greatly to his discredit if he did. The silence of Abul Fazl and Faizi Sirhindi probably signifies nothing more than that they thought the matter too unimportant to mention.

[23] *. . . qu'ils se tinssent coys un peu, jusques à ce que la cholere eut passé au Roy.* In the *Thesaurus* we find the following: *Idomi proinde se continerent donec ira regia detumuisset*, which Mr. Smith recklessly renders ". . . to wait at Idomi till . . ." A reference to the French original would, I think, have made it clear to him that the first 'i' of Idomi has crept in by mistake, and that what Matthia Martinez wrote, or intended to write, was, *Domi proinde se continerent, etc.*

[24] Abul Fazl says that the keys of the fortress were surrendered on the 7th of the month Bahman, i.e. about the 17th of January (1601). "I myself," he adds, "sate at the gate, and in four days 34,000 persons came out with their families and goods."

NOTES TO CHAPTER X

An Embassy to Goa

[1] This chapter is almost a literal translation from the *Relaçam* (Part I, ch. III).

[2] Perhaps a picture of the black image of the Virgin in the Santa Casa at Lorete.

[3] The Arabic word *Kalai*, meaning 'tin,' is in common use throughout India. The metal here referred to was probably tutenag, or the 'white copper' of China, which was frequently miscalled 'calai' by the Portuguese and other early writers. Tutenag (probably derived from the Sanskrit *tutiya*=sulphate of copper) is a Chinese alloy of copper, zinc and nikel (see *Hobson-Jobson*, pp. 145 and 932).

[4] I think that Guerreiro has here misplaced a conversation which Akbar had some years previously (it was at the close of the first Mission), not with Pinheiro, but with Rudolf Aquaviva. On that occasion, Monserrate tells us, Rudolf explained the ceremonial observed at papal interviews, and Akbar then bade him inform the Pope that he fully appreciated his holiness and dignity, and charged him to kiss his Holiness's toe on his behalf. "Intellexisse me, dices, quam ampla, atque augusta Summi Pontificis Romani, esse dignitas, quippe qui Christi loco in terris sit: et audiuisse me, reges omnes, ad ejus pedes accidere: denique te, a me mitti, ut ejus pedes meo nomine osculeris, quando ego præsens, osculari coram non possum" (*Memoirs*, *A.S.B.*, 1914, p. 628).

[5] See Introduction, p. xlv.

[6] This was Sultan Hamid (capitano di Cogi), referred to on p. 100.

[7] "Pour cette cause l'honneur Royal est encliné & a procuré, qu'vn de ses seruiteurs et courtisans ait esté enuoyé par forme d'Embassade, pour affermir d'auantage les fondemens de l'alliance; de maniere qu'il n'y ait aucune occasion de doubter d'icelle. A ceste occasion le P. Benoist de Goës a esté enuoyé, avec nostre bon serviteur Coget-qui Soldan Hama, vers vos quartiers: ou s'estant informé auec tout le soing et diligence possible des choses, comme elles passent, ils nous aduise auec assurance, afin que conformement à l'estat d'vn chacun, nostre fortune pouruoye d'y aller, ou enuoyer." The clue to these unintelligible lines is to be found in the *Relaçam* of Guerreiro, where

the corresponding passage runs : " Por isso a honra real se aplicou & procurou que hũ dos criados da cotte seja mandado por modo de embaxada, pera que faça firmes os allicesse da amizade, de modo que nam aja nenhũ escrupulo de duuida nella. Por esta causa o Padre Bento de Goës foy mandado em cõpanhia do bõ seruidor Cogetqui Soltaõ Sama pera essas partes *pera q̃ de certo sayba q̃ genero de peças raras sam estimadas em Portugal, & o modo do caminho, & o estilo, & maneira daquelles grãdes :* è informado cõ toda a diligẽcia, & certeza de todas as cousas como passão, nos auise cõ certeza q cõforme ao estado de cada hũ proueja nossa ventura de yr, ou mãdar." Or in English : " Therefore our royal honour has willed and provided that one of the servants of our court may be sent [i.e. to Portugal] as ambassador to confirm the treaty of friendship, so that there may henceforth be no cause for doubting it. For this reason the Father Bento de Goës is sent with out trusted servant Cogetqui Sultan Sama to your parts, in order that he may know with certainty what kind of rarities are highly esteemed in Portugal, the manner of journeying there, and the style and habits of the Portuguese grandees : and having diligently and accurately informed himself how everything is done, he may correctly advise us, so that out auspicious venture of going or sending may be conducted in accordance with the status of each one." It will be noticed that the portion of Guerreiro's version which I have italicised is missing from du Jarric's translation. Possibly his copy of the *Relaçam* was mutilated ; or he may have used a manuscript copy from which the words in question had been accidentally left out. Whatever the explanation, the omission renders the whole passage meaningless. Guerreiro's version is by no means free from obscurity, and I am far from guaranteeing the accuracy of my rendering ; but its general tenor is, I think, plain, and accords with what du Jarric has himself told us (*vide* p. 114), namely, that one of the objects of the mission to Goa was to make enquiries as to a suitable present for the King of Portugal, to whom it was proposed to send an embassy. The last clause is apparently corrupt, and my interpretation of it is little more than a guess. Father Colaço (Introduction, p. xxxiii) turned it into Spanish as follows : " y informado, con toda la diligẽcia y certeza de todas las cosas como passã, nos auise, para que conforme al estado de cada uno prouea nuestra ventura de yr ò embiar." The studious exactness of this and of du Jarric's version justify the assumption that neither writer knew the meaning of the clause. I know of no complete version of Akbar's letter other than that given in the *Relaçam*.

We hear nothing further of the proposed embassy to Portugal, which was probably, as du Jarric surmised, nothing more than an excuse on Akbar's part for sending his agent to Goa.

NOTES TO CHAPTER X

[a] i.e. the 9th day of Fauardi of the Ilahi, or 'divine,' era. This era was instituted by Akbar, and commenced with the first year of his reign. The Ilahi year was solar, and hence about ten days longer than the Hijri year, which is lunar. It began on the 11th March, Fauardi, or Faridun, being the first month. The names of the other months were Ardibihist, Khurdad, Tir, Mardad, Shahryar, Mihr, Aban, Azar, Dai, Bahman, and Isfandarmuz. These names were, according to Badaoni, the same as at the time of the old Persian Kings, and as given in the *Nicabuccibyan*. The same writer says that with the new era, "fourteen festivals also were introduced corresponding to the feasts of the Zoroastrians; but the feasts of the Musalmans and their glory were trodden down, the Friday prayer alone being retained, because some old, decrepit, silly people used to go to it" (*Ain*, I, p. 195). Ilahi dates are found on the coins of Akbar and his immediate successors; but the Divine Era was little used after his death, and is now, to all intents and purposes, obsolete.

[b] The 20th March by the new reckoning, and the 11th by the old (see note 2, ch. xx).

NOTES TO CHAPTER XI

Father Pigneiro at Lahore

[1] This chapter is an abridgement of chapter IV of the *Relaçam* (Part I).

[2] In the *Relaçam* he is called *justiça mayor*. The two officials referred to were apparently the *Sadr-i-jahan*, or Chief-Justice (see note 4, ch. XIV), and the *Diwan*, or Finance Minister.

[3] The first of the two friendly Viceroys was Khwaja Shamsuddin, whom Pinheiro calls Xamaradin (*vide* the extract from his letter of 1605 quoted in note 6, ch. XIX). Shamsuddin was appointed to the Punjab when Akbar set out for the Deccan in 1598. He died at Lahore in 1600. He is said to have been a man " of simple manners, honest and faithful, and practical in transacting business " (*Ain*, I, pp. 446–7). He was succeeded in his office by Zain Khan Koka, who was also friendly to the Fathers. When Akbar returned from Burhanpur in 1601, he summoned Zain Khan to Agra, and sent Qulij Khan, whom he had left in charge at Agra during his absence in the Deccan, to be Viceroy at Lahore. Zain Khan was one of the most famous of Akbar's generals. He was a commander of 5000, and a recipient of the high honour of the *Alam*, or ' Standard.' In 1597 his daughter was married to Prince Salim. He died at Agra in 1602. Why Shamsuddin and Zain Khan should be described as brothers I do not know. Probably the mistake arose from the fact that when Shamsuddin died, his brother Khwaja Mumim Khawafi was appointed Diwan of the Punjab (*Ain*, I, p. 447).

NOTES TO CHAPTER XII

The Confidence Trick

[1] The story told in this chapter is taken from Part I (ch. v) of the *Relaçam*.

[2] i.e. the seed of the Thorn-apple, *Datura Stramonium*, a drug much used by thieves in India to render their victims helpless. Its effect, says Yule, is "to produce temporary alienation of mind, and violent laughter, permitting the thief to act unopposed" (*Hobson-Jobson*, p. 298). 'Datura' is from *dhatura*, the Sanskrit name of the Thorn-apple.

[3] Probably a wooden shutter which it would not be a difficult matter to wrench off. "In their upper roomes they have many lights and doores to let in the ayre, but use no glass" (Purchas, Vol. II, p. 1470). The use of glass in windows was, however, by no means unknown. Abul Fazl tells us in the 86th *Ain* that the price of glass for this purpose was R.1 for 1¼ *sers*, or one pane for 4 *dam* (Blochmann, I, p. 224). He elsewhere (88th *Ain*) estimates 2½ *sers* of glass for a window, which would allow for about two dozen panes.

NOTES TO CHAPTER XIII

Some Notable Conversions

[1] The first four paragraphs of this chapter are taken from ch. vi (Part I) of the *Relaçam*, and the remainder from ch. vii.

[2] This must have been Zain Khan Koka (see note 3, ch. xi).

[3] *Shaikh* (lit. 'a venerable old man') is a title given to religious teachers, particularly to those of the Sufi sect. In India, however, the word is frequently used to denote a convert, or the descendant of a convert, to Islam.

[4] For a full discussion of the origin of the word 'pagoda,' and of its three significations, (1) an idol, (2) a temple, (3) a coin, see Yule's *Hobson-Jobson*, pp. 652–657, and Dalgado's *Glossario-Luso-Asiatico*, II, pp. 130–136. Of the various derivations suggested, the two most favoured are (1) the Sanskrit *bhagavat*, 'holy, divine,' or *bhagavati*, the name of the Goddess Durga, (2) the Persian *but-kada*, an idol temple. In Yule's view there is "little doubt that the origin really lies between these two."

[5] The Portuguese gave the name 'Serra' to the district of Malabar on account of its mountainous character. In Book VI of the *Histoire*, which deals with the activities of the Jesuits in Southern India, du Jarric frequently refers to Malabar as *La Serre, ou Montaignes du Malabar*, and sometimes simply as *La Serre*. As the prelate who lost his possessions and his life on this occasion appears to have been an Armenian Christian, he cannot have been destined to preside over the Syrian Christians of Malabar. Du Jarric seems to have mixed him up with another bishop, who was held up at Ormuz at this time, and who actually was on his way to Malabar, whither he had been despatched by the Patriarch of Babylon.

Ever since the establishment of the Inquisition at Goa in 1560, the Jesuits had been scheming to bring the Christians of Malabar into their fold. Their efforts had been vigorously opposed by Mar Abraham, the local Nestorian prelate; and it was not until two years after he died, that is, in the year 1599, that they held the synod of Diampre, which sealed, at any rate for a time, the fate of Nestorianism in Malabar. Before Mar Abraham's death, a request had been sent by the 'Malabarees' to the Patriarch at Babylon, that he would send them another bishop of the same sect. When this came to the ears of the Portuguese, the Archbishop of Goa, du Jarric tells us, " manda soubs griefues peines & censures au Capitaine d'Ormuz (qui est le lieu par lequel ils souloient venir en l'Inde) qu'il ne laissast passer aucun Ecclesiastique de Chaldée, de Perse, ou d'Armenie, sans son congé exprez " (*Histoire*, III, p. 513). These orders, he adds, were strictly enforced, and the Archbishop, who was on his way to Malabar, was turned back with his wife, his children, and his followers.

[6] In Father Pimenta's letter of 1st December, 1600, the same eclipse is mentioned, and we are told that the Brahmans of Vijayanagar ascribed the phenomenon to the eating up of the sun by Draco, the Dragon : " De Solis eclypsi, quæ 10 Iulii anni hujus 1600 incidit die Lunæ sub meridiem, cognouimus eos hominibus persuadere, eam accidere, quando Draco, quẽ illi inter signa cœlestia annumerant, mordet Solem aut Lunam, atque ideò Rex, aliiq́ ; ob dolorem & mærorem cibo omnique potu toto die abstinuerunt, dicentes. O miseros nos, quoniam Draco deuorat Solem." This myth is still current in many parts of India.

NOTES TO CHAPTER XIV

A Brave Champion

[1] This chapter is, for the most part, a literal translation of chs. VIII and IX (Part I) of the *Relaçam*.

[2] I cannot explain this word. Possibly one of the many Hindu names commencing with *bala* is intended, perhaps Baladeva or Baldeo, a name given to the brother of Krishna in the Hindu legends.

[3] *Sendi* or *Shendi* is the Marathi word for the 'top-knot' of the Hindu. Amongst the Portuguese spellings of this word are 'Xendy,' 'Xendi,' and 'Xendim.'

[4] The 'Nauabo' presumably held the office of *Sadr*, or *Sadr-i-jahan*, which Blochmann interprets as 'Chief-Justice and Administrator-General of the Empire' (*Ain*, I, p. vii). Guerreiro styles him *justiça mayor;* but he is not a safe guide, for elsewhere he confers the same title on the 'Catual.' The account of the Catechumen's case is, throughout, confused and rambling. The proceedings, had they been clearly described, would have thrown valuable light on a very obscure feature of Mogul administration. Unfortunately, however, we can do little more than guess at the nature of the various tribunals before whom the case was taken.

Blochmann (*ibid.*, p. 270) says that during the reign of Akbar the Sadr-i-jahan ranked as the fourth officer of the Empire. His power was immense. He was the highest law-officer, and had the powers which Administrators-General have amongst us; he was in charge of all lands devoted to ecclesiastical and benevolent purposes, and possessed an almost unlimited authority of conferring such lands independently of the King. He was also the highest ecclesiastical law-officer, and might exercise the powers of a High Inquisitor. The holder of the office at this time was Miran Sadr Jahan Mufti, whose name coincided with the title of his office. He was a member of the Din Ilahi, though he appears to have remained a Mussalman at heart. Badaoni thus scornfully refers to his conversion: "During the Muharram of 1004, Sadr Jahan, *mufti* of the Empire, who had been promoted to a Commandership of One Thousand, joined the Divine Faith, as also his two over-ambitious sons; and having taken the *Shact* of the new religion, he ran into the net like a fish, and got his *Hazariship*. He even asked

His Majesty what he was to do with his beard (see note 8, ch. vii), when he was told to let it be" (*Ain*, I, p. 208).

[5] The expression intended is *rahmat-i-Khuda*, 'may God's blessing be upon you,' not *Ghanimat-i-Khuda*, as suggested by Maclagan. The point is settled by the *Relaçam*, where the spelling is 'rhamathegoda.'

[6] The Persian word *be-din* signifies an unbeliever. *Be*='without,' and *din*='faith,' 'religion.'

[7] Guerreiro says that the Nawab *remeteo o casa aos Cateris, que he hu genero de gentios graves*. 'Cateri' is perhaps a corrupt form of *shastri*, a Sanskrit word signifying one skilled in Hindu law, or religious books. Maclagan interprets it as *Khatri;* but this does not seem to fit the context.

[8] Guerreiro's version does nothing to elucidate this involved and obscure passage.

[9] This is a somewhat inflated rendering of the words used by Guerreiro: *Coxi dos gentios, que he como seu provisor*, 'the Coxi of the Gentiles, who is, as it were, their provisor.' The young convert was probably taken before the chief *guru* of the town, or the head-man of his caste. I can offer no explanation of the word 'coxi,' unless it is one of the numerous Portuguese spellings of 'caxi' or 'cazique' (see note 6, ch. ii). I have, however, found no other instance of this word being used of a Hindu divine.

[10] The *sol tournois*, the common *sol* then in use, was usually taken as equivalent to a tenth of a shilling. Twenty-six *sols* would, therefore, be equal to about 2s. 7d. The value of the rupee was subject, in Akbar's day, to considerable fluctuations; but its normal value was about 2s. 3d.

[11] The *damri*, the smallest copper coin in circulation, was, in Akbar's time, equal to $\frac{1}{8}$ *dam*, or $\frac{1}{320}$ of a rupee. The word *dam* appears in our so-called profane expression, "I don't care a dam" (see *Hobson-Jobson*, p. 294).

[12] 'Cazique' here appears to be a mistake for Cazi (*Kazi*).

NOTES TO CHAPTER XV

An Imperial Farman

[1] This chapter is taken from Part II (Bk. III, ch. v) of the *Relaçam*.

[2] Akbar was recalled to Agra by the misconduct of his eldest son, Prince Salim, who had for some months been in open rebellion against him. The Prince had by this time established himself at Allahabad, where he was engaged in raising troops with a view to marching on Agra.

[3] Machado and Goës arrived at Agra during the hot season of 1602, i.e. probably in May or June. Goës, it will be remembered, had been sent to Goa in the previous year, in company with Akbar's ambassador, Sultan Hamid. It was whilst at Goa that he received instructions to proceed to Cathay. He remained only a short time at Agra, and then went to Lahore, whence he set out, in January, 1603, on his eastern travels, Machado taking his place at Lahore. The latter has already been mentioned as one of the Fathers who were selected to go to Cambay in 1595 (see note 13, ch. VII).

[4] As already stated, the two friendly Viceroys were Khwaja Shamsuddin and Zain Khan Koka. The next to hold the office was Qulij Khan. He was appointed in 1601. According to Abul Fazl, it was on the 16th of the month *Aban* that he " obtained leave to go to the Panjab. As there was no great officer there, this chosen servant was appointed there. It had been proposed that the government of Kabul should be entrusted to Shah Quli K. Mahram. He (Qulij Khan) asked for the charge of both places (the Panjab and Kabul), and this was granted, and an order was issued " (*Akbarnama*, tr. Beveridge, p. 1196). Qulij Khan was one of the most distinguished of Akbar's commanders. He had taken a leading part in the operations against Daman in 1581, and in the Gujarat campaign of 1583. He was appointed Governor of Kabul in 1594, and of Agra in 1599. In 1601, after the King's return from the Deccan campaign, he became Viceroy of Lahore and Governor of Kabul. It was during the operations in 1581 that he had been wounded. According to Danvers (*Portuguese in India*, II, p. 43), Qulij Khan challenged Ferdinand de Miranda, the commander of a certain Portuguese fort, to single combat. The latter accepted the challenge, and charged his opponent so furiously

that his spear "passed through Calichan's armour, wounding his breast, and flew into pieces. Being tied to the saddle, Calichan retained his seat on horseback, but, turning back, retired to his men. After this he broke up his camp and marched away. . . ." Besides being a man of learning, Qulij Khan was a staunch and orthodox Sunni, and, as such, looked with little favour on the Fathers and their mission. The latter had in consequence no love for Qulij Khan, whom they denounce in their letters as a second Nero, a tyrant who "thought no more of putting a man to death than of drinking a cup of water," and whose name was a terror even to his own people (*vide* Maclagan, p. 98). Qulij Khan, however, appears to have served Akbar well, and especially during the rebellion of Salim, when his powerful influence deprived the Prince of many supporters. In his letter of August 12th, 1605 (referred to on p. 276), Pinheiro wrote: "The Emperor does nothing in the whole kingdom but what is pleasing to the Governor, having need of him to govern in these parts in case of a war with his son, for he is the Prince's open enemy and publicly declares to the Emperor that he is his only faithful subject. . . . They looked on Calichão as a second Emperor and feared him as a magician, and through his arts the Emperor had been induced to put many friends to death, some of whom I knew, among others our friend Xencão (Zain Khan Koka), the prince's father-in-law, and the defender of our religion" (Maclagan, p. 99). The statement that Zain Khan was put to death by Akbar is not found elsewhere. According to Blochmann (*Ain*, I, 345), his death, which occurred in 1602–3, was partly caused by excessive drinking. 'Qulij' is the Turki word *qilij*, 'a sword.'

5. During the 16th century the Portuguese held undisputed command of the Indian seas, and controlled all traffic, from the Persian Gulf to Mozambique, and from Mozambique to Malacca. "Trade on certain routes, and in certain goods, was declared a State monopoly, and carried on for the benefit of the King of Portugal or his nominees; outside these limits private shipping was allowed to ply, provided that a license had been taken out and paid for, but unlicensed ships were treated as prizes of war, and sunk, burnt, or captured as circumstances might determine. The administration was, however, exceedingly corrupt when judged by modern standards: the high officers were as a rule concerned only to make money as quickly as possible, and consequently the practical working of the regulations was more elastic than is suggested by their terms; perhaps it is not too much to say that under Portuguese domination Indian merchants could carry on almost any trade they wanted to, provided they understood how to set to work, and were prepared to pay the sums demanded for the privilege" (Moreland, *India at the Death of Akbar*, p. 201). Even Akbar's

ships which carried pilgrims to Mecca were obliged to sail under Portuguese license.

[6] Guerreiro styles him *veador da fazenda*, equivalent perhaps to the Controller of the Household.

[7] i.e. the powerful Qulij Khan.

[8] Aziz Koka (see note 10, ch. xvi) at this time held the office of *Vakil*, or Prime Minister, to which he had been appointed in 1596 (*Ain*, I, p. 327).

NOTES TO CHAPTER XVI

A Miraculous Picture

[1] This chapter corresponds with chapter vi of Part II of the *Relaçam*.

[2] Maclagan quotes as follows from the Provincial's report of 1607: "When once he (Akbar) had listened to the Life of Christ written by Jerome Xavier in Persian, he began to reverence highly the pictures of Christ and to speak more respectfully of Christ himself, though several of the Muhammadans tried to persuade him that Christ's miracles were not due to any supernatural power, but to Christ's exceeding skill as a physician, dealing with natural methods." For an account of the work here referred to, which was called *Miratu-l-Quds* (The Mirror of Purity) or *Dastan-i-Masih* (Life of Christ), see *J.A.S.B.*, LXV, p. 110.

[3] i.e. Mirza Aziz Koka, Khan-i-Azam (see note 10 below).

[4] This presumably is the picture of the Virgin over the high altar in the Church of S. Maria del Popolo. Like that in the S. Maria Maggiore, it is supposed to be endowed with miraculous powers. It was brought from Lateran by Pope Gregory IX during an outbreak of plague in Rome. The Madonna del Popolo is another of the pictures ascribed to St. Luke.

[5] There was no actual church at Agra at this time. The services were held in a room of the Fathers' house which had been converted into a chapel, as had previously been done in Lahore. The building of the church at Agra was commenced in 1603 (? 4). In a letter dated 6th September, 1604, Xavier says: "The first stone was laid with great solemnity. Many Muhammadans were present, and were greatly edified by the ceremonial which Christians use on these occasions. These works are not so expensive here as in other places, being made of bricks, lead, and a great part of clay, which is made of a certain kind of earth. The chapel will be well finished, though perfect workmanship may be wanting. It will soon be finished, please God. It is badly needed, as the Christians are very crowded in our present small chapel" (*J.A.S.B.*, LXV, p. 93). The building was completed in the reign of Jahangir, and, according to Bernier, was pulled down by Shah Jahan.

[6] i.e. Bahadur Khan, who had been captured at Asirgarh, and was at this time a prisoner at Gwalior.

The Spanish *gabàn* is a rain-cloak with a hood attached. The garment in question was doubtless from the royal wardrobe. Akbar's partiality for European costumes has already been noticed.

[8] i.e. to her own apartments in the palace.

[9] Akbar's delight in and encouragement of the art of painting are referred to by Abul Fazl in the 34th *Ain* (Blochmann, I, pp. 107–8). "Most excellent painters," he says, "are now to be found, and masterpieces, worthy of a *Bihzád* [a famous Persian artist], may be placed at the side of the wonderful works of the European painters who have attained world-wide fame. More than a hundred painters have become famous masters of the art, whilst the number of those who approach perfection, or of those who are middling, is very large." The King, he adds, and all the grandees of the court, sat for their likenesses, and these were preserved in an immense album.

[10] This was Mirza Aziz Koka, better known by his title *Khan-i-Azam* (lord of magnificence). He had been brought up with Akbar, and became one of his greatest generals. "Though often offended by his boldness, Akbar would seldom punish him; he used to say, 'Between me and Aziz is a river of milk which I cannot cross'" (*Ain*, I, 325). For a long time Aziz, who had been brought up a strict Mussalman, openly expressed his disapproval of Akbar's religious views. In 1594, whilst Governor of Gujarat, he was called to court, but, disgusted with the King's contempt for his faith, he disobeyed the summons, and set out on a pilgrimage to Mecca. During his stay in the holy city he was so badly fleeced, that he returned to India with his zeal for Islam considerably abated. He made his peace with Akbar, and soon resumed his former position at court. He subsequently embraced the Din Ilahi. Aziz was made a commander of 5000 in 1580. In 1587 his daughter was married to Prince Murad, and a few years later another of his daughters was married to Prince Khusru. "Aziz," says Blochmann, "was remarkable for ease of address, intelligence, and his knowledge of history. He also wrote poems. Historians quote the following aphorism from his 'pithy' sayings: 'A man should marry four wives—a Persian woman to have somebody to talk to; a Khurasani woman, for his housework; a Hindu woman, for nursing his children; and a woman from Mawarannahr, to have some one to whip as a warning for the other three'" (*Ain*, I, 327).

[11] This, as Maclagan points out, must mean the son of Muzaffar Husain Mirza (note 5, ch. VII), as, according to Blochmann (*Ain* I, 314), Muzaffar died in 1599–1600.

[12] i.e. Abdullah Khan Usbeg, the powerful ruler of Turan or Transoxiana, who, throughout his long reign of forty-two years (1556–1598), was an active and dangerous rival of the Great Mogul.

NOTES TO CHAPTER XVII

EVENTS OF THE YEAR 1602

[1] This chapter is taken from Part II (chap. VII) of the *Relaçam*.

[2] *Rum*, the Arabic form of the Latin *Roma*, was the name given to the Seljukian empire, which extended from the Euphrates to Constantinople and from the Black Sea to the confines of Syria; and the word 'Rumes' was accordingly used to designate both the Turks of Europe and those of Asiatic Turkey. Du Jarric follows Guerreiro in confining this designation to the Turks of Europe. But other writers have used it in a similarly restricted sense (see *Hobson-Jobson*, p. 768).

[3] Inayatu-lla, the author of the supplement to the *Akbarnama* of Abul Fazl, refers to Manuquer's departure as follows: "Manucihr the ambassador of the ruler of Persia received valuable presents and was allowed to depart. Numerous productions of India were sent along with him as presents for his Sovereign, and at the time of his departure Manucihr received four lakhs of *dams* in addition to what had already been given to him" (*Akbarnama*, tr. Beveridge, p. 1223).

[4] This circumstance is referred to by Xavier in his letter of Sept. 6, 1604, as follows: "A young man from the realm of the Emperor, captive to a Turk who made him prisoner in the late wars, came hither with his master, who set him free, but even when at liberty his fear of being retaken was so great that he trembled at every step. The Fathers sent him to us at Agra, and we received him and placed him with João Battista Vechiete who will take him back to his own land" (*J.A.S.B.*, LXV, p. 98). Vechiete was apparently a Florentine merchant who visited Akbar's court in 1604 (*ibid.*, p. 95). I have found no mention elsewhere of the Turkish embassy here referred to.

[5] The story of the release of the prisoners, which took place in December, 1603, is told in Xavier's letter of 6th September, 1604.

NOTES TO CHAPTER XVIII

Prince Salim

[1] This chapter is taken from Part II (ch. viii) of the *Relaçam.*

[2] The account in the *Akbarnama* (supplement) is as follows: "Meanwhile news came that he was proceeding towards the court with evil intentions and accompanied by 30,000 horse. A Fate-like order was issued from the antechamber of wrath and severity to the effect that 'He should recognise that his peace and prosperity lay in returning to Allahabad. If a desire for service had seized his collar, he should come to court unattended.' In as much as his disposition was not sincere, he on receipt of this order lost the thread of plan, and was mortified, and turned back from Etawah towards Allahabad. In reply to the order he used expressions of lamentation, and represented his ashamedness, and made excuses unworthy of being heard and sent them to the court by the *Sadr-i-jahan*" (*Akbarnama*, tr. Beveridge, p. 1211).

[3] This is a somewhat inaccurate account of the murder of Abul Fazl, though du Jarric appears to have been ignorant of the victim's identity. Abul Fazl was not in the neighbourhood of the Prince when Akbar sent for him, but in the Deccan; and it was near Gwalior, whilst on his way to obey the King's summons, that he was waylaid and killed by the Prince's hired assassins. In the *Thesaurus* the translator has made du Jarric's mistake much worse by rendering the words *qui estoit auprez de son fils* by *qui filio adhærebat.* Guerreiro's expression is *que perto delle* (i.e. the Prince) *estava.* Details of the murder are given by Asad Beg (*E. & D.*, VI, pp. 154–160) and in the *Akbarnama* of Innayatu-llah (*ibid.*, p. 107). For Jahangir's unblushing account of his own crime, see the *Tuzuk-i-Jahangiri*, I, pp. 24, 25.

[4] The *marc* was equivalent to about 8 oz.

[5] Hamida Begam was not more than seventy-seven years old at this time (1604). She was married to Humayun, at the age of fourteen, in the year 1541 (see Smith's *Akbar*, p. 13). Guerreiro not only states that she was ninety years old, but adds that she left behind her *hum filho de quarenta & noue annos de Rey, & bisnetos* (great-grand-children) *ia casados & com filhos.* Khusru, the son of Salim, and great-grandson

of the Queen-Mother, was born in 1587. He was, therefore, seventeen years old at this date (1604); so that Guerreiro's statement that he already had children of his own is quite possibly correct. Salim was only eighteen years of age when Khusru was born.

[6] cf. *Akbarnama* (supplement), p. 1244: "Suddenly news came of the illness of Miriam Makani. As she did not approve of the expedition, H.M. did not believe in her illness. He thought her illness was feigned and did not contemplate returning. Till heart-striking news came, and trustworthy persons reported that she was seriously ill and that the physicians had given up using medicines. Of necessity the loving sovereign gave up the journey and hastened to see his mother."

[7] In adopting these signs of mourning Akbar followed the custom of the Hindus. In the supplement to the *Akbarnama* (p. 1245) we read: "He (Akbar) shaved his hair, moustaches, etc., and cast off his turban and donned the garb of woe. He was the first to bear the body on his shoulder, and then the grandees conveyed it in turn. The cortege proceeded to Delhi. When H.M. had accompanied it some distance, he returned to the palace. . . . The body was conveyed to Delhi in the period of eleven watches, and laid in the tomb of H.M. Jinnat Ashiyam [His Majesty who has his abode in Paradise]."

[8] Such I take to be the meaning of the phrase, *ou il l'enserre avec beaucoup de douceur.* The *Thesaurus* has *huic laudis illum verbis includit*, a rendering which naturally puzzled Mr. Smith (*vide Akbar*, p. 330). Guerreiro's words are, *o fechou em hua casa com muita mansidao.* In the supplement to the *Akbarnama*, the Prince's arrest is thus described: "He had the prince arrested and conveyed to the female apartments. He first reproached him, and after enumerating his transgressions gave him many censures. The prince cast his eyes on the ground and answered with streaming eyes. Then an order was given to the servants to put the prince into a closet and to deprive him of wine. This was the hardest of punishments. The prince grieved greatly and was much heart-broken. His sisters came and went and sympathised with him and comforted him. They also represented the contrition and repentance of the prince to H.M. After ten days H.M.'s innate kindness prevailed and an order was given for his release. By H.M.'s orders he went to his house. H.M. wanted that the prince should remain there alone. But as he was specially hopeless about prince Daniel, he stayed the retribution of his acts at this point, and allowed him his fief and his ranks as before" (*Akbarnama*, tr. Beveridge, p. 1248).

[9] Presumably the *Miratu-l-Quds* (see note 2, ch. XVI), which Xavier completed in the year 1602.

NOTES TO CHAPTER XIX

Persecution of the Fathers

[1] This chapter is taken from Part IV (Bk. III, ch. III) of the *Relaçam*. The primary authority for the first six paragraphs is the letter written from Agra by Father Xavier, dated September 6th, 1604. The remaining paragraphs are based on a letter addressed to the Provincial at Goa by Father Pinheiro, dated August 12th, 1605. The originals of both these letters are amongst the Marsden MSS. in the British Museum library. Extracts are given by Maclagan (*J.A.S.B.*, LXV, pp. 89–106).

[2] This was Mirza Lahauri, the favourite son of Qulij Khan. Lahauri's depraved habits and discreditable conduct are referred to by Blochmann (*Ain*, I, 500).

[3] i.e. Abdullah Khan Usbeg, the late ruler of Transoxiana (note 12, ch. XVI).

[4] i.e. Qulij Khan.

[5] In his letter of 6th September, 1604, Xavier wrote that, shortly after this outburst, the Viceroy, finding that Father Corsi was going on a visit to Agra, and fearing an ill report of his behaviour might reach the King, sent for Father Pinheiro, and said to him : " Father, I am a friend to you and to the Lord Jesus : no one knows Him better than I do. He had the spirit of God and neither prophet nor angel could speak as he spoke " (*vide* Maclagan, p. 97).

[6] This date which du Jarric took from the *Relaçam* is clearly a mistake on Guerreiro's part for 1604. In the letter referred to in note 3, ch. XI, Father Pinheiro gives what purports to be an extract from one of these Gentile communications, though how it came into his hands does not appear. Or perhaps he is merely stating what he had been told was the general tenor of such communications. The passage, as translated by Maclagan (p. 100), runs as follows : " As concerns the Nawab, it will be sufficient to accuse the Father every day of grievous things which even if they are not believed will be enough to throw discredit on him. We can do this the more easily that his friends the Nawabs Xamaradin and Xencão are dead, and the present Nawab Calichicão is hostile to him, as he has shown on many occasions because of the religion he preaches. So we shall get

the Father driven from Lahor and the church, which we hate, destroyed."

[7] Maclagan's suggestion that some frontier disturbance is here referred to is probably correct, as Qulij Khan was Governor of Kabul as well as Viceroy of the Panjab (*vide* note 4, p. 268). The fugitive son was most likely Zaifullah (*Ain*, I, p. 500), who had seen considerable military service in Afghânistan. The Jesuit account is, however, extremely vague, its main purpose being to emphasise, or exaggerate Qulij Khan's confusion and disgrace. During the latter's absence, affairs at Lahore were temporarily in the hands of his son Chin Qulij, and it was probably to him that the farman mentioned in the next paragraph was presented. Chin Qulij is stated to have been "an educated, liberal man, well versed in government matters" (*Ain*, I, p. 500).

[8] *Ils estant presentés au Viceroy avec le sceau, ou approbation du Prince* (*chose qui ne se fait guere*). Guerreiro's version is equally obscure. The letters, he says, were presented to the Viceroy 'together with an order from the Prince': *juntamente com a portaria do Principe, que he cousa muy raramente se faz*. Pinheiro's letter, on which the account is based, states that Akbar first ordered a letter to be written to the Viceroy, and that when this proved ineffective, it was followed by a regular farman of which the Prince himself was the 'porvanazi' (*vide* Maclagan, p. 102). Pinheiro then goes on to define 'porvanazi' (*parwanchi*) as 'he who gives an order for a firman.' This is, of course, incorrect. The word *parwanchi* signifies a secretary who drafts a *parwana* or a *farman*. What part the Prince actually played in the preparation of this farman is not clear; but the document evidently carried his seal as well as that of the King. This procedure, though new, was probably quite regular; for very considerable authority in state affairs, and particularly in regard to the issue and sealing of royal grants, appears to have been conferred on the Prince after his submission. In the supplement to the *Akbarnama* it is stated that at this time "an order was given that the diwans should manage the affairs of the kingdom in accordance with the advice of Prince Sultan Salim, and that his seal should be affixed to the grants of the officer's mansab" (*Akbarnama*, tr. Beveridge, p. 1257).

[9] Though nominally reconciled to his father, the Prince was throughout this year under suspicion. Akbar knew that, in the event of any further trouble with his son, he could rely on the loyal support of Qulij Khan. It seems very unlikely, therefore, that he had any intention of putting the latter to death; and still more unlikely that he ever contemplated sending an armed force to Lahore under Salim's command.

NOTES TO CHAPTER XX

The Death of Akbar

[1] This chapter is taken from Part IV (Bk. III, ch. iv) of the *Relaçam*.

[2] This is according to the new reckoning. The reformed calendar came into use in Roman Catholic countries in 1582, in which year October 15th was made to follow October 4th. According to the old style, which remained in force in Great Britain till 1752, Akbar died on October 17th, 1605.

[3] According to the Provincial's report of 20th December, 1607, the Fathers announced themselves the bearers of healing medicines (Maclagan, p. 107).

[4] This was Shaikh Farid, more generally known as Mir Murtaza Khan. The chief supporters of Khusru were Aziz Koka and Raja Man Singh. Asad Beg says that Aziz Koka, on realizing that Salim's succession was assured, came "in great shame, and paid his respects. The Prince took not the least notice of his ill-conduct, and bestowed all royal kindness upon him" (*E. & D.*, VI, p. 171). Raja Man Singh, says the same writer, took Khusru with him to his own palace, and prepared boats, intending to escape to Bengal. The next day, however, having received a solemn assurance from Salim that no harm should befall the Prince, he returned to court, "and brought Sultan Khusru to the feet of his royal father."

[5] 'Iorda' is evidently a mistake for *sijdah*; the spelling is Guerreiro's. This account agrees substantially with that given by Asad Beg. The King, says this writer, was still breathing when the Prince arrived. The latter, on entering, "bowed himself at the feet of his Majesty. He saw that he was in his last agonies. The King opened his eyes, and signed to them to invest him with the turban and robes which had been prepared for him, and to gird him with his own dagger. The attendants prostrated themselves and did homage; at the same moment that sovereign, whose sins are forgiven, bowed himself also and closed his life" (*E. & D.*, VI, p. 171).

[6] There seems no reason for doubting the truth of this simple statement, which is in accord with all that we know of Akbar's attitude towards religion. Attempts were doubtless made to conceal the fact that Akbar did not die in the profession of Islam; and such attempts

would be quite sufficient to account for the stories told by Sir T. Roe and Father Botelho, both of whom state that he died as he was born, a Muhammadan. That those present at the last sought to remind the dying monarch of their Prophet has no special significance. It is the custom throughout Islam for watchers beside a death-bed to repeat the *Kalimah*, or creed. Hughes (*Dictionary of Islam*, p. 80) quotes the following from Herklot's *Qanun-i-Islam*: "The Kalimutu 'sh-shahadah is also read with an audible voice by those present. They do not require the patient to read it himself, as at such times he is in a distressing state, and not in a fit state of mind to repeat the Kalimah. Most people lie insensible, and cannot even speak, but the pious retain their mental faculties and converse till the very last. The following is a most serious rule amongst us (Muslims), viz. that if a person desire the patient to repeat the Kalimah, and the sick man expire without being able to do so, his faith is considered dubious: whilst the man who directed him to do so thereby incurs guilt. It is therefore best that the sitters-by read it, in anticipation of the hope that the sick man, by hearing the sound of it, may bring it to his recollection, and repeat it either aloud or in his own mind."

[7] In the 72nd *Ain* (Blochmann, p. 155) we read: "His Majesty abstains much from flesh, so that whole months pass away without his touching any animal food, which, though prized by most, is nothing thought of by the sage. His august nature cares but little for the pleasures of the world. In the course of twenty-four hours, he never makes more than one meal." From what Abul Fazl states elsewhere, however, we may infer that Akbar's one meal was by no means unsubstantial. There was, he says, no fixed time for it; "but the servants have always things so far ready, that in the space of an hour after the order has been given, a hundred dishes are served up." The same writer's description of the imperial kitchens, and the elaborate dishes which were daily prepared by "cooks from all countries," shows that, if Akbar himself was an abstemious eater, his table was supplied with the choicest luxuries that the wealth of a Mogul emperor could command (see *Ain*, I, pp. 56–61).

[8] cf. the Provincial's report for 1607, quoted in note 2, ch. XVI.

[9] Du Jarric follows the spelling of the *Relaçam*. I conclude the province referred to is Khandesh. The commoner Portuguese distortion of this name was 'Xhandes.'

[10] By solar reckoning, Akbar died during the fiftieth year of his reign. He ascended the throne in February, 1556, being then fourteen years of age. According to Hijri reckoning, he reigned for just over fifty-one years, i.e. from Rabi II 963 to Jumadi II 1014.

[11] "The obsequies of the dead lion," says Smith (*Akbar*, p. 327),

"were hurried and perfunctory"; and the Fathers were evidently of the same opinion. Guerreiro concludes his account with these words: "Sic transit gloria mundi: hum ordinario fidalgo nosso fora levado com mais ordem & apparato funeral." But this is, I think, to ignore the customs and traditions of Islam. It must be remembered in the first place that, amongst the Sunni Muhammadans of India, the wearing of mourning is exceptional; nor is it enjoined by Islamic law. We are told that Akbar, on the death of his mother, shaved off his beard, his eyebrows, and the hair of his head, and clad himself in blue garments. But in matters of this kind Akbar was a law unto himself. Jahangir, on the other hand, was professedly a Mussalman; and hence his omission of such outward signs of mourning was not in itself a mark either of indifference or disrespect. Again, amongst Muhammadans, a funeral is never regarded as an occasion for a display of grandeur: the proceedings are usually conducted with the utmost simplicity. And, lastly, it is strictly enjoined that the obsequies of the dead should be performed with haste. "Unlike our Christian custom of walking slowly to the grave, the Muhammadans carry their dead quickly to the place of interment; for Muhammad is related to have said that it is good to carry the dead quickly to the grave, to cause the righteous person to arrive soon at happiness, and if he is a bad man, it is well to put wickedness away from one's shoulders" (Hughes, *Dictionary of Islam*, p. 46). For like reasons, it is deemed improper that a corpse should be kept long in the house (*ibid.*, p. 80). The hurried nature of the proceedings, the absence of 'apparato,' and the fact that many of the mourners did not assume a mourning garb, do not, therefore, justify the conclusion that Akbar's funeral rites were scamped, though they may easily have given that impression to the Fathers, who took little trouble to inform themselves of the significance of Muhammadan religious customs. The haste that characterized the obsequies of the Queen-mother appears to have given them a similar impression. But Akbar was far too devoted a son to show disrespect for his mother's remains; and the speed with which the deceased lady was carried to her last resting-place was in strict accordance with Islamic custom. According to Asad Beg, a reliable chronicler, Akbar was buried with all the ceremonies due to his rank (*E. & D.*, VI, p. 172). It is true, as Smith observes, that Asad Beg was absent in the Deccan when Akbar died; but he must have had ample opportunities of obtaining correct information. Moreover, if his absence in the Deccan is a sufficient reason for discrediting his account of Akbar's funeral, it would seem to be an equally good reason for discrediting his account of the death-scene, which Smith would have us regard as authoritative.

INDEX

(*N.B.* The letter "A" stands for Akbar.)

Abdullah Khan, Usbeg, 171, 195, 272, 276

Abdur Rahim Mirza, Khan-khanan, 47, 98, 230, 234, 235, 249, 251

Abul Fazl, 31, 33, 36, 183, 224, 234, 274

Abul Maali, 211

Acosta, E., xxvi, 232

Adil Khan (Idalcan), of Bijapur, 98, 113, 152, 249

Agra, A's first residence at, 8; haunted by evil spirits, 214; A moves from Lahore to, 88–89; returns from Deccan to, 152; building of church at, 191, 271; other references, 173, 174, 182, 189, 192, 194

Ahmadabad, 48, 59, 60, 235, 236

Ahmadnagar, sieges of, 234, 235, 242, 249

Aina-i-Haqq-numa, 248

Ain-i-Akbari (tr. H. Blochmann), 212, 214, 215, 216, 219, 224, 225, 229, 237–238, 261, 263, 266, 272

Akbar, Intercourse with the Fathers, xli; his attitude towards the Portuguese, xlv–xlvi; his descent, 1, 210; his name, 3; his court, 4: his wealth and military strength, 5–7, 212–213; costume and temperament, 8, 205–207, 215; amusements, 9; methods of hunting, 10; public audiences, 11; first acquaintance with Christianity, 14, 217; sends for Julian Pereira, 15; invites Jesuit Fathers from Goa, 17; welcomes 1st Mission, 18; hears religious debates, 20–21; his children, 24; visits the oratory, 25; his admiration for Christianity, 26–28; his doctrinal difficulties, 30–31; his march to Kabul, 33, 213, 225; defends his Mullas, 34; his friendship with Aquaviva, 38–40; celebrates the Assumption, 44; sends 2nd invitation to Fathers at Goa, 45; arranges for their journey, 46–47; his letter to the Fathers, 48–49; sends 3rd invitation to Goa, 51; welcomes 3rd Mission, 62; his library, 63; receives a vassal prince, 64; visits the Fathers' chapel, 66; worships the sun, 68, 72, 74, 241; visits Kashmir, 75–79; gives audience to the Fathers, 82–84; moves from Lahore to Agra, 88; marches to the Deccan, 97; enters Burhanpur, 102; besieges Asirgarh, 102–109; does homage to picture of Virgin, 110–111; sends embassy to Goa, 113–115; his

INDEX

letter to the Portuguese Viceroy, 116; issues edict permitting his subjects to embrace Christianity, 155–159; honours the Madonna di Popolo, 165–169; releases Portuguese prisoners, 180, 273; prepares for war with Salim, 182–183; his mother's illness and death, 188, 275; reconciliation with Salim, 189; his sickness and death, 203, 278; funeral rites, 208, 279–280; Jahangir's portrait of, 214; subject to epilepsy, 9, 215; his religious speculations, 68–69, 242; the belief that he died of poison, 96, 204, 247; his abstemious diet, 279; his age, 279

Akbarnama, of Abul Fazl, referred to, 215, 217, 218, 222, 224, 225, 229, 243, 244, 246, 251, 253–256, 258, 268, 274, 275, 277

Albuquerque, 154

Alcala, xxvi, 232

'Alcorana,' 44, 67, 227–228

Ali, Khalifa, 3, 211

Ali Khan, of Khandesh, 231, 251

Allahabad, 183, 274

All Souls College, xxxiii

Aquaviva, Cardinal, 18

Aquaviva, Father Claud, 18

Aquaviva, Father Rudolf, family of, 18; appointed leader of 1st Mission, 18, 220; exhorts A to embrace Christianity, 23; alone at A's court, 38–43; plots against his life, 39; his austerities, 40, 226; sickness and return to Goa, 41; death of, 220; other references, xlvii, 52, 62, 215, 219, 223, 225, 229, 259

Arachosia, 2, 211

Armenians, 60, 135

Army, of Akbar, 6, 7, 212–213

Arras, xxxv

Asad Beg, *Waqaya*, 274, 278, 280

Asirgarh (Syr), siege of, 103–109, 152, 173, 249, 251–258, 271

Atria, duke of, 18

Aurangzeb, xlviii

Ayres de Saldagna, 154

Aziz Khan Koka (Agiscoa), 158, 169, 269, 271, 272, 278

Babur, 3

Babylon, Patriarch of, 264

Badakshan, 239

Badaoni, History of, referred to, 212, 223, 224, 229, 237, 241, 246, 247

Bahadur Khan, of Khandesh, 102–105, 108, 164, 235, 249, 251, 253–258, 271

Bajazet, 1, 210

Baluchistan, 211

Banians, 99, 250

Barbosa, Duarte, 245

Baroche, 100, 212

Bartoli, Father D., *Missione al Gran Mogor*, 219, 220

Barzé, Father Gaspar, 228

Bassein, 232

Beas, river, 5, 212

Bengala, 4, 14, 15, 208, 218

— islands of, 3, 4, 211

— revolt in, 32–33, 213, 225

Berar (Barara), 102, 234, 251

Beretari, Father Sebastian, 243

Bernier, François, 271

Besse, Fr. L., xxviii

Bible, the Royal, 19, 221

Bihzad, artist, 272

INDEX

Bijapur, 249
Bikanir, 48, 230
Bordeaux, xxiii, xxx, xxxv
Botelho, Father Anthony, 279
British Museum Library, xxxiii, xxxvi, 210, 276
Broecke, P. van den, 247
Buchwald, G. von, xxxiii–xxxiv
Buda Pesth, 178
Burhanpur (Breampur), 98, 101, 102, 152, 175, 249
Burhanu-l Mulk, 234

Cabral, Antoine, 14, 217
Calaim, 111, 259
Calicut, 4
Cambay, 2, 4, 46, 48; 3rd Mission at, 52–57; Father Corsi at, 99, 180, 230, 233–234, 239, 240, 268
Caravan, travelling by, 58, 59
Cateris, Hindu judges, 146, 267
Cathay (Catai), 99; 152, 229, 232–233, 268
Catrou, F. F., *Histoire*, 210, 242, 250
Caziques, 15, 49, 219, 267
Chagatai (Chaquata), 2, 132, 211
Chambal, river, 5
Chand Bibi, 102, 234, 249
Chatigam, 116
Chaul, 73, 107
Chenab, river, 5
China, xxiv, xxix, 74, 111, 233, 243
Chinghis Khan, 211
Chin Qulij, 277
Cochin, 232
Coimbra, xxx, 228, 241
Colaço, Antonio, S. J., xxxiii, 260
Corsi, Father Francis, joins 3rd Mission, 99; his journey to Burhanpur, 99–101, 250; at Lahore, 152; his difficulties, 153–155; his intercourse with Sir T. Roe, 249
Coxi, Hindu divine, 146–148, 219, 267
Cranganore, 232
Crasbeeck, Pedro, xxxiii

Dalgado, S. R., *Glossário*, 228, 264
Daman, 18, 52, 99, 220, 268
Damaris, coin, 148, 267
Danvers, F. C., *Portuguese in India*, 268
Danyal, Prince, 25, 74, 219, 223, 249, 275
Datura, 123, 263
De Backer, A., *Bibliothèque*, xxviii, xxxii
Deccan, campaign in the, 57, 73, 88, 90, 97–98, 102–109, 182, 234, 249
Delhi, 7, 275
De Noronha, Don Antonio, 217
De Sousa, Father F., *Oriente Conquistado*, 219, 220, 221
Diampre, Synod of, 264
Dias, Father Peter, 218
Din Ilahi, 219, 224, 226, 237–238, 247, 257, 266, 272
Divine Era, 117, 261
Du Jarric, Father P., career and work of, xxiii–xxxi, xxxvii; origin and description of the *Histoire*, xxiii–xxiv; materials used, xxxi–xxxii; publication, xxxv–xxxvi; scarcity of, xxxvi–xxxvii; Latin version, xxxvii; character and purpose, xxxviii–xl; historical value of, xl–xliii; references to, xxix, xxxix, 219, 221, 228, 232, 240, 247, 265

INDEX

Elephants, use of, in war, 6–7, 213–214
Ethiopia, 18, 84, 245
Evora, xxxiii, 241

Faizi Sirhindi, *Akbarnama* of, 249, 251, 253, 255–257
Faria y Sousa, Manoel, xxviii
Fathpur (Pateful), 8; Father Pereira at, 15–16; 1st Mission arrives at, 18; 214, 217, 220
Felix, Father, *Mughal Farmans*, 239, 240
Finch, William, 233
Firishta, *History*, 253
Fitch, Ralph, xliii, 211, 233
Foster, Sir W., *Early Travels*, 211, 235

Gama, Vasco da, 228
Ganges, river, 5, 102; sanctity of, 148, 211
George, Father Abraham, 84, 245
Ghazi Beg, Mirza, 247
Gladiators, 9, 215
Goa, xxviii, xliv, 4, 17; Leon Grimon's embassy to, 45–49, 51, 52; House of *Profes* at, 52, 232; 57, 83, 90, 102, 113; political embassy to, 114–117; 178, 224
Godavery, river, 251
Goës, Benoist de, joins 3rd Mission, 52; accompanies A to Kashmir, 75; 80, 85; accompanies A to the Deccan, 97; 109; accompanies embassy to Goa, 115–116, 259–260; returns to Agra, 152; his mission to Cathay, 229, 232–233, 268
Goga, 250
Golconda, 249
Goldie, Father F., *First Jesuit Mission*, 220, 221, 225
Gregory IX, Pope, 271
Grenville, Hon. Thomas, xxxvi
Grimon, Leon, 45–49, 229
Guerreiro, Father Farnam, du Jarric's correspondence with, xxvii; supplies materials for *Histoire*, xxviii–xxix; account of, xxxii; mistaken for a missionary, xxxiv
— *Relaçam* of, du Jarric's use of, xxxi, xxxii; publication of, xxxii; scarcity of, xxxiii; misuse of, xxxiv–xxxv; references to, 241, 248, 251–252, 259, 260, 262, 263, 264, 266, 267, 268, 271, 273, 276, 277, 278, 280
Gujarat, 52, 59, 73, 101, 153, 189, 211, 233, 235, 238, 253, 268
Guzman, Father Luis de, xxvi, xxvii
— *Historia* of, account of, xxvi; translated by du Jarric, xxvii–xxix; references to, 210, 216, 218, 223, 226, 227, 240, 241, 243, 248
Gwalior, 221, 249, 271, 274

Haig, Sir T. Wolsey, 258
Hakim Ali, 225
Hamida Bano Begam, A's mother, 43, 167–168; death of, 188, 275, 280; 211, 274
Hasan and Husain, sons of A, 214
Hawking, 10
Hawkins, William, xlviii, 233
Hay, John, *De Rebus Japonicis, etc.*, 210, 241, 244
Henriques, Father F., 18, 221
Herbert, Sir T., *Travels*, 227
Hosten, Rev. H., writings of, 209, 211, 220, 221

INDEX

Hughes, T. P., *Dictionary of Islam*, 236, 279, 280
Humayun, 3, 211, 215, 274
Hunting, A's method of, 10
Hydaspes, river, 212

Ibrahim Husain Mirza, 250
'Idomi,' 258
Indus, river, 5, 102

Jahangir, Emperor, xxxiv, xlvi, 214, 246, 248, 257, 271, 280
Jains, 239
Japan, xxvi, xxviii, 29, 82, 243
Jesuit Missions, xxxi
Jesuit Fathers, their missionary zeal, xxxix; their intimacy with A, xli; their political activities, xlvi–xlviii; their contempt for alien creeds, 224, 228, 236, 280
Jesuit writings, character of, xxxix–xl; xliii–xliv
Jhilam, river, 5, 212
Jumna, river, 5, 212

Kabul, 2, 225, 268
Kabul, Prince of (Muhammad Hakim), 2; A's campaign against, 6, 32–33, 212–213, 216, 225
Kandahar, 164, 211, 237
Kashmir (Caximir), 5; visited by A, 75–79; description of, 75–76; 208, 231, 244
Khandesh (Xhander), 164, 208, 221, 249, 251, 279
Khan-khanan, see Abdur Rahim Mirza
Khusru, Prince, 237, 272, 274, 278
Kutbu-l Mulkiya (Golconda), 249

Laertius, Father Albert, xxviii, xxxii, 215
Lahauri, Mirza, 276
Lahore, A's residence at, 8; 2nd Mission at, 48–50; arrival of 3rd Mission at, 61; destructive fire at, 74–75, 243; A moves to Agra from, 88; Father Pignero at, 91–96; events at, in 1602, 173–181; plots against the Fathers at, 195–200; other references, 71, 79, 87, 88, 240, 262, 268
Le Grand, Albert, xxiii
Leïoton, Father Edward, 49–50, 230
Linschoten, J. H. van, 224, 245
Lisbon, xxvii, 59, 220
Lorete, Notre Dame de, 111, 259
Loyola, Father Ignatius, 82
Lucena, Jean de, xxviii–xxx, xxxii
Luke, St., 221, 271

Macedon, Philip of, 108
Machado, Father Anthony, 152, 240, 268
Maclagan, Sir E. D., *Missions to Akbar* (J.A.S.B. lxv), 213, 220, 223, 226, 230, 232, 234, 237, 239, 245, 248, 269, 271, 273, 274, 276, 277
Madonna di Popolo, 160–171, 271
Maffeus, Joannes P., xxv, xxx
Mah Chuchak Begam, 211
Mahmudi (Manude), coin, 56, 235
Malabar, xxviii, 5, 102, 135, 228, 241, 264
— Christians of, 135, 264–265
Maligarh, fortress, 254
Malik Ambar, 234
Malik Yakub (Abyssinian Governor of Asirgarh), 105–106, 253, 257–258
Mansabdari System, 6, 212–213
Man Singh, Raja, 278

INDEX

Manuquer, Persian ambassador, 177–178, 273
Mar Abraham, 264
Martinez, Matthia, xxxvi
Mecca, 15, 60, 132, 153, 172
Menezes, Dom Diogo de, 217
Mildenhall, John, xlvi, xlviii, 233
Millanges, S., xxiii, xxxv
Miran, King of Khandesh, see Bahadur Khan
Miranda, Ferdinand de, 268
Miratu-l Quds, 271, 275
Mir-i-Arz, 215
Mir-ul-Hajj (Soldan of Mecque), 15, 219
Mogor, 1, 210
Monserrate, Father A., joins 1st Mission, 18, 220; tutor to A's sons, 36, 223; captivity of, 83, 221; accompanies A to Kabul, 212, 225; returns to Goa, 226, 245
— *Commentarius* of, 209, 214, 215, 216, 219, 220, 221, 224, 225, 259
— *Relaçam* of, 209, 210, 211, 213, 214, 217, 218
Montanus, Father B. Arias, 221
Moreland, W. H., *India at the Death of Akbar*, xlv, 224, 245, 269
Mubarak Shah, of Khandesh, 251
Muhammad Hakim, Mirza, see Kabul
Multan, 48
Mundy, Peter, 247
Muqarrib Khan, 105–106, 253, 257
Murad, Prince, a pupil of the Fathers, 24–25, 223; meets 3rd Mission at Cambay, 54–57; on service in the Deccan, 54, 234, 235, 242; sends present to A from Gujarat, 65; defeat and death of, 73-74,88,242; was subject to epilepsy, 215; married to daughter of Aziz Khan, 272
Murray, Hugh, *Discoveries*, 221
Muzaffar Husain Mirza, of Kandahar, 64–65, 164, 171, 237, 272
Muzaffar Husain Mirza, son of Ibrahim Husain Mirza, 101, 250
Muzaffar Khan, Governor of Bengal, 225
Muzaffar Shah, of Gujarat, 234

Narbada, river, 5, 211
Narsingha, 4, 5, 211
Nau-roz, 65, 74, 242
Nizam-ul Mulkiya, 234, 249
Noer, Count von, vii, xxxiii, xxxv, 210
Notre Dame la Maieur, 20, 221
Nuniz, Farnão, *Chronicle*, 213
Nur-ul Haqq, *Tawarikh*, 244

Ogilby, John, *Asia*, vi, 234, 235, 243, 244, 247, 251
Ormuz, 58, 135, 228, 265
Osorius, writings of, consulted by du Jarric, xxx

Pagoda, 133, 264
Pahari, see Murad, Prince
Painting, the art of, 169, 272
Pattan, 60, 236
Paul, St., College of, at Goa, 17, 219, 220
Pegu, 116
Pekin, 233
Pereira, Father Julian, sent for by A, 15; disputes with Mullas, 15–16; 209, 214, 218
Peres, Dominic, 17, 219
Persia, 3, 5, 6, 178